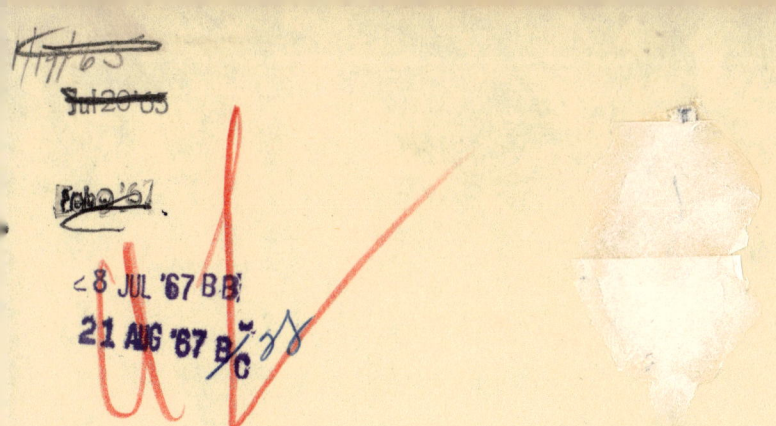

Simplified Techniques for
PREPARING VISUAL INSTRUCTIONAL MATERIALS

Simplified Techniques for

Preparing Visual Instructional Materials

Ed Minor
Director, Communications Services
Florida A. & M. University

McGRAW-HILL BOOK COMPANY, INC.   1962
New York   San Francisco   Toronto   London

Simplified Techniques for PREPARING VISUAL INSTRUCTIONAL MATERIALS. Copyright © 1962 by the McGraw-Hill Book Company, Inc. All Rights Reserved. Printed in the United States of America. This book, or parts thereof, may not be reproduced in any form without permission of the publishers.

Library of Congress Catalog Card Number:
62-18055

To
Harvey Raymond Frye, who over the years has so generously shared his knowledge and philosophy with me and hundreds of other persons from all over the world, this manual is gratefully dedicated.

PREFACE

Never in the history of civilization have visual instructional materials played such an important role in the communication processes. It was mainly upon this premise that this manual was conceived as a means of presenting, under one cover, simplified techniques for preparing visual instructional materials.

The manual is restricted to the techniques necessary for the preparation of modern visual instructional materials, and has been written both for the person without skills in art, graphic art, and photographic techniques, and for the professional seeking new approaches to production problems.

Throughout the manual, simplified approaches to the preparation of visual instructional materials are emphasized, utilizing modern materials, equipment, and techniques the author has found to be sound and most practical. This manual has been written with the belief that excellence need not be predicated upon complexity; therefore complicated directions and terminology, often associated with art, graphic art, and photographic techniques, have been avoided.

The manual is divided into five sections. Section one deals with mounting techniques as they apply to mounting and preserving instructional materials. Section two includes twelve of the most practical easy-to-use lettering techniques available today. Section three is made up of simplified techniques for preparing various types of visuals (drawings, illustrations, etc.). Also included in this section are a number of drawing and lettering devices and cutting aids. Section four treats several unique techniques for adding color and texture to visual materials. Section five includes a number of new techniques for preparing slides and large transparencies. Also included in this section are techniques for binding, mounting, and masking slides and transparencies. Finally, up-to-date comprehensive listings of publications, visual aids, and glossary and sources of materials and equipment related to the techniques presented in the manual have been included.

The manual itself is designed for the working area and not a bookshelf. The pages are so arranged that they can lie back flat, making it easy to follow the clear step-by-step directions and illustrations for each technique. Cross references play an important part in the manual, as many of the techniques involve the use of similar steps, materials, and equipment.

Actually, space forbids including all of the techniques, materials, and equipment available today. However, what has been presented here is believed to be one of the most practical approaches to the preparation of modern instructional materials. It is hoped that these techniques will serve as a springboard of ideas for the creation of instructional materials yet to come.

A task almost as pleasant as writing this manual is that of expressing appreciation to those whose endeavors have made it possible. Dedicating this manual to Harvey Frye by no means expresses complete appreciation to a person who is responsible for much of the training and experiences of the author in this area. Particular thanks are due James Bruton who served as typographer for the manual and provided valuable technical assistance; Howard Lewis for a large portion of the artwork; Sadie Gaither and Oswald Lampkins for editing the manuscript and giving valuable suggestions; Robert Hammond for typing and editing; Archie Hannon for the typesetting; Harvey Robinson for the proofing; June Brown for many hours on photographs and artwork; and finally Bertha Minor, whose contributions exceed those of the author in so many ways.

CONTENTS

Preface vii

SECTION 1   MOUNTING TECHNIQUES 1

    Rubber Cement Mounting 2
    Dry Mounting Tissue 4
    Double-Coated Acetate 6
    Self-Sealing Acetate 8
    Sealamin Laminating Film 10
    Thermo-Fax Lamination 12
    Dry Mounting Cloth 14
    Wet-Mounting 16
    Passe Partout Mounting 18
    Hook N' Loop Board 20
    Display Easels 22
    Finishing and Displaying Cloth Mounts 23
    Miscellaneous Mounting Techniques 24

SECTION 2   LETTERING TECHNIQUES 27

    Rubber Stamp Lettering 28
    Stenso Lettering Guides 30
    Pre-Cut Letters 32
    Spray-On-Lettering 34
    Planotype Letters 36
    Dry-Transfer Letters 38
    Transparent Type Paste-Up Letters 40
    Paper Type Paste-Up Letters 42
    Wrico Lettering 44
    Letterguide Lettering 46
    LeRoy Lettering 48
    Varigraph Lettering 50

SECTION 3   VISUAL TECHNIQUES 53

    Visuals by Projection 54
    Enlarging and Reducing Visuals 56
    Visuals by Tracing 58
    Drawing and Lettering Devices 60
    Cutting and Drawing Aids 62
    Inks and Liquid Colors 64

SECTION 4 COLOR AND TEXTURE TECHNIQUES 65
    Color Adhesive Sheets 66
    Texture Adhesive Sheets 68
    Craftint Doubletone Shading 70
    Color and Pattern Self-Adhering Tapes 72
    Transparent Liquid Colors 74

SECTION 5 PHOTOGRAPHIC AND NON-PHOTOGRAPHIC
    TRANSPARENCIES 77
    Picture-Transfer—
        Rubber Cement 78
        Seal Process 80
        Thermo-Fax Colof-Lift 82
        Self-Sealing Acetate 84
    Diffusion-Transfer-Transparencies 86
    Thermo-Fax Transparencies 88
    Diazo Transparencies 90
    Polaroid Transparencies 92
    Electronic Stencil Transparencies 94
    Fluid Duplicator Transparencies 95
    Beseler Slide-O-Film Slides 96
    Slide Binding and Mounting 98
    Large Transparencies—Masking and Mounting 100

REFERENCES

    A—Publications 103
    B—Visual Aids 105
    C—Materials and Equipment
        Glossary and Sources 107
    D—Addresses 118
    E—Visual Index 122

SECTION 1

MOUNTING TECHNIQUES

MOUNTING TECHNIQUES

Many visual instructional materials, such as maps, charts, graphs, posters, diagrams, etc., can now be mounted or preserved on cardboard, cloth, wood, paper, plastic, acetate, and other similar materials

Until recently, however, several of the mounting techniques presented in this section were associated only with industrial users. Such techniques included plastic lamination, dry mounting tissue, dry mounting cloth, etc. Recently these same techniques, along with newer ones, have been simplified and made accessible to the non-professional user.

Ten of the most modern mounting or preserving techniques are illustrated and discussed in this section. Included among these techniques are several unique mounting aids, ideas for making display easels, and for finishing and displaying materials that have been mounted on cloth.

Only the more practical and easy-to-use mounting and preserving techniques have been presented here. These techniques, properly selected, can be used to enhance the most modern instructional materials.

▶ RUBBER CEMENT MOUNTING

▶ DRY MOUNTING TISSUE

▶ DOUBLE-COATED ACETATE

▶ SELF-SEALING ACETATE

▶ SEALAMIN LAMINATING FILM

▶ THERMO-FAX LAMINATION

▶ DRY MOUNTING CLOTH

▶ WET-MOUNTING

▶ PASSE PARTOUT MOUNTING

▶ HOOK N' LOOP BOARD

▶ DISPLAY EASELS

▶ FINISHING AND DISPLAYING CLOTH MOUNTS

▶ MISCELLANEOUS MOUNTING TECHNIQUES

RUBBER CEMENT MOUNTING

Rubber cement mounting is a quick, easy and clean technique. It is ideal for mounting many flat instructional materials, such as prints, photographs, drawings, pre-cut letters, etc.

Rubber cement is a clean, easy-spreading adhesive for joining paper to paper, cloth, leather, glass, metal, wood, and other surfaces. Good quality cement is non-wrinkling, non-curling, and easily removed by rolling it off with fingers or eraser.

To thin or soften cement, use rubber cement thinner.

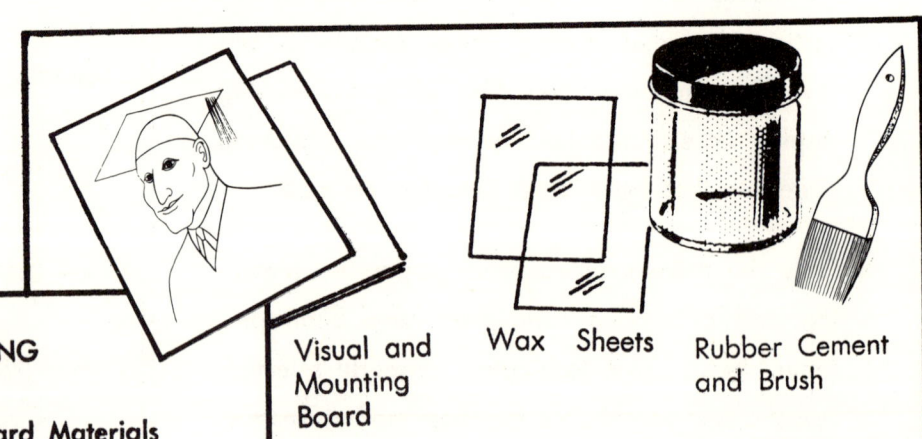

FOR MOUNTING
- Artwork
- Bulletin Board Materials
- Drawings
- Exhibit Materials
- Photographs
- Pre-Cut Letters

Visual and Mounting Board

Wax Sheets

Rubber Cement and Brush

1-1 To 1-7

DIRECTIONS

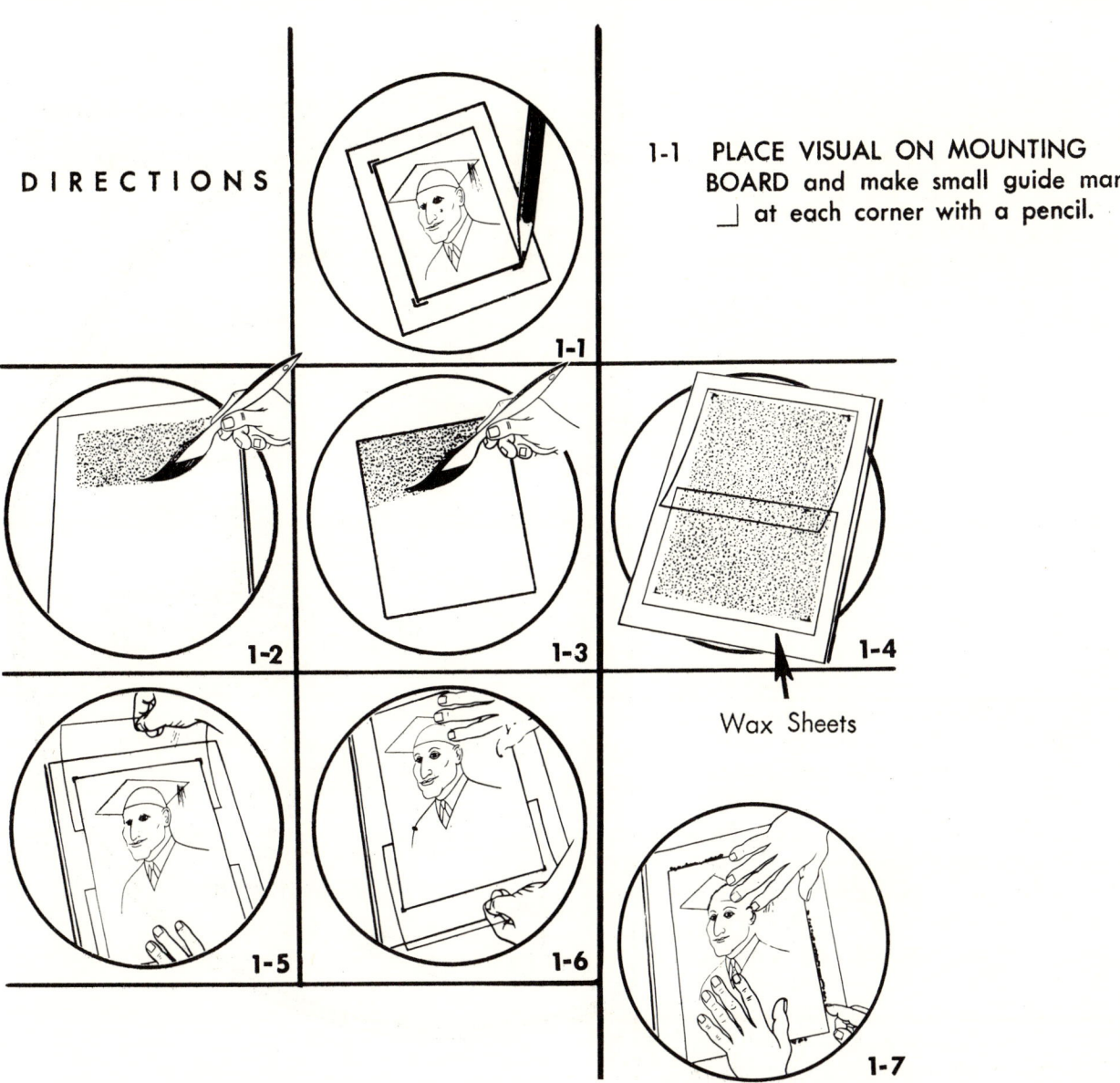

1-1 PLACE VISUAL ON MOUNTING BOARD and make small guide mark ⌐ at each corner with a pencil.

Wax Sheets

1-2 APPLY A THIN EVEN COAT OF RUBBER CEMENT over the marked area of the mounting board. Allow the cement to extend a little beyond the guide marks.

1-3 APPLY A THIN EVEN COAT OF RUBBER CEMENT to the back of the visual. A protective sheet under the visual will prevent cement from getting on the working surface.

1-4 PLACE TWO ORDINARY TRANSLUCENT SHEETS OF WAX PAPER on the cemented surface of the mounting board, slightly overlapping them at the center. These sheets will prevent visual from adhering to the board during positioning.

1-5 PLACE VISUAL ON TOP OF WAX SHEETS with cemented side down. Position visual within guide marks. REMOVE TOP WAX SHEET with a "snap" while holding the bottom portion of the visual in place.

1-6 REMOVE THE BOTTOM WAX SHEET with a "snap" while holding the top portion of the visual in place.

1-7 SMOOTH DOWN THE SURFACE OF VISUAL with palm of hand. Remove excess cement and guide marks by rubbing around the edges of visual with the finger.

DRY MOUNTING TISSUE

This dry mounting technique is ideal for mounting many flat instructional materials without the use of liquid adhesives.

Dry mounting tissue is a thin sheet of paper, similar to a sheet of wax paper, which is coated on both sides with a coating of high grade thermo-plastic adhesive. By applying heat and pressure with a dry mounting press, fotowelder, or hand iron, to the dry mounting tissue, it forms a strong bond between the materials to which it has been applied. Materials can be mounted in a matter of a few seconds.

Dry mounting tissue is available in rolls and sheets.

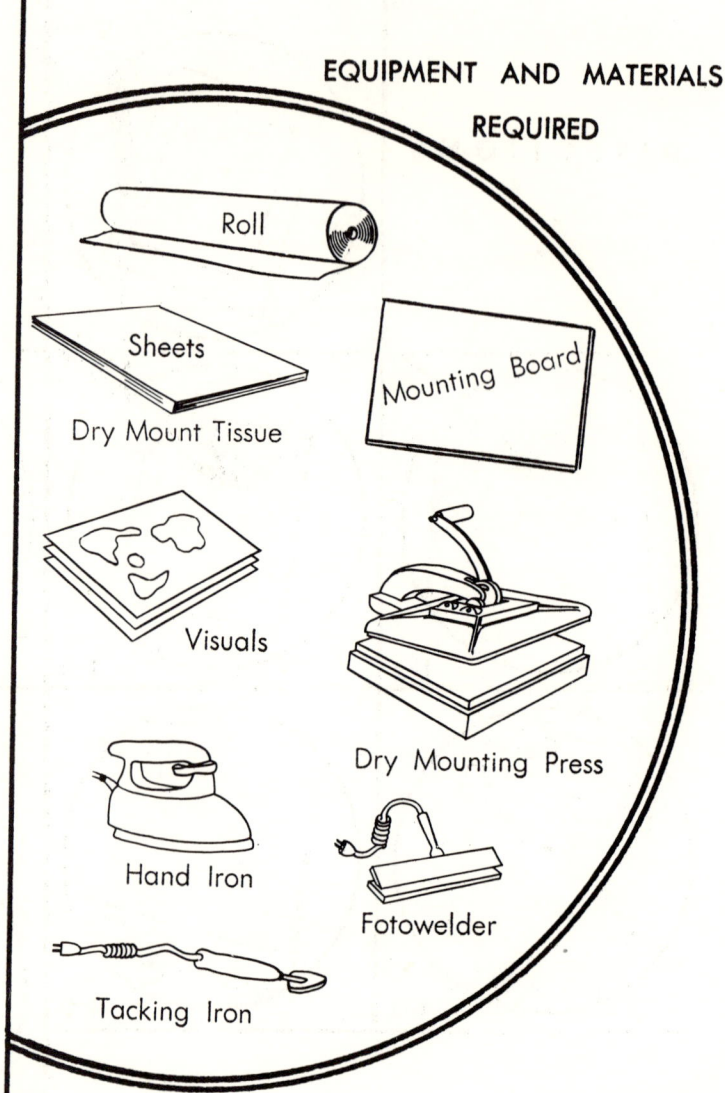

EQUIPMENT AND MATERIALS REQUIRED

- Roll
- Sheets — Dry Mount Tissue
- Mounting Board
- Visuals
- Dry Mounting Press
- Hand Iron
- Fotowelder
- Tacking Iron

FOR MOUNTING

Artwork
Bulletin Board Materials
Documents
Drawings
Exhibit Materials
Photographs
Pre-cut Paper Letters

DIRECTIONS

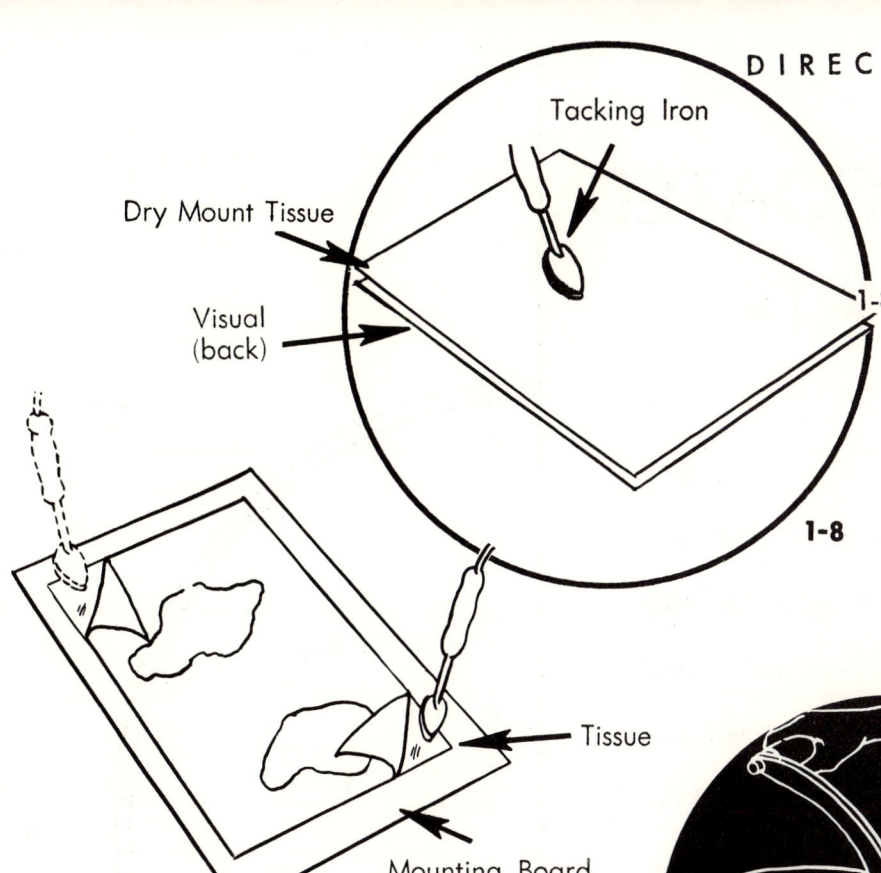

1-8 VISUAL SHOULD BE DRY and free of all wrinkles; if not, insert in heated press (225° F.) with a protective sheet on top for about 10 seconds.

ATTACH SHEET OF DRY MOUNTING TISSUE TO BACK OF VISUAL. The tissue should be exactly the same size as the visual or a bit larger so that it can be trimmed with the visual after it has been "tacked" in place. "Tack" the tissue two or three places in in the center with heated tacking iron or tip of hand iron.

1-9 ATTACH VISUAL AND TISSUE TO MOUNTING BOARD. Since the tissue is not sticky, it can be positioned as desired on the board. "Tack" it onto the board by lifting any two opposite corners and by touching the tip of the tacking iron or hand iron to the tissue. This will keep the visual in place during the actual mounting.

1-10 INSERT IN HEATED PRESS (225° F.) with a clean sheet of paper on top of the visual to protect the surface. Close press for recommended time. Thicker visuals will require more time in the press.

1-11 USE AN ORDINARY HAND IRON as a substitute for the press. Use a heat-absorbing paper as a protective sheet. The surface of the iron should be just hot enough to "sizzle" when touched with a moistened finger. Keep the iron in motion during the mounting. In mounting large visuals, do a small section at a time.

DOUBLE-COATED ACETATE

Double-coated acetate or plastic is a thin acetate sheet with pressure-sensitive adhesive on both sides for easy dry mounting without heat and special mounting equipment. Double-coated acetate is ideal for mounting a variety of flat materials; it is available in tape form also (see 1-82).

FOR MOUNTING

Artwork

Charts, Graphs, and Maps

Documents

Exhibit and Display Materials

Photographs

MATERIALS REQUIRED

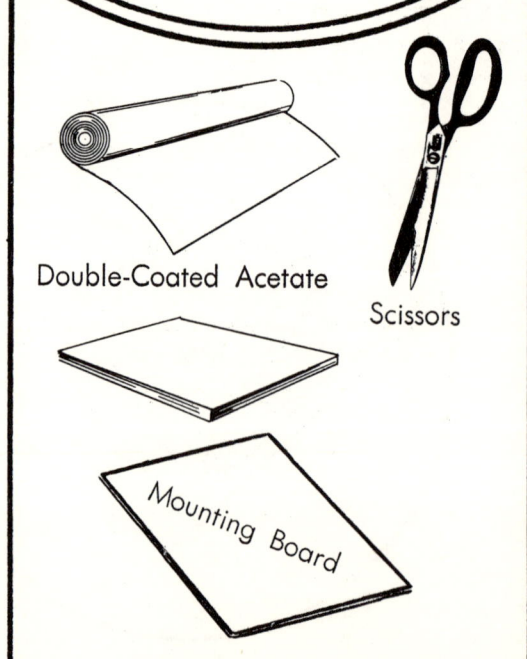

Double-Coated Acetate

Scissors

Mounting Board

1-12 To 1-15

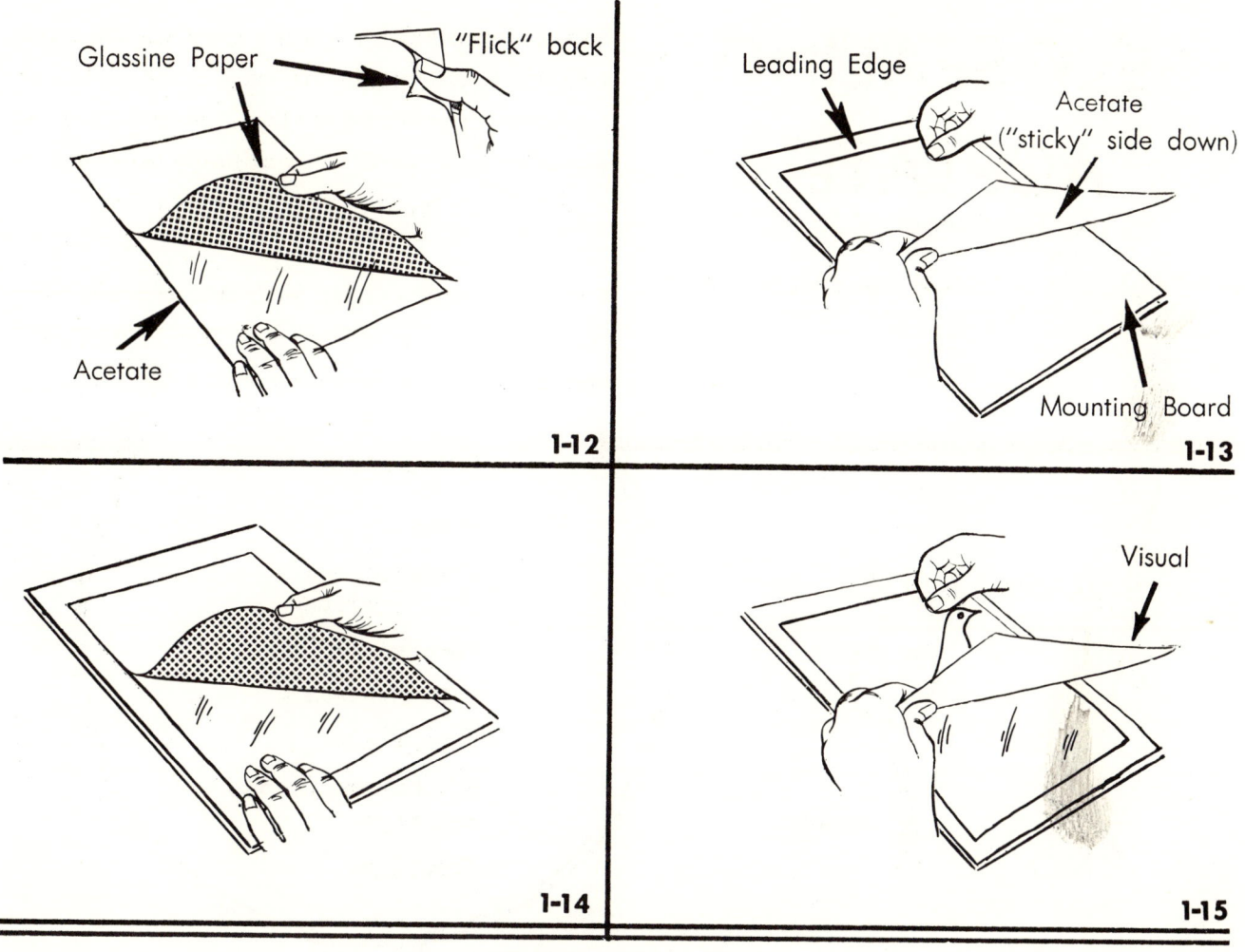

DIRECTIONS

CUT DESIRED PORTION OF ACETATE with scissors or paper cutter. Both acetate and visual should be cut the same size.

1-12 **PEEL GLASSINE PAPER** from one side of the acetate by first 'flicking' the upper corner. This will release the paper and allow for easy peeling, and will expose one "sticky" side of the acetate.

1-13 **APPLY "STICKY" SIDE OF ACETATE** to surface of mounting board by positioning the leading edge of the acetate on the board first; then slowly lower, at an angle, until acetate is completely flat. Rub down surface with the hand to insure perfect adhesion. Do not test the adhesive qualities of the acetate by lifting, as it will come off readily when first applied. The adhesive has been designed to work slowly.

1-14 **PEEL GLASSINE PAPER** from remaining side of acetate. Follow the directions in 1-12.

1-15 **APPLY VISUAL TO "STICKY" SIDE OF EXPOSED ACETATE** by positioning the leading edge even with the acetate; then slowly lower the visual at an angle until it is completely flat. Rub down with the hand to insure perfect adhesion.

SELF-SEALING ACETATE
(For Lamination)

Self-sealing acetate is a transparent acetate sheet with a pressure-sensitive adhesive on one side that permanently bonds on contact. This technique requires no heat, press, or additional adhesives. It is ideal for preparing many flat printed materials.

Lamination is the process of applying a sheet of plastic film or acetate to a printed sheet.

Materials that have been laminated with self-sealing acetate can be marked on with marking pencil (see 3-45) and easily erased with a soft cloth.

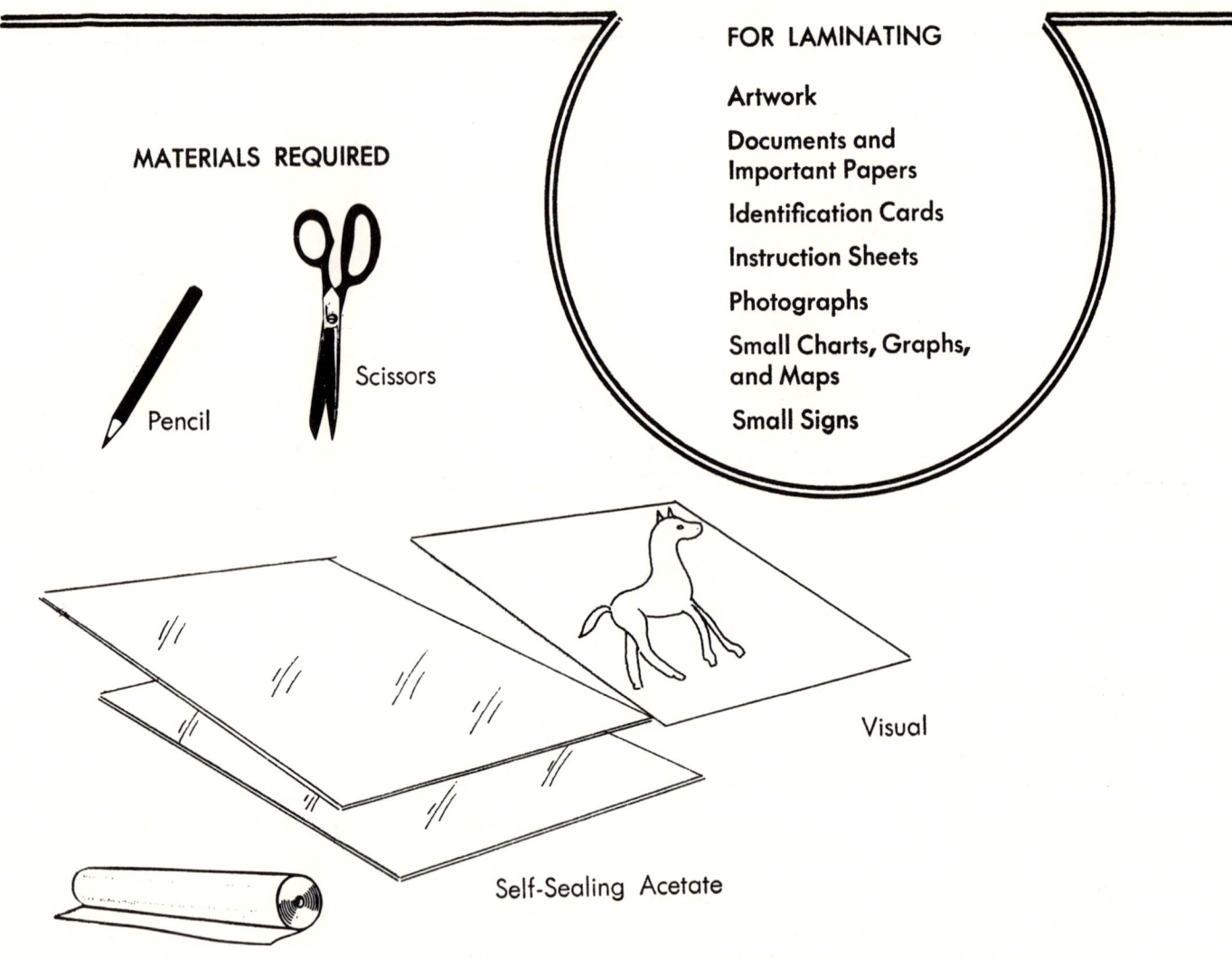

MATERIALS REQUIRED

Pencil   Scissors

FOR LAMINATING

Artwork
Documents and Important Papers
Identification Cards
Instruction Sheets
Photographs
Small Charts, Graphs, and Maps
Small Signs

Visual

Self-Sealing Acetate

1-16 To 1-19

DIRECTIONS

CUT TWO PIECES OF ACETATE large enough to allow for a transparent margin if desired.

1-16 PEEL GLASSINE PAPER from one of the sheets of acetate by first "flicking" the upper corner; this will release the paper and allow easy peeling. Acetate should be actual size of material to be laminated unless a transparent margin is desired.

1-17 APPLY VISUAL OR MATERIAL to be laminated to the "sticky" side of the acetate by contacting the leading edge down first; then lower at an angle until it is completely flat. Rub down with the hand to insure perfect adhesion. Do not test the adhesive quali-

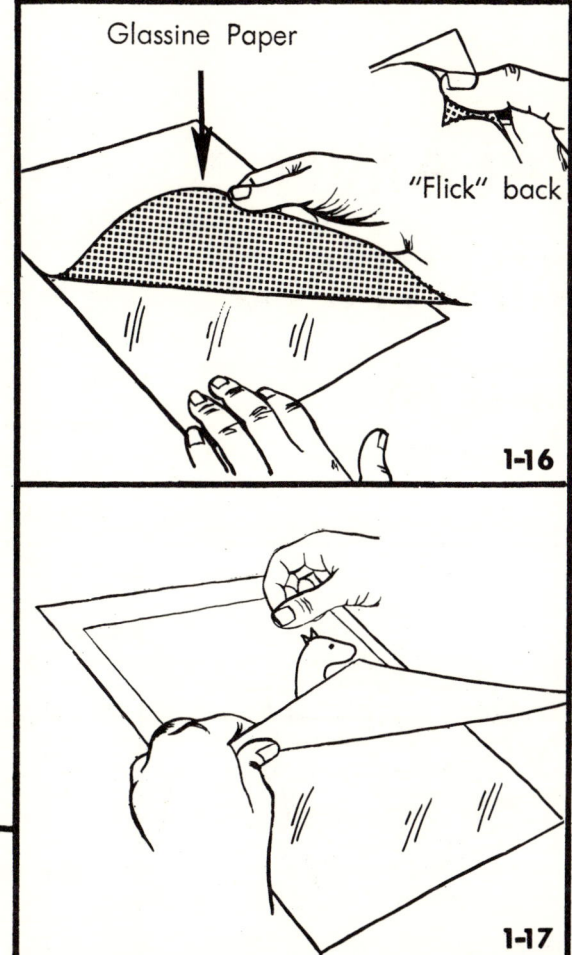

ties of the acetate by lifting, as it will come off readily when first applied. The adhesive has been designed to work slowly.

1-18 APPLY SECOND SHEET OF ACETATE, after removing glassine paper (see 1-16), to face of visual by positioning the leading edge of acetate (adhesive side down) even with the first sheet of acetate. Slowly lower at an angle until completely flat. Rub down with the hand to insure perfect adhesion.

1-19 TRIM IF DESIRED; or, if a margin of acetate is intended, run the round end of a pencil or a similar device around the edges of the visual to complete the laminating.

SEALAMIN LAMINATING FILM
(ACETATE)

Sealamin is a thin, transparent, laminating film that requires heat and pressure to adhere to uncoated papers.

In the past, laminating flat materials required expensive equipment and technical know-how. Now this new product, Sealamin, makes it possible to laminate flat printed materials in less than a minute. A dry mounting press and Sealamin laminating film are all that is needed.

EQUIPMENT AND MATERIALS REQUIRED

FOR LAMINATING

Artwork

Documents and Important Papers

Identification Cards

Instruction Sheets

Charts, Graphs and Maps

DIRECTIONS

PHOTOGRAPHIC AND SHINY SURFACED PAPERS should be wiped off with a piece of cotton, moistened with regular rubbing alcohol, before laminating.

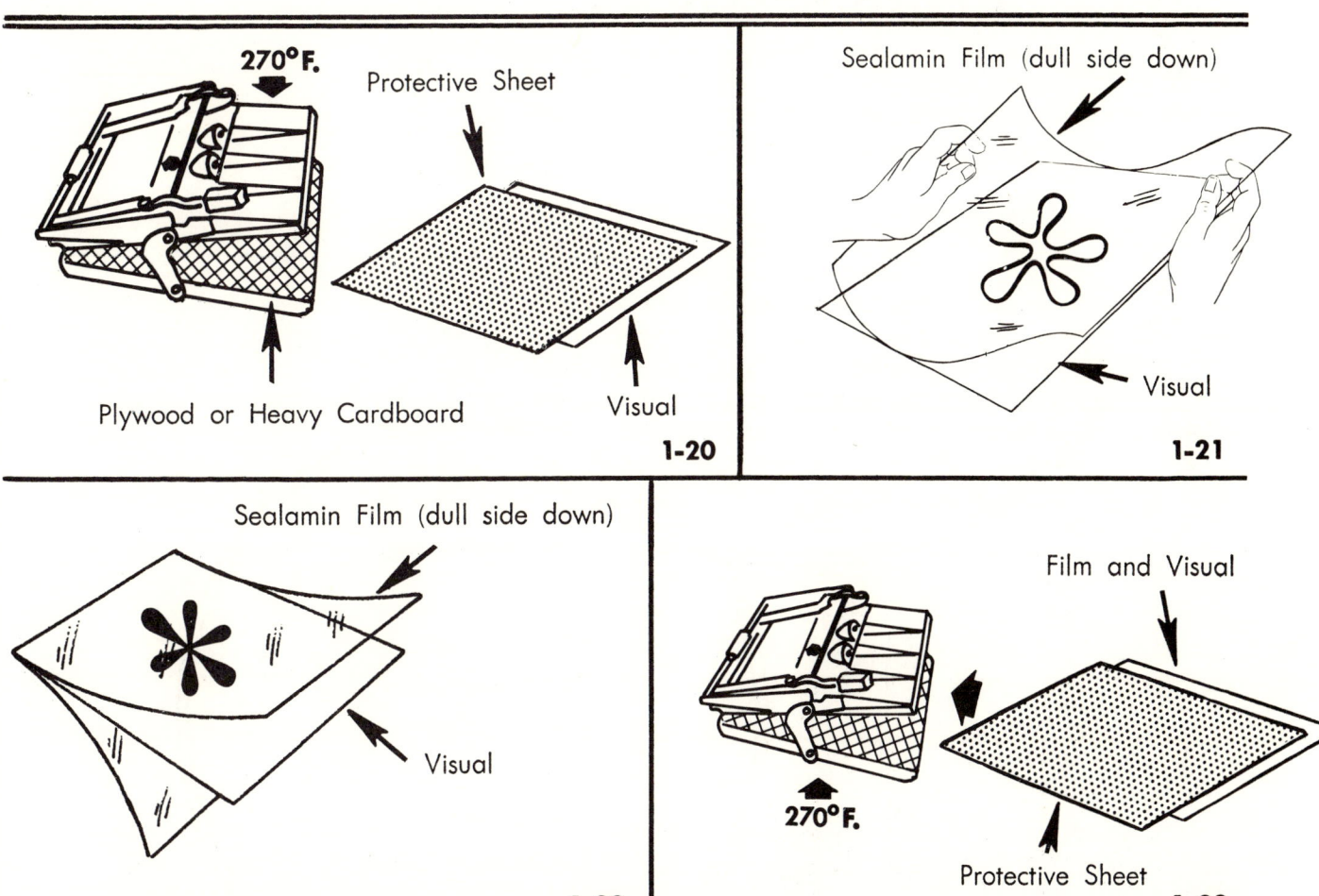

1-20 PRE-HEAT MATERIAL TO BE LAMINATED, with protective sheet on top, to remove as much moisture as possible. Insert in heated press for about 30 seconds.

1-22 FOR THIN SHEET MATERIALS, fold film to form a "jacket" in which to insert the sheet to be laminated.

1-21 CUT SEALAMIN FILM the size of the material to be laminated; or, if the material is a thin sheet, cut film long enough to cover both sides of the sheet (see 1-22).

PLACE A PIECE OF MASONITE plywood, or heavy cardboard in the press on top of the rubber pad to help increase pressure of press during the laminating.

1-23 PLACE FILM AND VISUAL IN THE PRESS for about 15 seconds. Make certain a sheet of onion skin or tissue paper is placed on top of film before inserting in press.

IF FILM FAILS TO ADHERE return to press for additional heating.

THERMO-FAX LAMINATION

Many flat printed materials, such as documents, photographs, etc., can now be laminated with the Thermo-Fax Copying Machine and a special laminating film.

Heavy weight originals, sixteen pound bond weight up to and including some card stock, work best. Originals may be printed or written on both sides. Lighter weight materials, ten to fifteen pound bond weight, can also be laminated. Material to be laminated must conform to size and thickness accepted by the machine.

FOR LAMINATING

Artwork

Documents and Important Papers

Instruction Sheets

Photographs

Small Charts, Graphs, and Maps

EQUIPMENT AND MATERIALS REQUIRED

Thermo-Fax Copying Machine

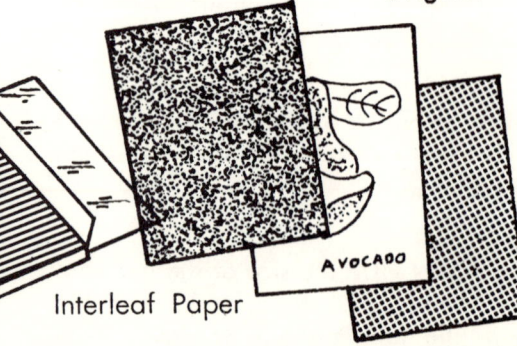

Thermo-Fax Laminating Film

Interleaf Paper

Original

Laminating Card

12

DIRECTIONS

1-24 SET DIAL CONTROL AT DARKEST SETTING. When laminating several sheets without interruption, gradually turn the dial to a lighter setting.

1-25 ASSEMBLE MATERIALS AS ILLUSTRATED. Make certain the materials to be **laminated** is not folded, creased, or crumpled.

1-26 INSERT ASSEMBLED MATERIALS IN THE MACHINE. Make certain the olived-colored interleaf paper is on top.

1-27 A FINISHED LAMINATED ORIGINAL. TO LAMINATE SMALL "OFF-SIZE" SHEETS, pre-trim the laminating film, leaving about 1/8 inch excess on each side. Follow instructions 1-25.

TO LAMINATE THE REVERSE SIDE, assemble the materials as illustrated in 1-25, making certain the original is reversed to prevent laminating the same side twice.

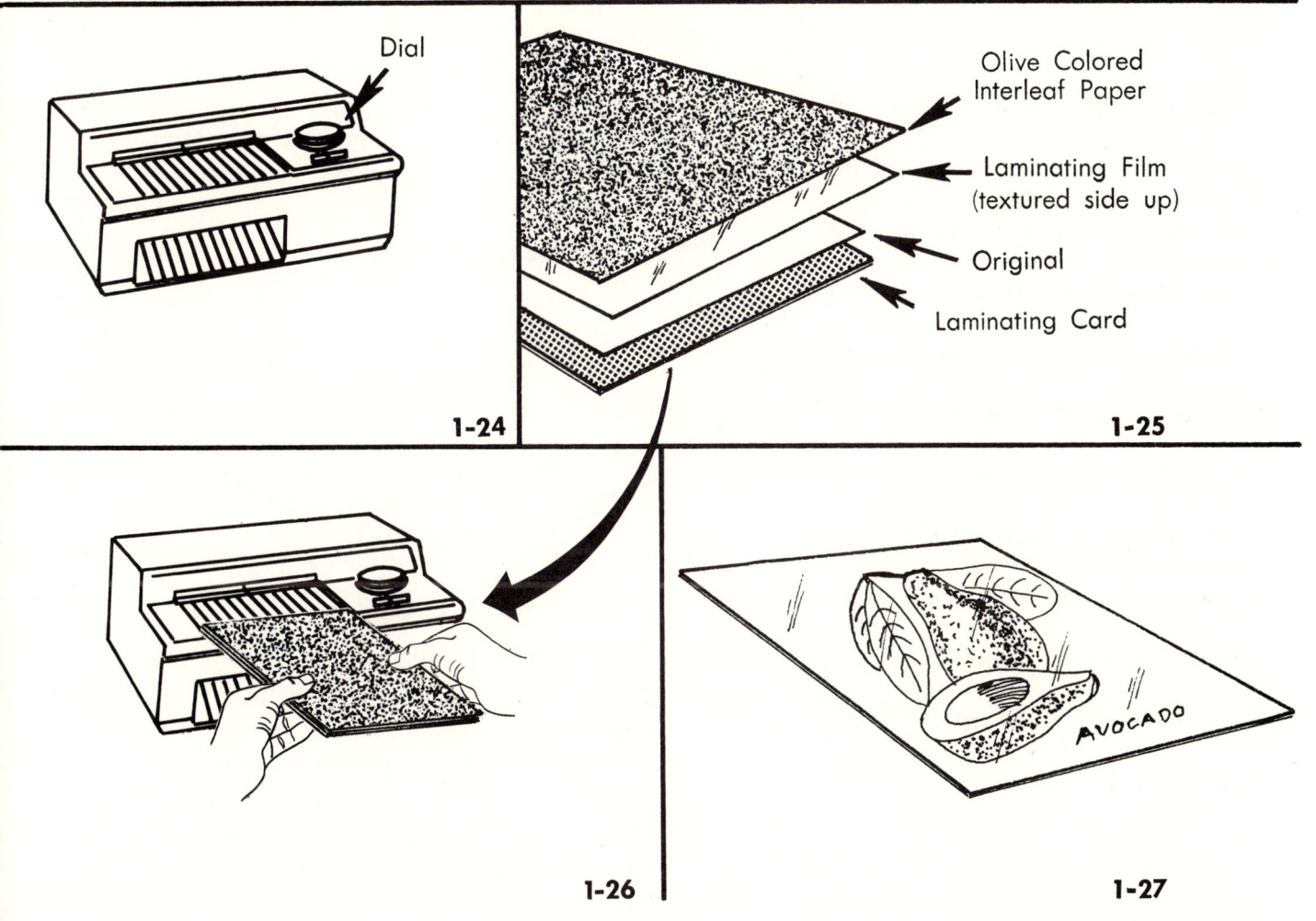

DRY MOUNTING CLOTH

Dry mounting cloth is a modern cloth backing which is applied dry to maps, charts, photographs, etc. All that is required is to place a sheet of the cloth on back of the material to be cloth-backed and to apply heat and pressure, and the job is finished. The complete operation takes less than a minute. A unique feature of this mounting technique is that no special equipment is required, nor is there any mess to clean up after the job has been completed. An ordinary hand iron can be used to apply the cloth. However, a dry mounting press does a much faster and better job. A photographic print dryer can also be used to mount the cloth.

FOR MOUNTING

Charts, Graphs, and Maps
Photographs
Picture Books
Picture Scrolls

EQUIPMENT AND MATERIALS REQUIRED

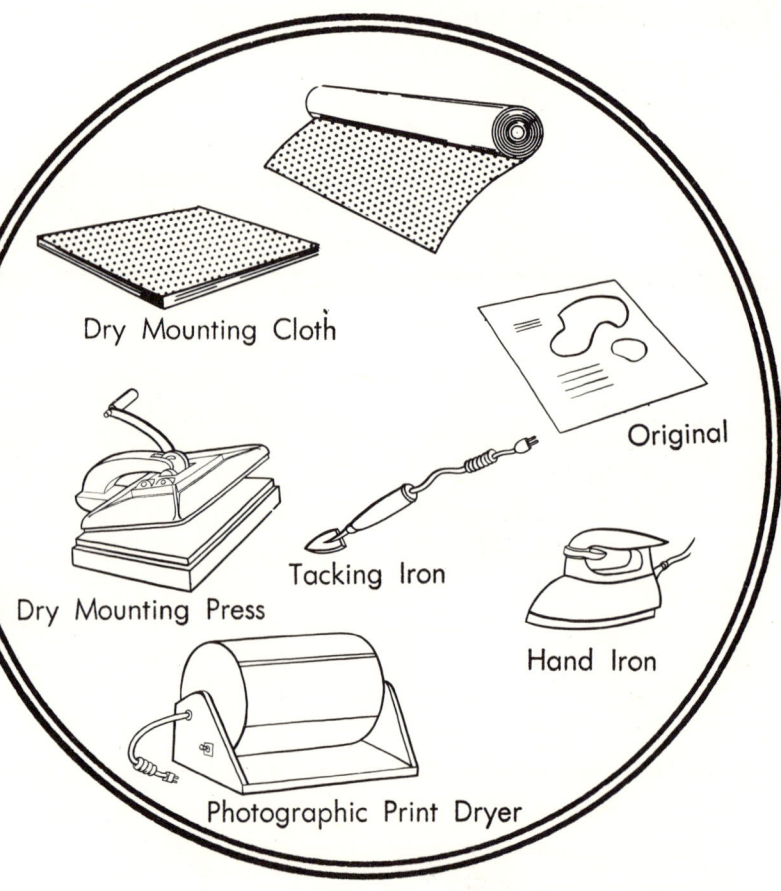

Dry Mounting Cloth
Original
Dry Mounting Press
Tacking Iron
Hand Iron
Photographic Print Dryer

HELPFUL HINTS

Store cloth in a cool place.

Should "blisters" or 'bubbles" appear after mounting, re-apply heat or rub down flaw with a print roller or a wadded piece of cloth.

Cloth's adhesive can be removed with naptha. If cleaning adhesive off heating unit, allow unit to cool off first.

DIRECTIONS

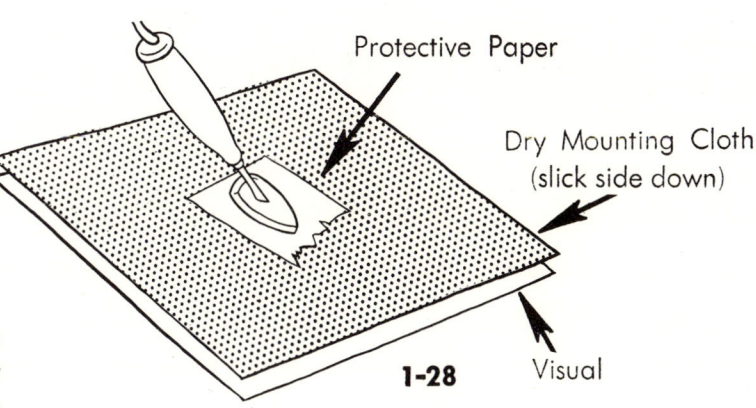

1-28

MAKE CERTAIN THE MATERIAL TO WHICH CLOTH IS TO BE ATTACHED is flat and thoroughly dry. (See 1-20).

1-28 PLACE VISUAL FACE DOWN on a clean sheet and attach a sheet of dry mounting cloth (slick side down). "Tack" cloth in place through a piece of clean paper. Use a heated tacking iron or the tip of a hand iron. Trim cloth and visual together if necessary. Never allow the cloth to extend beyond the edge of the visual.

1-29 INSERT CLOTH AND VISUAL IN PRESS (set at 225° F.) for about five seconds. If the press is not equipped with a heat control, the heating surface should be hot enough to "sizzle" when touched with a moistened finger. Make certain a protective sheet is placed on top of the cloth during the mounting.

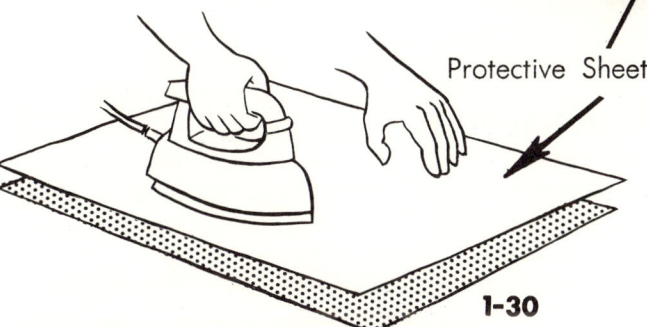

1-30

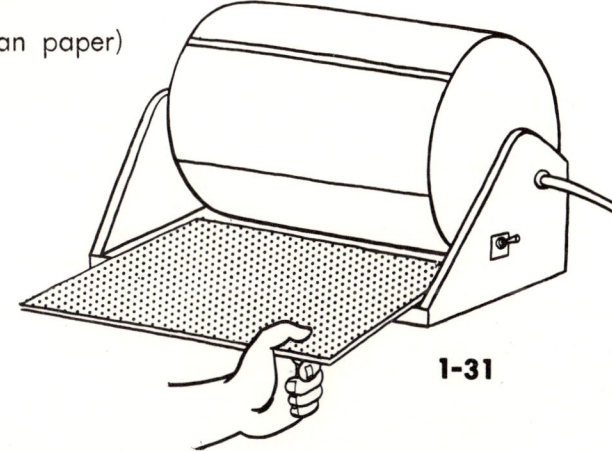

1-31

1-30 MOUNT CLOTH WITH A HAND IRON. Follow directions in 1-28. The surface of the iron should be hot enough to "sizzle" when touched with a moistened finger. Place a protective sheet on top of the cloth and "iron" the cloth on the back of the visual. Keep the iron in motion. If mounting a large visual, do a small section at a time.

1-31 USE A PHOTOGRAPHIC PRINT DRYER TO MOUNT THE CLOTH. Follow directions in 1-28. Make certain dryer is hot, then insert cloth and visual in dryer the same as drying an ordinary photographic print.

WET-MOUNTING

Wet mounting is a simple technique for backing paper instructional materials with cloth, usually unbleached muslin. Here is a mounting technique that is ideal for preserving large visual materials such as charts, maps, posters, etc. Materials to be mounted must be waterproof; if not, spray with clear plastic spray. Ideas for finishing and displaying mounts can be seen on page 23.

EQUIPMENT AND MATERIALS REQUIRED

FOR MOUNTING
- Charts
- Graphs
- Maps
- Picture Scrolls
- Opaque Projector Strips

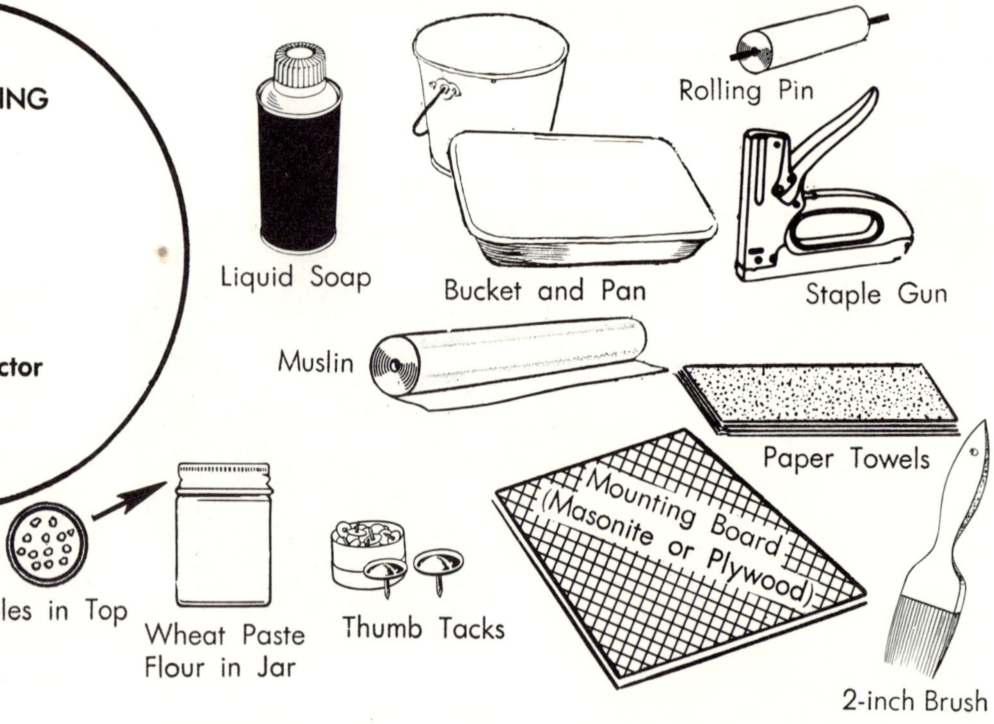

Liquid Soap

Bucket and Pan

Rolling Pin

Staple Gun

Muslin

Paper Towels

Punch Holes in Top

Wheat Paste Flour in Jar

Thumb Tacks

Mounting Board (Masonite or Plywood)

2-inch Brush

DIRECTIONS

1-32 Wash SURFACE of mounting board or table to assure a clean mount.

1-33 SOAK CLOTH THOROUGHLY to remove sizing. New cloth has a tendency to resist water.

1-34 MIX FLOUR WITH WATER. Allow about one cup of water for each lagre visual. Sift flour from jar and stir into water until paste looks like thick soup.

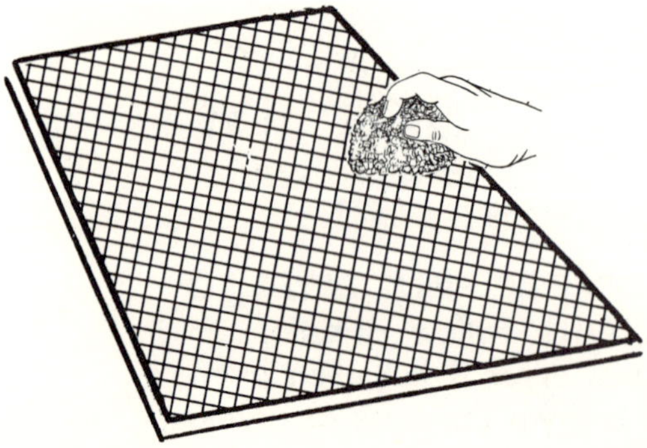

ADD LIQUID ADHESIVE if visual is thick or has a hard finish surface.

1-32   1-33   1-34

16

1-32 To 1-42

1-42 LIFT PAPER AWAY, wipe away excess paste, and check for flaws. Allow mount to dry before removing from **board.**

1-41 PLACE PAPER TOWELS OR STRIPS over all edges of visual and repeat all rolling patterns. This time roll beyond edges of visual.

1-40 ROLL FROM CENTER TO EACH CORNER, after lifting each corner to relieve tension created during the first rolling pattern. Start at the center and roll to each corner. Avoid rolling beyond the edges of visual.

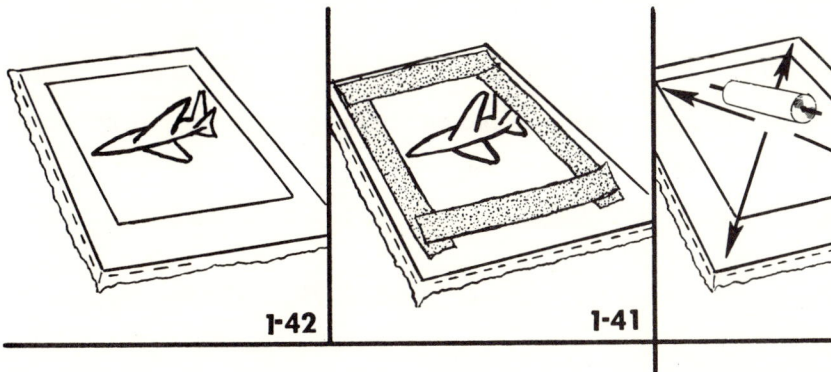

First, roll from the center to the nearest edge. Follow the rolling pattern illustrated. ➡

1-39 POSITION VISUAL, printed side up, on the cloth, within the guide marks, and smooth down with the hand. Use rolling pin to roll down the visual. Do not roll over the edges of visuals, as paste will stick to rolling pin.

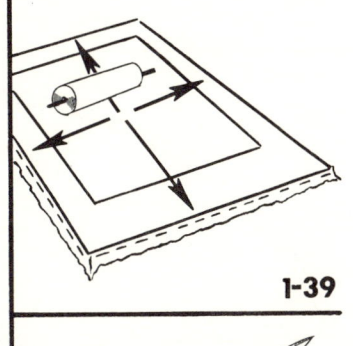

REMOVE CLOTH FROM BUCKET and squeeze out excess water.

1-35 STRETCH CLOTH EVENLY ON THE FLAT SURFACE and fasten one corner; then stretch the cloth firmly and fasten the two adjoining corners. Insert additional tacks or staples about three inches apart.

1-38 APPLY AN EVEN COAT OF PASTE over the area on which the visual is to be mounted. Apply paste slightly beyond guide marks.

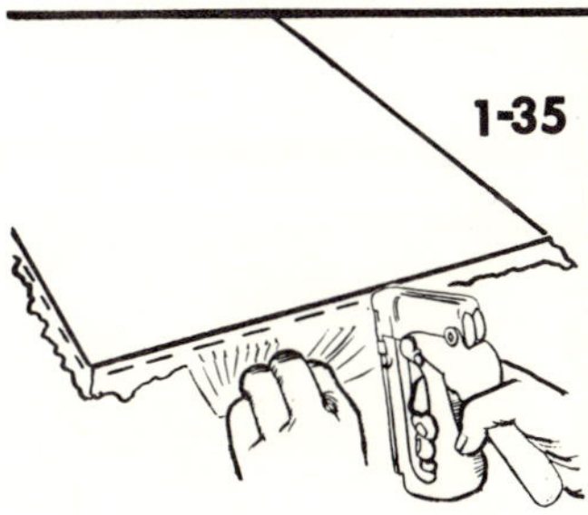

1-37 SOAK BACK OF VISUAL by placing it face down on a clean surface. Using a sponge or cloth, wet the back until it is completely soaked.

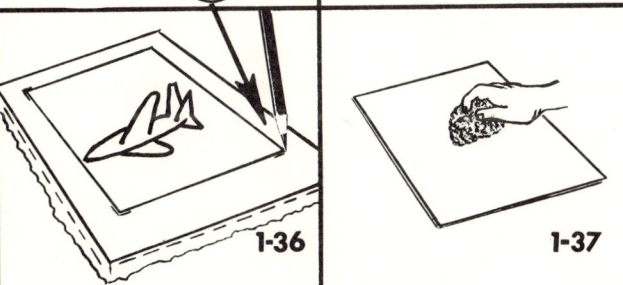

1-36 MAKE PENCIL GUIDE MARKS ON CLOTH. Place visual on the cloth and make L-shaped marks to show the area the visual will cover. ➡

17

PASSE-PARTOUT MOUNTING

Passe-partout mounting is a unique technique for preserving flat and three-dimensional instructional materials that require mounting under glass or thick plastic. Colored cloth, paper, or plastic base tapes, along with a sheet of glass or plastic, and a piece of thick mounting board are all that is required to produce an attractive mount.

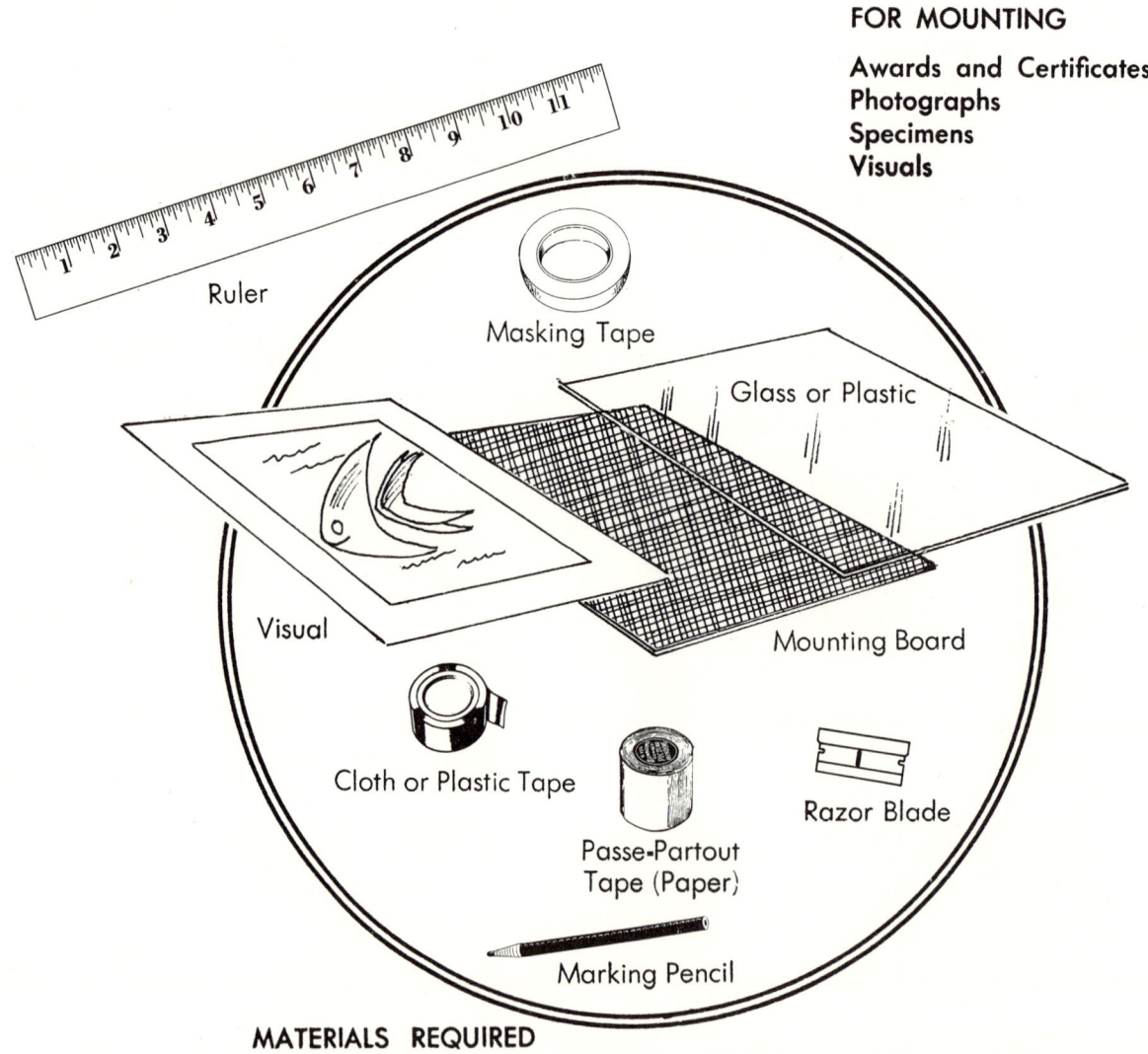

FOR MOUNTING

Awards and Certificates
Photographs
Specimens
Visuals

MATERIALS REQUIRED

1-43 To 1-49

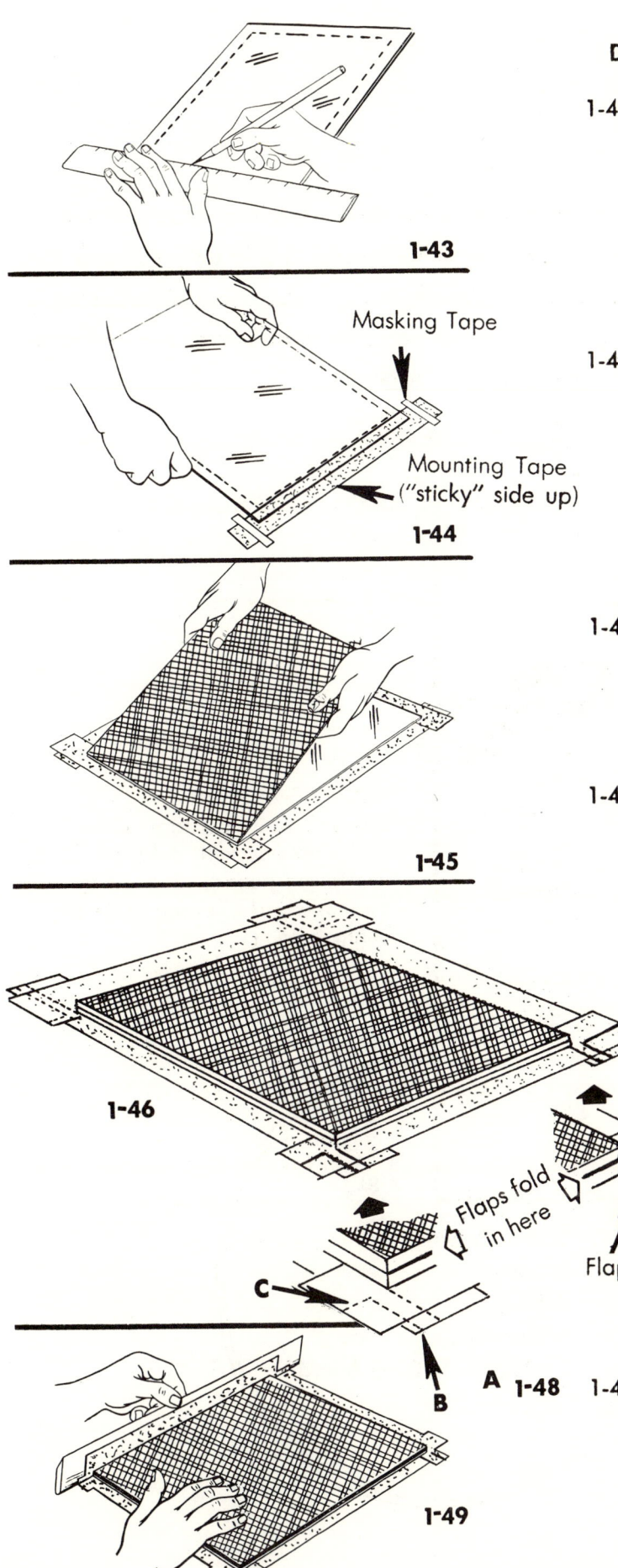

DIRECTIONS

1-43 MARK GUIDE LINE FOR TAPE on one side of the glass or plastic with a marking pencil (see 3-45).

CUT FOUR STRIPS OF TAPE, two for the horizontal sides and two for the vertical sides. Cut each strip two inches longer than the side's dimension.

1-44 POSITION GLASS, marked side up, on "sticky" side of mounting tape held in place with pieces of masking tape. Allow one inch of mounting tape to extend beyond side edge of glass. Line up guide marks with edge of tape. Repeat for remaining three sides. Wipe off guide marks and dirt.

1-45 MOUNT VISUAL ON CARDBOARD (see pages 3, 7, 24, and 25). Position mounted visual, face down, on the glass. Measure total thickness of glass and mounted visual to determne cutting of tape at each corner.

1-46 CUT TAPE CORNERS FOR FOLDING. Position mount, face down, and cut the right corner first. Place a small piece of cardboard under each corner during the cutting.

1-47 RIGHT CORNER CUT. Make cuts (A), (B), and (C) as illustrated. The distance of cut (B) from cut (A) is determined by the total thickness of mounted visual and glass.

1-48 LEFT CORNER CUT is the same as right corner cut.
TURN MOUNT AROUND so that uncut corners replace the position of cut corners, and repeat 1-47.

1-49 FOLD OVER SIDES to adhere tape to back of mount. Fold over vertical sides first. Bottom and top flaps fold in to reenforce corners. Fold over horizontal sides. A ruler under tape will help make a neater fold. See page 22 for making display easels.

HOOK N' LOOP BOARD

Hook N' Loop is a new concept in display and presentation boards. Unlike flannel or magnetic boards, Hook N' Loop boards have many times the holding power of these boards. This holding power is due to the teaming of quick-applying nylon hooked tape with countless tiny nylon loops—interlocking to anchor virtually any size or shape material or product with almost unbelievable strength. To make this board more versatile, symbols and cut-out letters are now available.

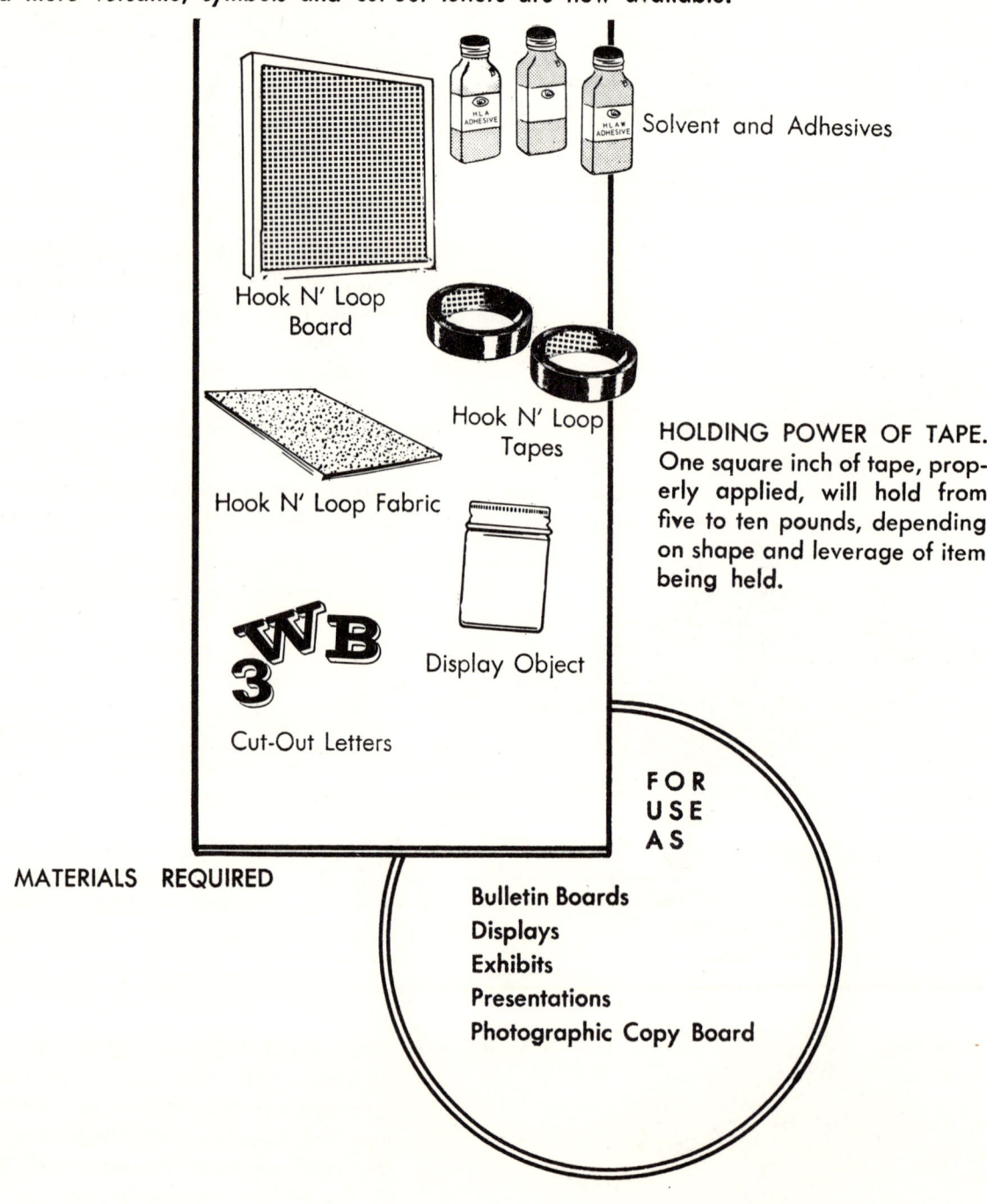

HOLDING POWER OF TAPE. One square inch of tape, properly applied, will hold from five to ten pounds, depending on shape and leverage of item being held.

MATERIALS REQUIRED

FOR USE AS
Bulletin Boards
Displays
Exhibits
Presentations
Photographic Copy Board

20

1-50 To 1-56

DIRECTIONS

1-51 FOR DISPLAYING PLASTIC OBJECTS, use a special solvent activated tape. Pieces of tape are dipped into CD-2 Hook N' Loop Tape Solvent, then attached to the plas- object. Object can then be mounted on Hook N' Loop Board.

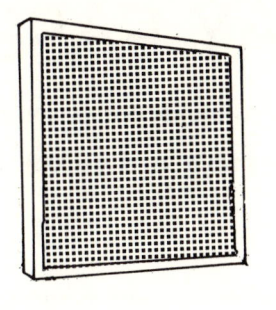

1-50

1-50 HOOK N' LOOP BOARDS are available in several styles: Add-A-Board, flat wall pannels, and folding boards.

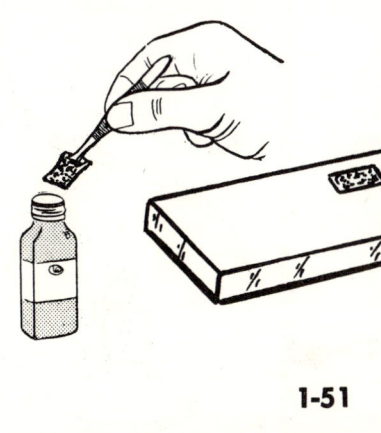

1-51

1-52

1-53

1-52 FOR GENERAL MOUNTING, use HLAW adhesive. Apply a thin coat of the adhesive to both tape and surface. Let dry for about ten minutes, then press tape to coated spot on material or object to be mounted on the board.

1-54

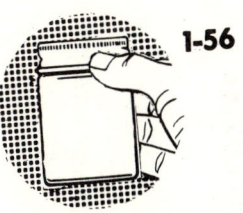

1-55

1-55 ATTACH RECOMMENDED TAPE ON OBJECT.

1-56

1-53 FOR MOUNTING MATERIALS WITH POROUS SURFACES, use HLA adhesive. This adhesive will set up on porous surfaces in about four hours. Excess adhesive may be removed with warm water.

1-54 DRY ADHESIVE BACKED TAPE is a new general purpose tape. Cut tape to correct size, immerse in room temperature water from ten to sixty seconds and position on the object to be mounted on the board. Press the tape down until the adhesive "oozes" from around the edges of the tape.

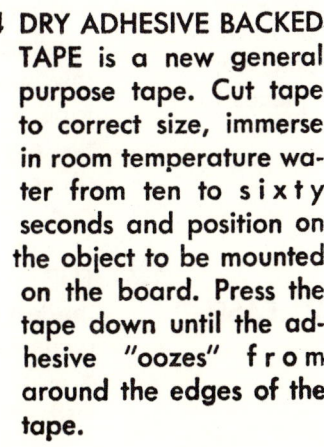

1-56 POSITION OBJECT ON HOOK N' LOOP BOARD. To release object, rotate clockwise or counterclockwise.

DISPLAY EASELS

FOLDING EASEL

ATTACHED EASEL

Here are two easy-to-make easels for displaying mounted pictures, exhibits and display items, etc.

1-57 **FINISHED EASEL** displaying a picture.

1-62 **FINISHED EASEL** attached to back of picture.

DIRECTIONS

1-58 **MAKE A PAPER PATTERN OF EASEL** (see pages 56 and 57 for directions). Cut out finished pattern.

1-59 **TRACE PATTERN TWICE** on heavy cardboard. Cut out both pieces.

1-60 **CONNECT BOTH PIECES** as illustrated. Allow 1/16-inch between pieces to permit easel to be folded. Use binding tape to hinge pieces together.

1-61 **FINISHED EASEL**

1-63 **MAKE A PAPER PATTERN OF EASEL** (see pages 56 and 57 for directions). Cut out finished pattern.

1-64 **TRACE PATTERN** once on heavy cardboard. Cut out easel.

1-65 **DRAW A LIGHT PENCIL LINE** down the back center of the picture.

1-66 **POSITION EASEL NEXT TO PENCIL GUIDE LINE.** Secure easel in place with binding or masking tape. Allow half of the tape to adhere to the easel and the other half to the back of picture.

1-67 **FLIP EASEL** over to the left side of the picture and apply a strip of tape as instructed in 1-66.

22

Materials mounted on cloth can be finished and displayed in a variety of ways. Here are a few suggested techniques for finishing and displaying materials that have been mounted on cloth. See pages 15, 16, and 17 for cloth mounting techniques.

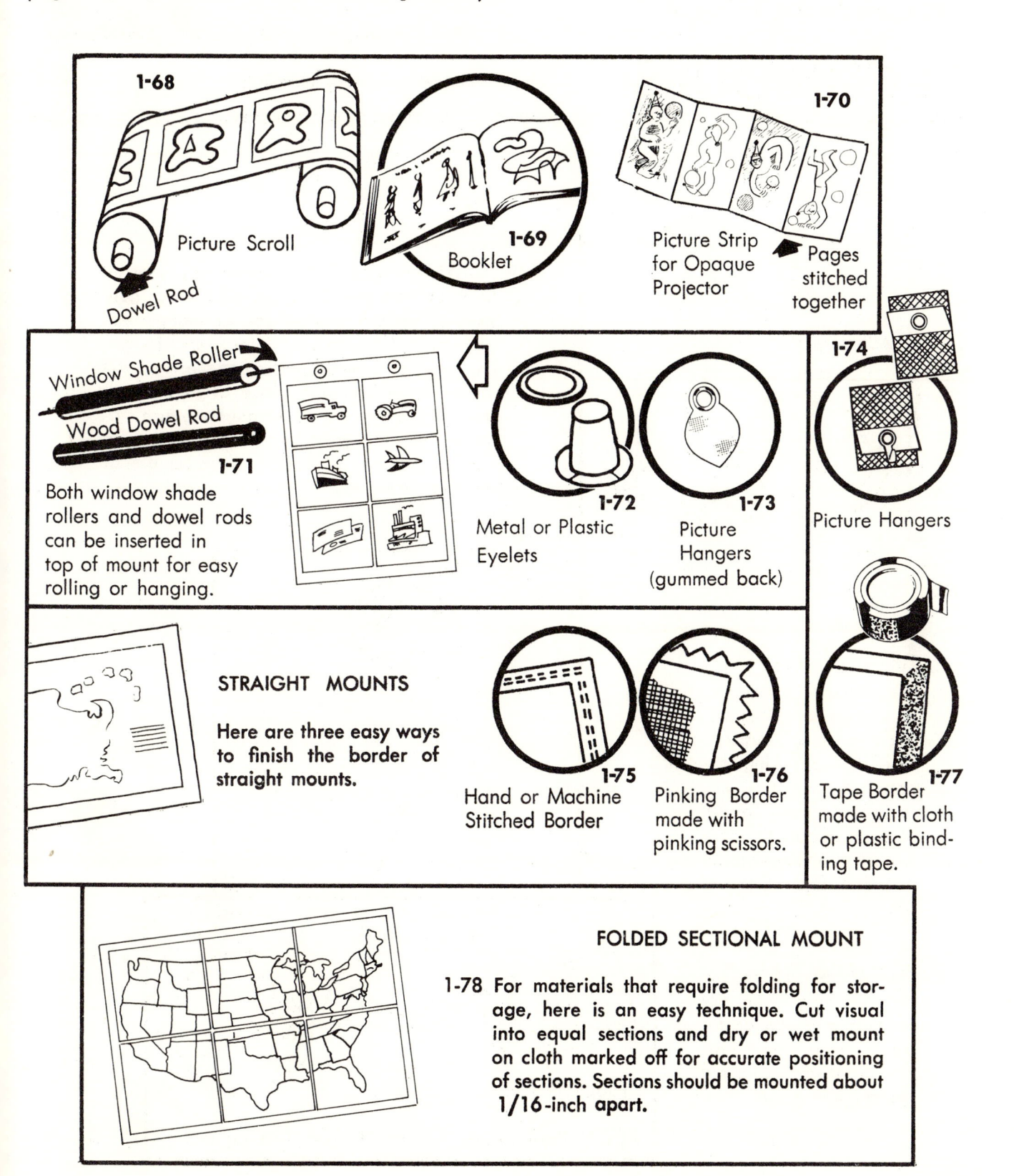

1-68 Picture Scroll — Dowel Rod

1-69 Booklet

1-70 Picture Strip for Opaque Projector — Pages stitched together

1-71 Window Shade Roller / Wood Dowel Rod — Both window shade rollers and dowel rods can be inserted in top of mount for easy rolling or hanging.

1-72 Metal or Plastic Eyelets

1-73 Picture Hangers (gummed back)

1-74 Picture Hangers

STRAIGHT MOUNTS

Here are three easy ways to finish the border of straight mounts.

1-75 Hand or Machine Stitched Border

1-76 Pinking Border made with pinking scissors.

1-77 Tape Border made with cloth or plastic binding tape.

FOLDED SECTIONAL MOUNT

1-78 For materials that require folding for storage, here is an easy technique. Cut visual into equal sections and dry or wet mount on cloth marked off for accurate positioning of sections. Sections should be mounted about 1/16-inch apart.

MISCELLANEOUS MOUNTING TECHNIQUES

There are many quality mounting materials on the market today, designed to simplify mounting problems. Illustrated and described are several recommended mounting materials.

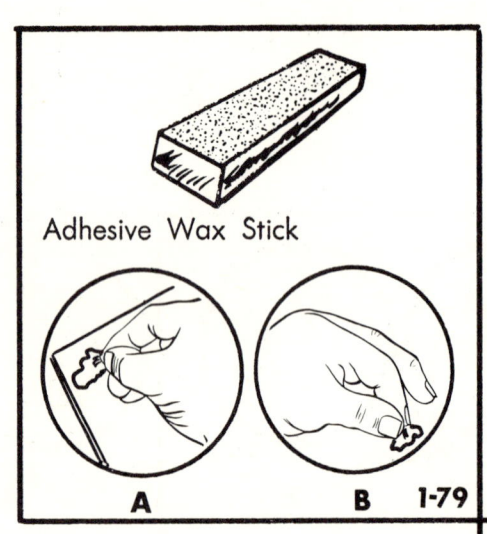

Adhesive Wax Stick

A   B   1-79

1-79 ADHESIVE WAX STICK, sometimes referred to as bulletin board wax, is a colorless, non-staining wax. It is ideal for mounting small objects, pictures, pre-cut letters, etc. To use, (A) pinch off a small portion of the wax; roll into a small ball and place at the contact point of the material to be mounted; turn material over and press firmly into position on desired surface. (B) Remove wax for use at another time.

Mounting Wax Discs

1-80

1-80 MOUNTING WAX DISCS are circular plastic discs coated on both sides with adhesive wax. They are ideal for attaching paper, pre-cut letters, etc. to most surfaces. To use, place a disc at the contact point of object to be mounted. Press object in place.

1-81 PLIABLE ADHESIVE will stick to most clean dry surfaces and can be re-used. It is ideal for mounting objects and pre-cut letters.

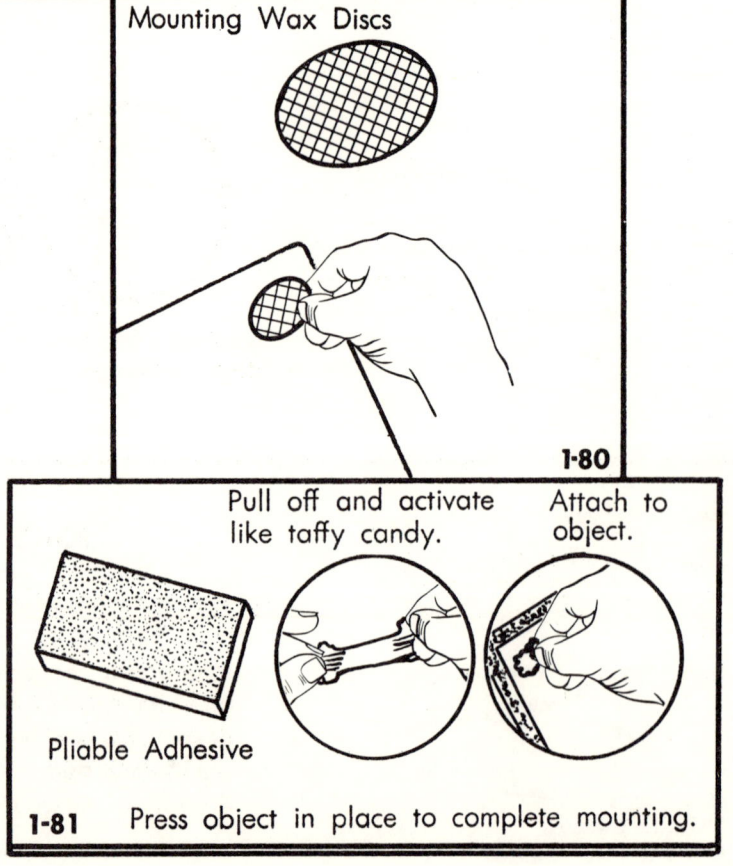

Pull off and activate like taffy candy.   Attach to object.

Pliable Adhesive

1-81   Press object in place to complete mounting.

1-79 To 1-85

Double-Coated Adhesive Tape

1-82

Adhesive Spray

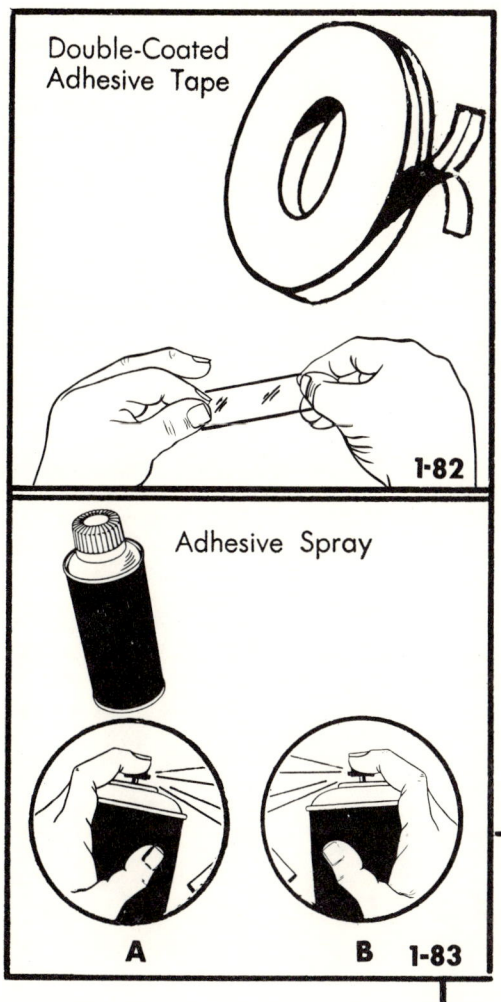

A   B   1-83

1-82 DOUBLE-COATED ADHESIVE TAPE is a thin acetate tape with pressure-sensitive adhesive on both sides. Tape will stick to most clean dry surfaces, such as metal, wood, glass, etc. To use, pull protective paper off both sides and apply to back of material to be mounted.

1-83 ADHESIVE SPRAY is a liquid adhesive in spray-can form that will stick paper and other light materials to most clean surfaces. To use, (A) spray adhesive on back of material to be mounted; (B) to assure greater adhesion, spray adhesive on second surface; allow both adhesived surfaces to dry; then join together.

1-84 LIQUID PLASTIC ADHESIVE is a fast-setting white or clear all-purpose liquid that holds on wood, paper, pottery and most porous and semi-porous materials. Apply like glue.

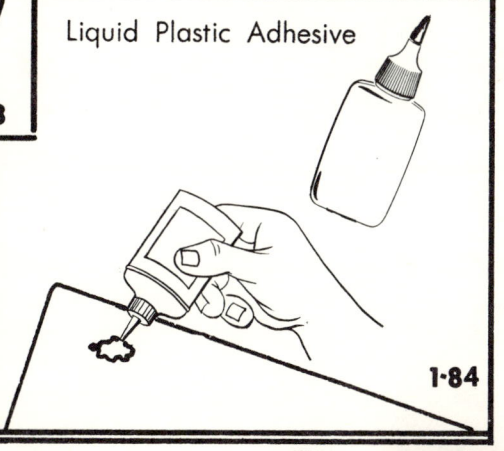

Liquid Plastic Adhesive

1-84

1-85 DRY MOUNTING CEMENT SPRAY (SPRAY MOUNT) is a thermoplastic spray-on dry mounting tissue cement that permanently bonds prints to paper, wood, glass, leather or metal. To use, spray lightly over back of material to be mounted; allow a few seconds for drying; mount like dry mounting tissue (see page 5).

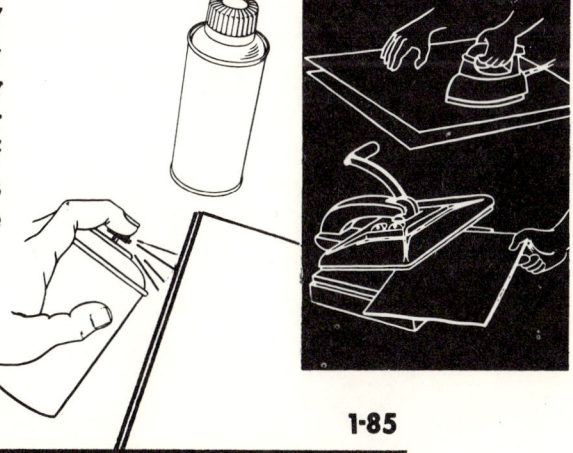

1-85

SECTION 2

LETTERING TECHNIQUES

LETTERING TECHNIQUES

There are many lettering techniques and aids on the market today, each designed to assist the user in producing legible characters on charts, graphs, maps, posters, signs, transparencies, etc.

Out of over a hundred lettering techniques and aids, twelve have been selected and presented in this section. These twelve techniques have been thoroughly tested with non-professional users and have proven to be the most practical and easy-to-use. Moreover, these techniques can be used to help solve any lettering problem.

By carefully following the directions and illustrations, one can, with a little practice, produce "professional looking" lettering on transparent and opaque instructional materials.

- ► RUBBER STAMP LETTERING
- ► STENSO LETTERING GUIDES
- ► PRE-CUT LETTERS
- ► SPRAY-ON-LETTERING
- ► PLANOTYPE LETTERS
- ► DRY-TRANSFER LETTERS
- ► TRANSPARENT TYPE PASTE-UP LETTERS
- ► PAPER TYPE PASTE-UP LETTERS
- ► WRICO LETTERING
- ► LETTERGUIDE LETTERING
- ► LEROY LETTERING
- ► VARIGRAPH LETTERING

RUBBER STAMP LETTERING

Rubber stamp letters are now being produced with technical accuracy and with features that insure correct spacing, straightness of line, and solid, clear printing. Rubber stamp sets are available in a variety of styles and sizes. Different color ink pads help provide a letter variety when using this technique.

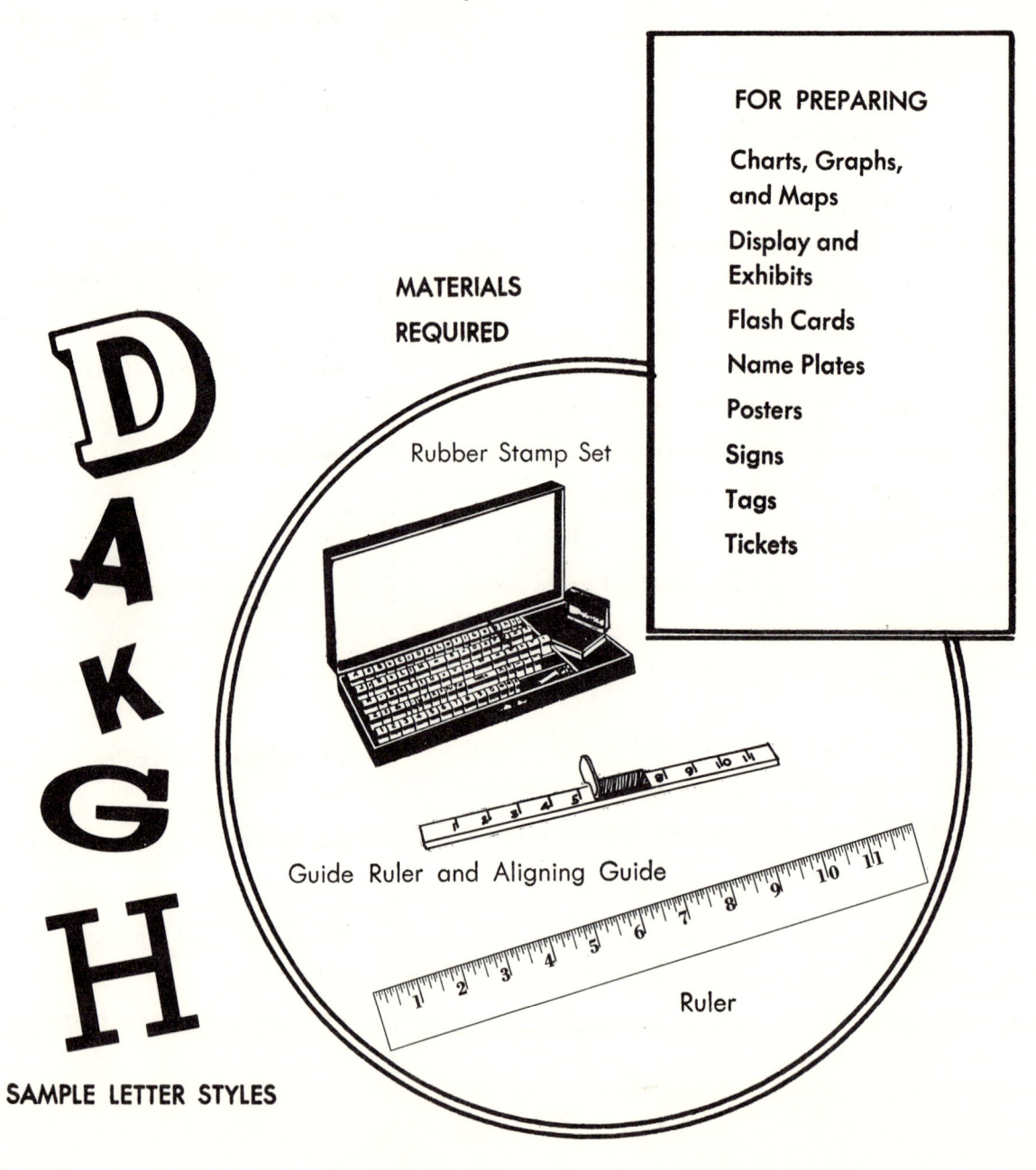

FOR PREPARING

Charts, Graphs, and Maps

Display and Exhibits

Flash Cards

Name Plates

Posters

Signs

Tags

Tickets

MATERIALS REQUIRED

Rubber Stamp Set

Guide Ruler and Aligning Guide

Ruler

D A K G H

SAMPLE LETTER STYLES

2-1 To 2-4

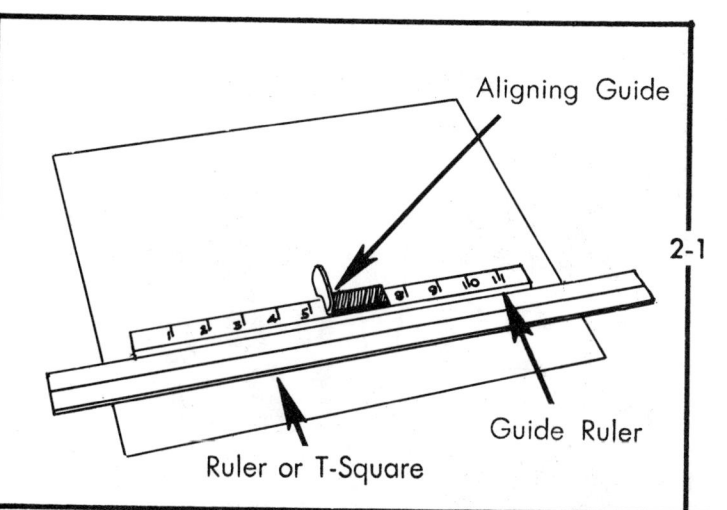

DIRECTIONS

2-1 **POSITION GUIDE RULER AND ALIGN GUIDE** for use. Make certain poster board and ruler, or T-square, are attached to working surface (see 2-51 and 2-52).

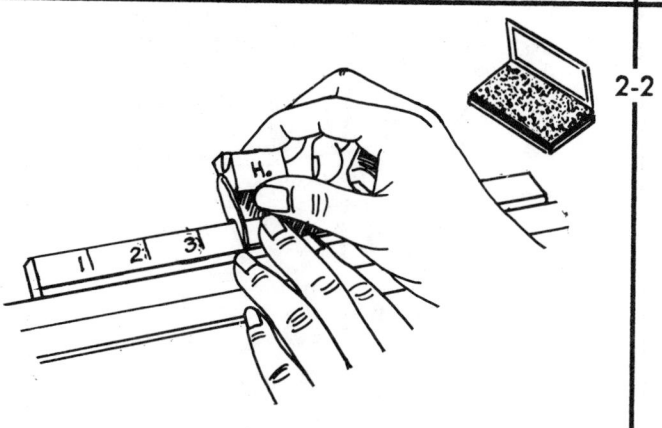

2-2 **PRINT THE FIRST LETTER** by first inking it on ink pad; then positioning against the guide ruler and next to the aligning guide. Make certain the letter is at an angle toward the guide ruler to prevent letter from making an impression before properly located. Next, move the aligning guide and letter to desired location of the first letter: then press letter down on the surface with a firm "rocking" motion. This will insure a complete letter impression.

2-3 **PRINT SECOND LETTER** and remaining letters by shifting the aligning guide and letter to next letter position and repeating step 2-2. **CORRECT LETTER SPACING** can be accomplished by using the calibrations on the guide ruler.

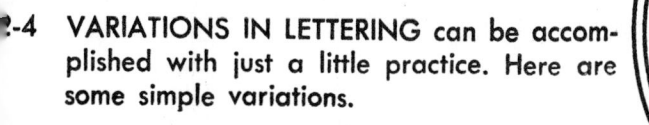

2-4 **VARIATIONS IN LETTERING** can be accomplished with just a little practice. Here are some simple variations.

29

STENSO LETTERING GUIDES

Stenso lettering guides are made of sturdy oiled cardboard, die-cut with Roman, Frontier, Modern Script, Gothic, or Old English letter styles. Letters range in size from one-half inch to twelve inches. The guides have indicator holes which make spacing and alignment easy. Each guide is perforated to fit all loose-leaf binders.

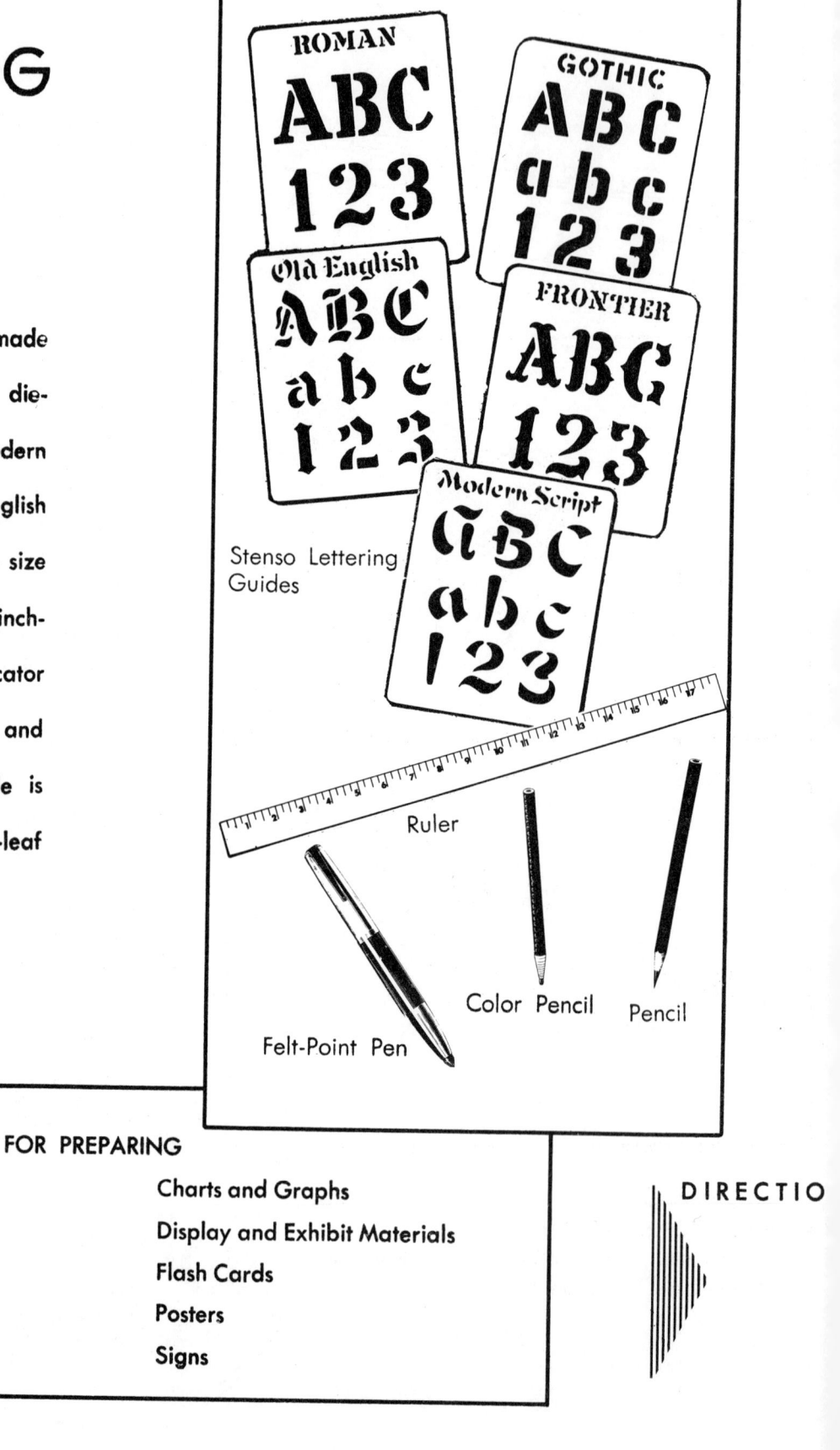

MATERIALS REQUIRED

Stenso Lettering Guides

Ruler

Felt-Point Pen

Color Pencil

Pencil

FOR PREPARING

Charts and Graphs
Display and Exhibit Materials
Flash Cards
Posters
Signs

DIRECTIO

2-5 To 2-8

2-5

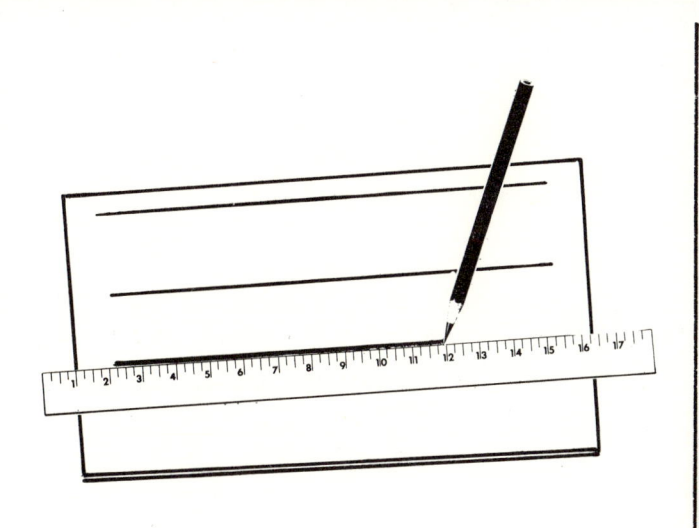

2-6

2-5 **DRAW LIGHT PENCIL GUIDE LINES** on the material to be lettered. Guide lines will be erased after lettering has been completed.

Indicator Hole — Pencil dot after tracing letter

2-6 **POSITION GUIDE ON LETTERING SURFACE** and line up indicator holes on pencil guide lines. **TRACE FIRST LETTER;** then make a light pencil dot through indicator hole at upper right of letter traced.

2-7 **MOVE STENCIL TO THE NEXT DESIRED LETTER**, lining up indicator holes on guide line. Make certain the pencil dot from the previously traced letter appears in the indicator hole at the upper left of desired letter. Repeat step 2-6 until each letter has been traced, skipping one set of indicator holes before starting the next word.

2-8 **FILL IN OPEN AREA OF LETTERS** if desired. A variety of drawing and lettering devices can be used (see pages 60 and 61). **ERASE PENCIL GUIDE LINES** and neat clear letters remain.

Dot from previous letter

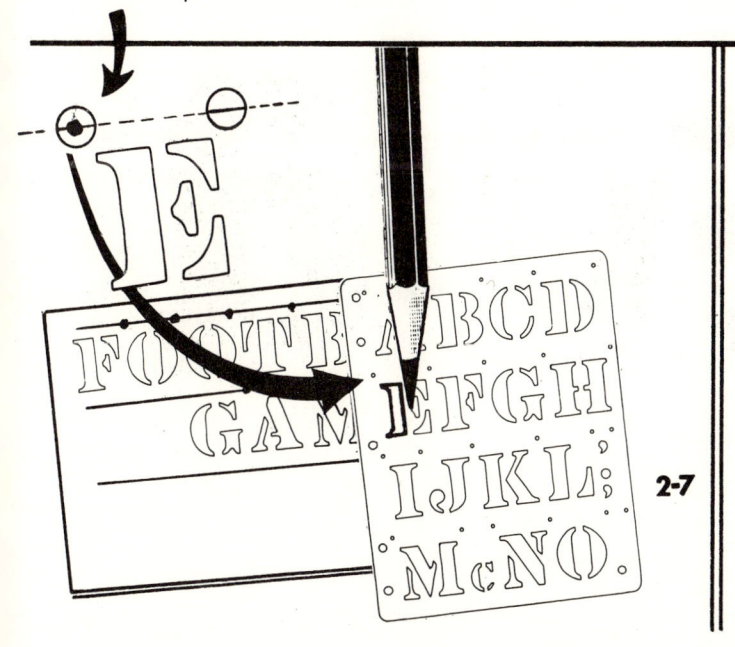

2-7

2-8

31

PRE-CUT LETTERS

Professional-looking results can be obtained with pre-cut letters. These letters are available in a variety of materials, such as cork, cardboard, paper, felt, wood, plastic, etc. A selected number of pre-cut letters are illustrated and discussed here.

2-9 GUMMED PAPER AND CARDBOARD LETTERS. Die-cut, gummed-back paper and light weight cardboard letters; applied like a postage stamp. Available in a wide range of colors, sizes, and styles.

FOR PREPARING

Charts, Graphs,
and Maps
Displays
Exhibits
Posters
Projection Titles
Signs
TV Titles

2-10 PLIABLE PLASTIC LETTERS Made of pliable plastic that will adhere to non-porous surfaces without any adhesive. Available in a variety of colors, sizes and styles.

FOR PREPARING

Displays

Exhibits

Projection Titles

Transparencies

2-11 SELF-ADHERING LETTERS Die-cut paper or cardboard letters with a pressure-sensitive adhesive backing. To use, peel off backing protective sheet and apply directly to most surfaces.

FOR PREPARING

Charts, Graphs,
and Maps
Displays
Exhibits
Posters
Projection Titles
Signs
TV Titles

2-9 To 2-13

2-12 CARDBOARD LETTERS. Die-cut from heavy cardboard. Available in color or uncolored stock, and in a wide range of sizes and styles. Ideal for preparing displays, exhibits, posters, magnetic and flannel board materials, projection and television titles, signs, etc.

2-13 PLASTIC OR TILE LETTERS. Molded plastic or tile letters. Available with pin or sanded back and with a lug base to fit into groove. Letters are usually white and can be colored for effect. Designed for displays, exhibits, posters, projected and television titles, etc.

CARDBOARD LETTERS

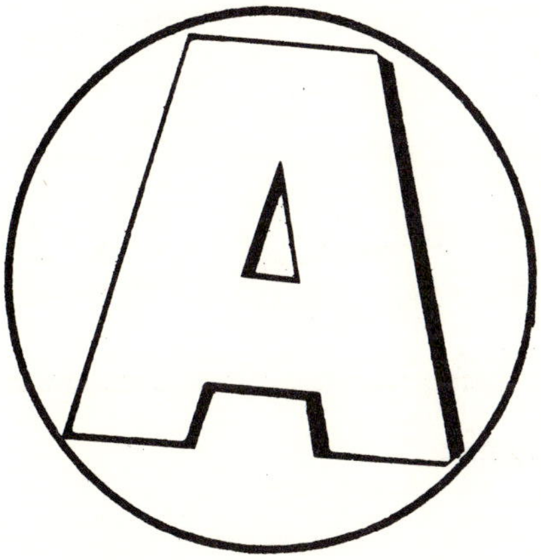

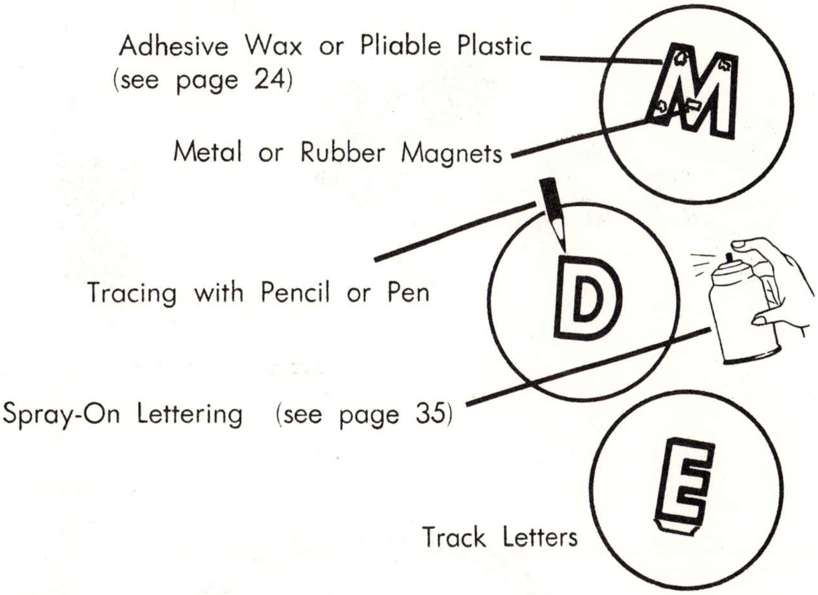

2-12

Adhesive Wax or Pliable Plastic (see page 24)

Metal or Rubber Magnets

Tracing with Pencil or Pen

Spray-On Lettering (see page 35)

Track Letters

PLASTIC OR TILE LETTERS

2-13

Pin Back

Letters easily pin into soft surfaces, such as cellotex, homosote, wallboard, cork, etc.

Sand Back

Can be glued on hard surfaces, such as glass, metal, wood, etc.

Track Letters

Lug base fits into wood or metal grooved bases.

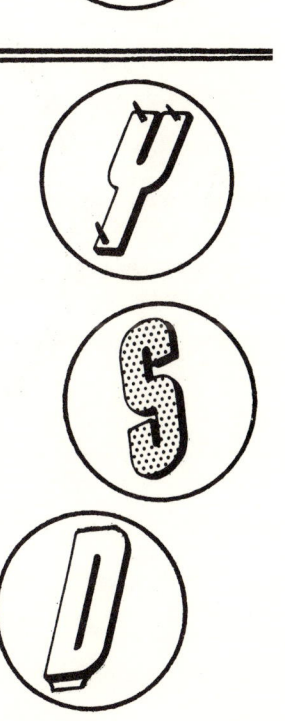

33

SPRAY-ON-LETTERING

Quick, attractive posters and signs can be made with pre-cut letters, numbers, symbols, etc., and spray-can colors. A variety of enamels and flourescent paints are now available in easy-to-use spray-cans. Here are a few easy steps for preparing colorful visual materials.

MATERIALS REQUIRED

Pre-Cut Letters and Symbols

Spray-Can Colors

Protective Cardboard

Poster Board

FOR PREPARING

Displays
Exhibits
Posters
Signs

IDEAS!

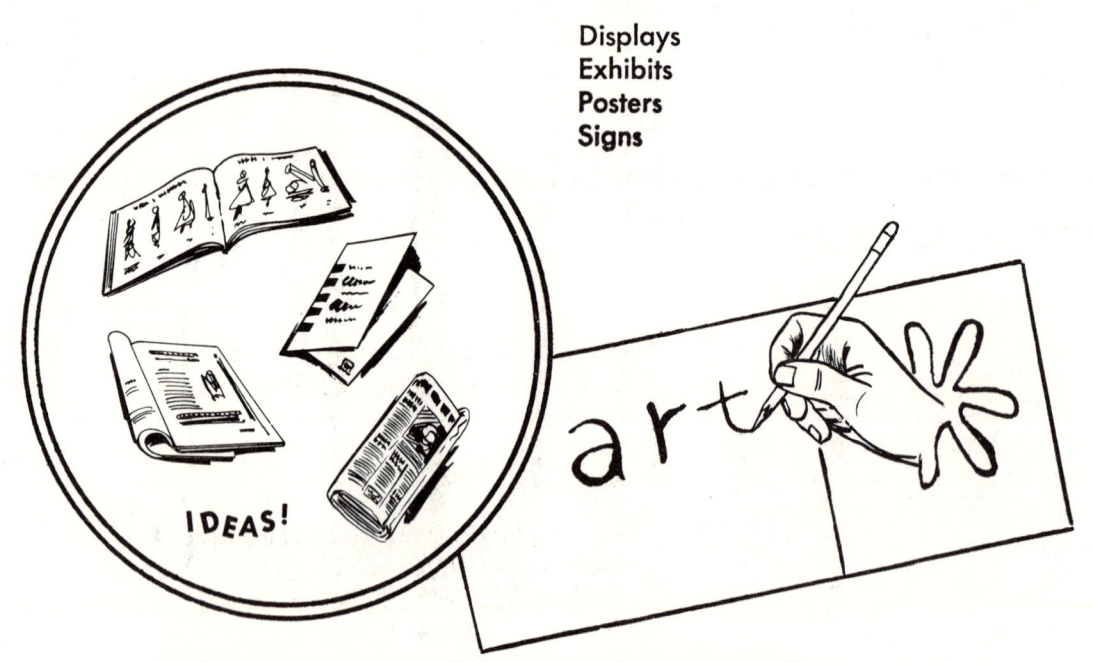

PREPARE A ROUGH SKETCH OF POSTER OR SIGN. Ideas can come from magazines, newspapers brochures, etc. **CUT OUT VISUALS** from cardboard or heavy construction paper (see Section 3 for visual techniques).

34

2-14 To 2-19

DIRECTIONS

2-14 POSITION LETTERS ON SURFACE to which lettering is to be sprayed. Use a straight piece of cardboard or ruler as a guide for aligning letters.

2-15 SPRAY FIRST COLOR on desired section of poster board, using a piece of cardboard to protect the surface on which second color is to be sprayed. Hold spray can about fifteen inches above the letters and spray back and forth to assure even coverage of paint. Allow letter to dry before removing from poster board.

2-16 POSITION VISUAL OR SYMBOL on the unpainted section of the poster board. Place a piece of cardboard on the lettered section to prevent the second color from spraying on the first color.

2-17 SPRAY SECOND COLOR on unpainted surface. Follow directions in 2-15.

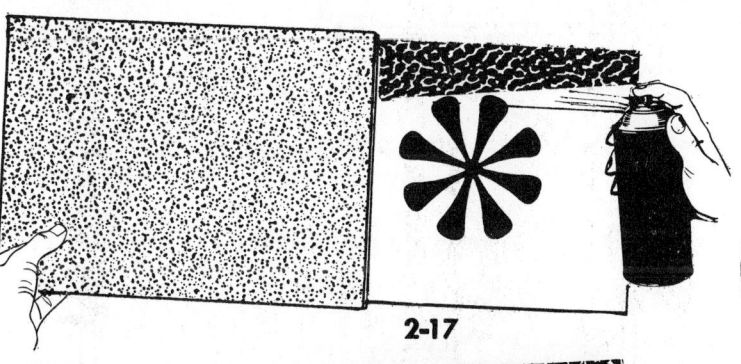

2-18 AVOID POSSIBLE CLOGGING OF SPRAY CAN by turning can upside down and spraying short jets of clear gas after completing job.

2-19 FINISHED SIGN!

PLANOTYPE LETTERS

Planotype letters are made of easy-to-use pliable plastic. Letters and symbols have a pressure-sensitive adhesive back and will adhere, on contact, to such materials as paper, cardboard, plastics, wood, glass, stone, metals, chalkboards, etc. No additional glue or adhesive is necessary. Four type faces in ten sizes (5/32-to 1½-inch) plus six colors in opaque and transparent plastic are available.

MATERIALS REQUIRED

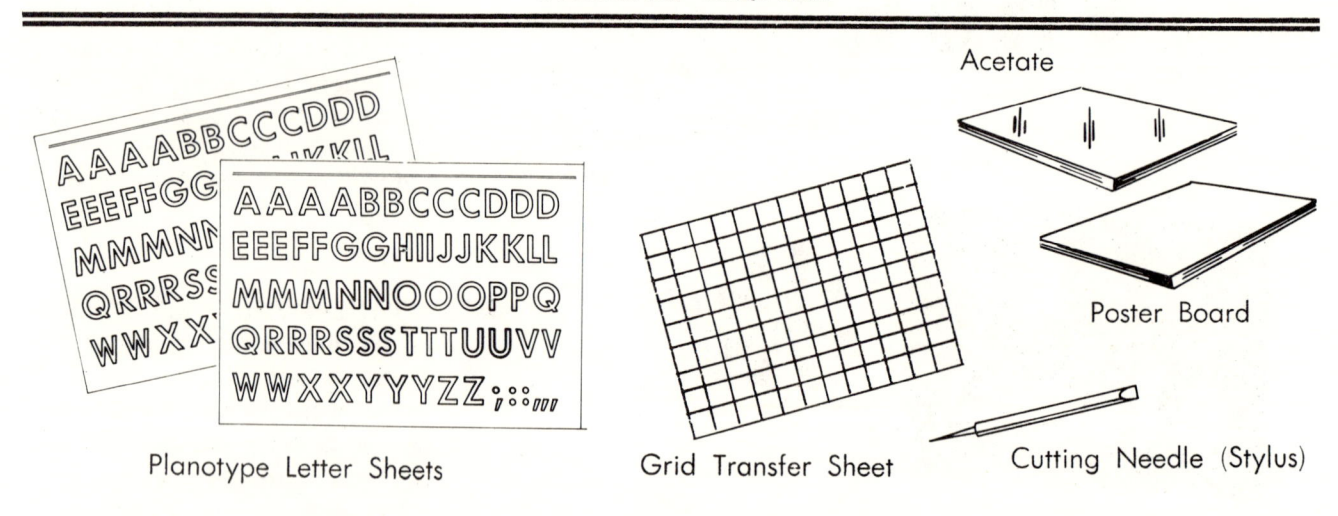

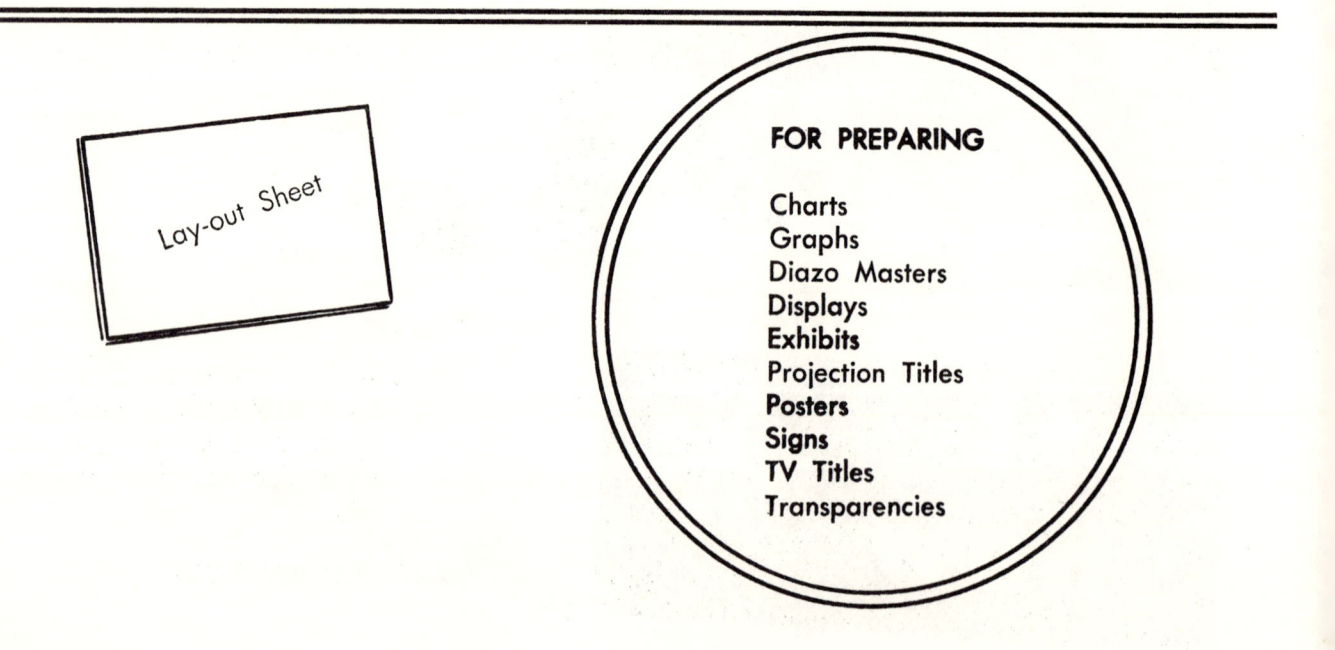

Planotype Letter Sheets

Grid Transfer Sheet

Acetate

Poster Board

Cutting Needle (Stylus)

Lay-out Sheet

FOR PREPARING

Charts
Graphs
Diazo Masters
Displays
Exhibits
Projection Titles
Posters
Signs
TV Titles
Transparencies

36

DIRECTIONS

2-20 PEEL DESIRED LETTERS off aluminum sheet with a cutting needle or similar device. Press index finger against part of letter already lifted and peel away.

PLACE REMOVED LETTER face up on blank side of lay-out sheet, preferably in desired order and lined up.

2-21 PICK UP EACH LETTER in proper sequence with the grid transfer sheet. Hold it over first letter to be picked up. Then, when letter appears in desired position, press transfer sheet against the letter. Letter will transfer from lay-out sheet to transfer sheet. Repeat the same procedure for remaining letters.

2-22 PLACE LETTERS IN DESIRED POSITION by taking the transfer sheet with the letters on it. Hold the sheet directly above the area on which the letters are to go and press the sheet against it. Carefully peel away the transfer sheet. Unless removed, the letters will stay indefinitely.

DRY-TRANSFER LETTERS

Dry-Transfer letters are pressure-sensitive letters printed on an acetate sheet and are easily transferred to most clean, dry surfaces. Letters are sharply defined and of high reproduction quality. Letters will adhere to paper, wood, cardboard, glass, metal, film, etc. There are over fifty styles in black, white, and colors.

FOR PREPARING

Artwork
Charts, Graphs, and Maps
Diazo Masters
Displays and Exhibits
Paper Offset Masters
Posters
Projection Titles
Television Titles
Transparencies

MATERIALS REQUIRED

Dry-Transfer Letter Sheets

Ruler

Pencil

38

DIRECTIONS

Figure 2-23: Pencil Guide Line

Figure 2-24: Printed Guide Line

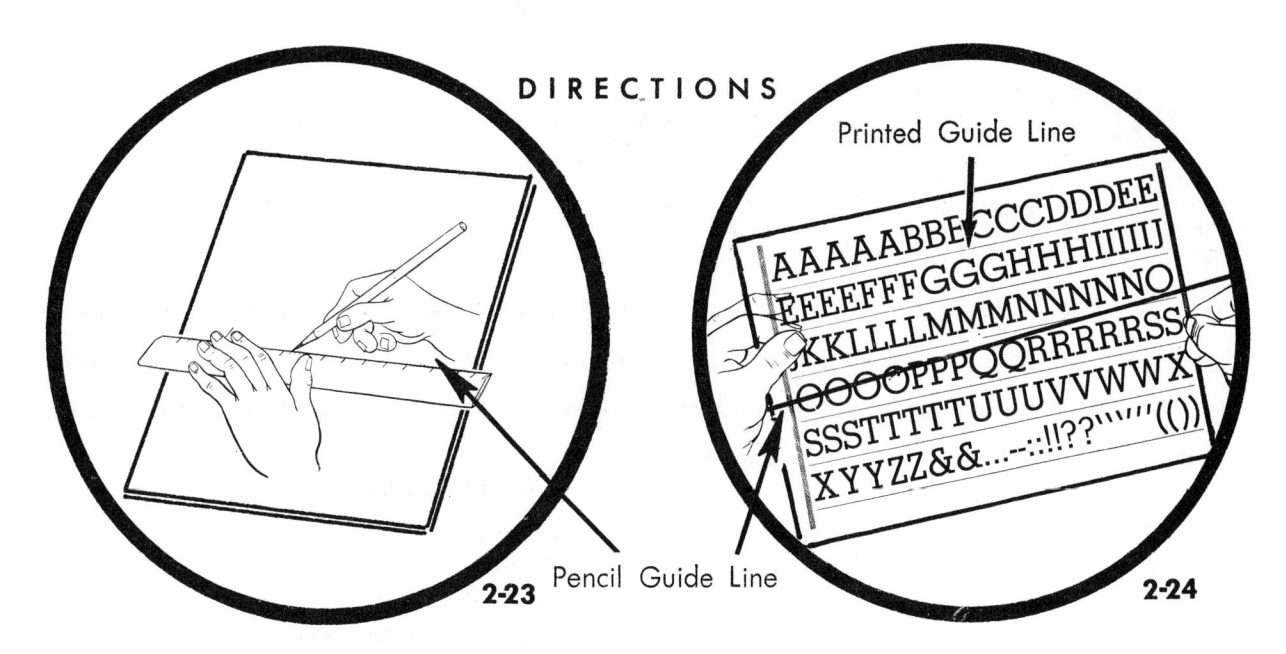

2-23 DRAW A LIGHT PENCIL GUIDE LINE on the surface to which lettering is to be applied. Some transfer letters make use of their protective sheet as a guide for aligning the letters. IF LETTERING ON ACETATE, draw the guide line on a sheet of paper or cardboard and place under the acetate. REMOVE BACKING SHEET.

2-25 RUB LETTER DOWN with the thumb nail or pencil point. Try to confine rubbing to letter area only.

2-24 POSITION LETTER SHEET over surface to be lettered on so that the first letter is in the desired location. Align guide line of letter sheet with pencil guide line. This will assure perfect alignment.

2-26 CAREFULLY PEEL OFF THE LETTER SHEET, leaving the desired letter in place. If letter fails to completely transfer, return sheet to surface and repeat the rubbing. CAREFULLY REMOVE PENCIL GUIDE LINES.

LETTERS APPLIED TO PAPER OFFSET MASTER SHOULD be gone over with a soft cloth saturated with rubber cement thinner.

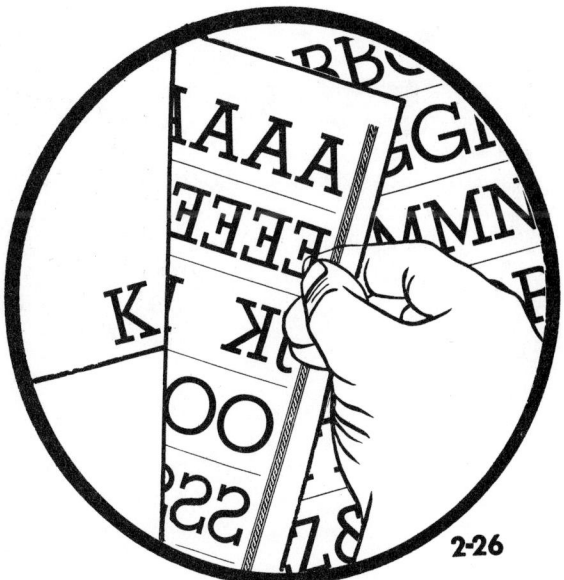

TRANSPARENT TYPE PASTE-UP LETTERS

Transparent paste-up letters, printed on the back side of a thin acetate sheet, provide a rapid convenient way of affixing letters to the desired surface, and are designed mainly for work where paste-up letters are desired. There are over two hundred letter styles and sizes in black, white, and colors. Each letter has its own guide line for perfect alignment.

FOR PREPARING

Artwork
Charts
Diazo Masters
Displays and Exhibits
Graphs
Maps
Photographic Posters
Projected Titles
Television Titles
Transparencies

Sample Letter Styles

MATERIALS REQUIRED

Frisket Knife

Cutting Needle (Stylus)

Paste-Up Letter Sheets

Pencil

Razor Blade

DIRECTIONS

2-27 LAY LETTER SHEET FACE DOWN. Loosen backing sheet by peeling away from letter sheet. Replace loosely and turn sheet over.

2-28 DRAW LIGHT PENCIL GUIDE LINE on surface to be lettered. If lettering is to be done on acetate or glossy surface (see 2-23) for making guide line.

2-29 LIGHTLY CUT AROUND DESIRED LETTER, including the printed guide line. Cutting can be done with point of stylus, razor blade, or frisket knife. Do not cut through the backing sheet.

REMOVE CUT OUT LETTER FROM SHEET by inserting the point of cutting instrument under the leter and press it against the point. Lift it away from sheet.

2-30 LINE UP PRINTED GUIDE LINE with drawn pencil guide line and press the letter in place. Burnish lightly with beveled end of stylus so that changes can be made before final burnishing.

2-31 WHEN LETTERING IS COMPLETE and corrections have been made, use beveled end of stylus to burnish firmly all letters, except the printed guide line. Cut away the printed line and complete the burnishing until all edges become invisible. Erase pencil guide line.

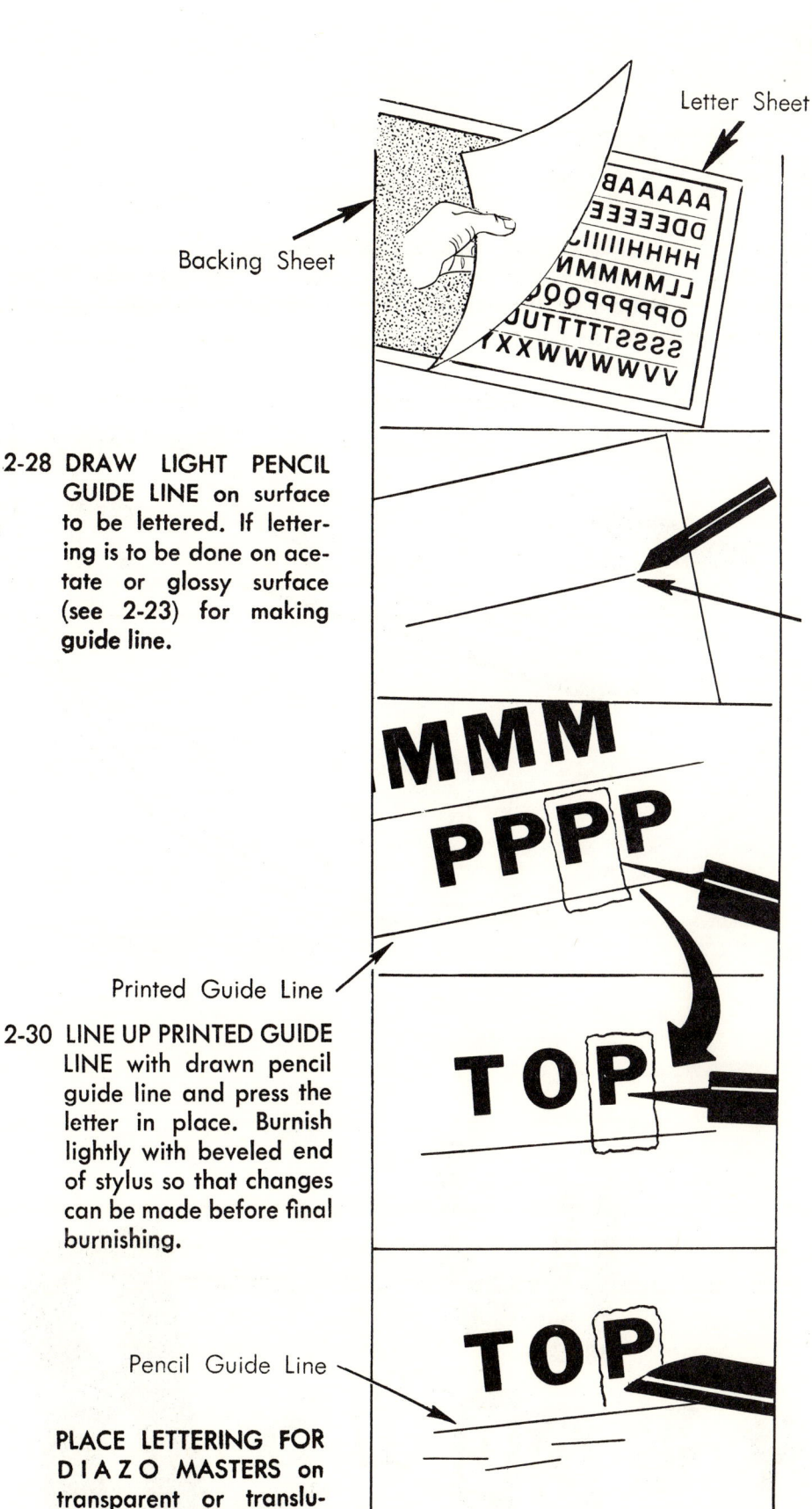

PLACE LETTERING FOR DIAZO MASTERS on transparent or translucent surface (clear or frosted acetate).

PAPER TYPE PASTE-UP LETTERS

Paper type paste-up letters are printed on paper or light weight cardboard. Here is an ideal lettering technique where precision typesetting is desired. Paper type usually comes in individual tabs having a character printed on it in relation to the bottom of the tab and within a margin to the right. Typesetting is achieved with the aid of a composing device or ruler.

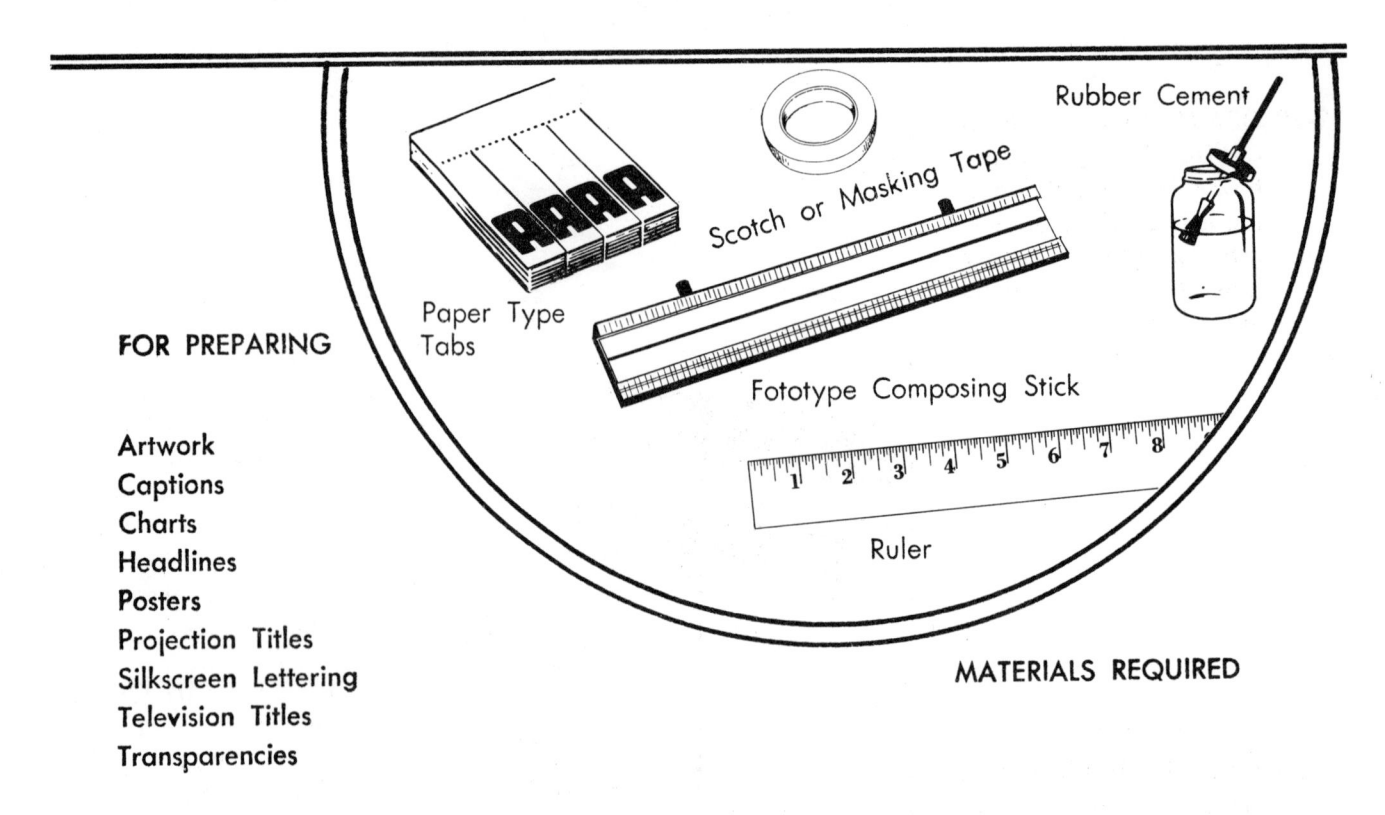

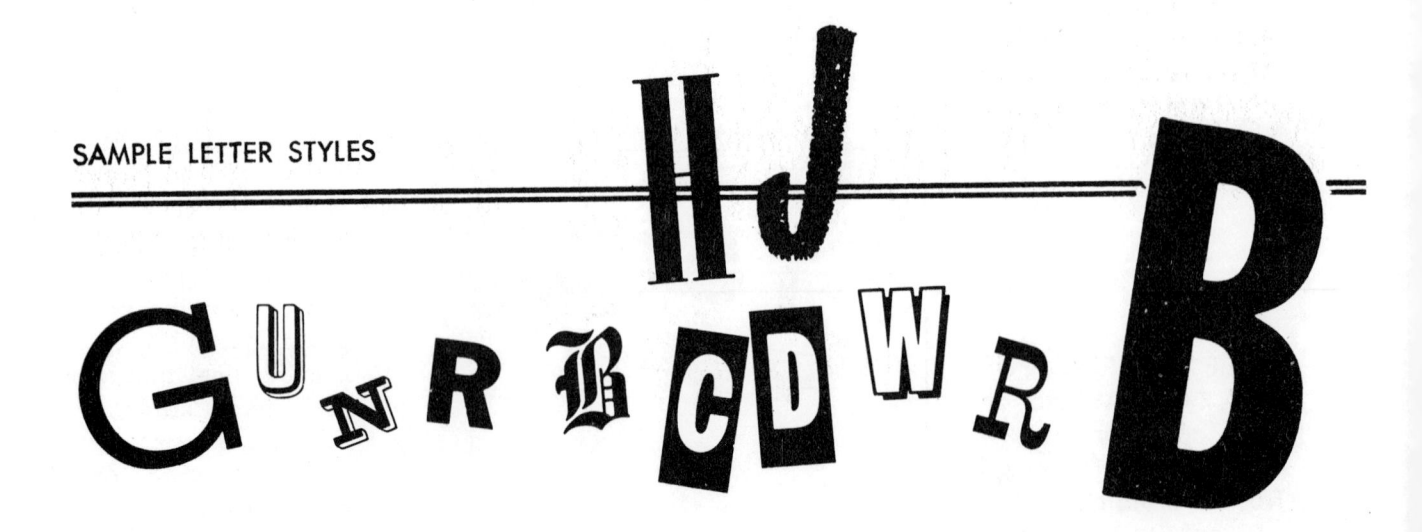

FOR PREPARING

Artwork
Captions
Charts
Headlines
Posters
Projection Titles
Silkscreen Lettering
Television Titles
Transparencies

MATERIALS REQUIRED

- Paper Type Tabs
- Scotch or Masking Tape
- Fototype Composing Stick
- Ruler
- Rubber Cement

SAMPLE LETTER STYLES

42

DIRECTIONS

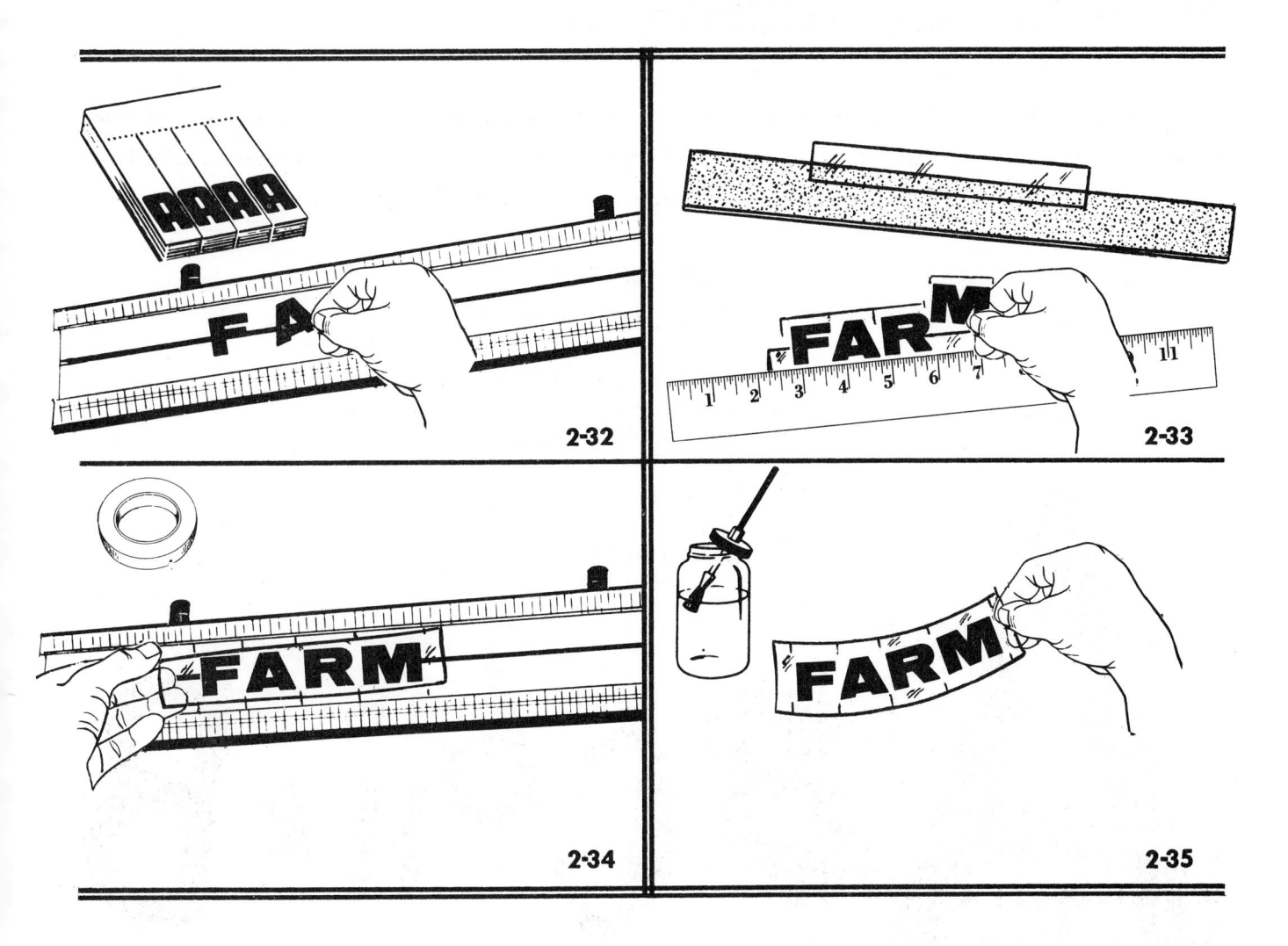

2-32 **PULL OFF CHARACTERS FROM TABS** and assemble, spelling one word at a time.

SNAP EACH LETTER IN PLACE IF A FOTO-TYPE COMPOSING STICK IS USED. This device aligns and spaces letters automatically. Blue side of letter should be facing up.

2-34 **APPLY TAPE TO COMPLETED LINE OF LETTERING.** Use double-coated adhesive tape if rubber cement is not desired for adhering letters to new surface.

2-33 **USE A RULER TO ALIGN AND SPACE THE LETTERS** if a composing stick is not available. First, place a strip of tape on back of ruler. If double-coated adhesive tape is used, rubber cement will not be needed for adhering letters to new surface. Next, anchor each letter against ruler. After word has been completed, lift from ruler.

2-35 **MOUNT COMPOSED LETTERS ON DESIRED SURFACE** with rubber cement, or if double-coated tape has been used, simply press the letters in place.

WRICO LETTERING

Wrico lettering sets consist of a transparent plastic lettering guide, guide holder, and a variety of lettering pens. Professional looking letters in a variety of styles, sizes and colors can be produced with just a little practice. Wrico lettering guides range in letter size from 1/16-inch to four inches.

FOR PREPARING

Charts, Graphs, and Maps
Diazo Masters
Displays and Exhibits
Flash Cards
Paper Offset Masters
Posters
Projected Titles
Signs
Television Titles
Transparencies

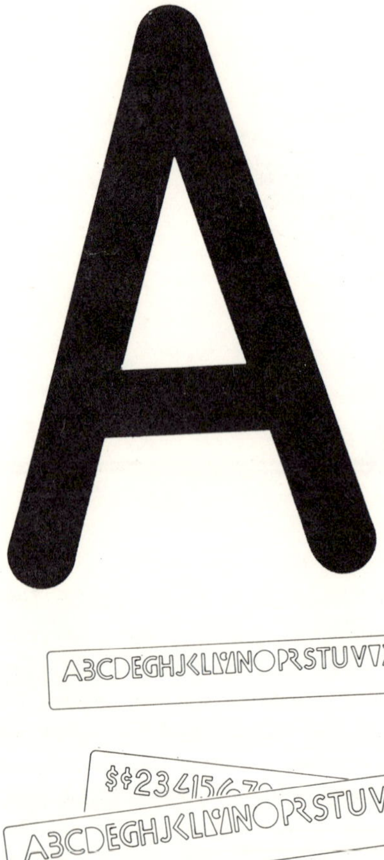

SAMPLE LETTER STYLES

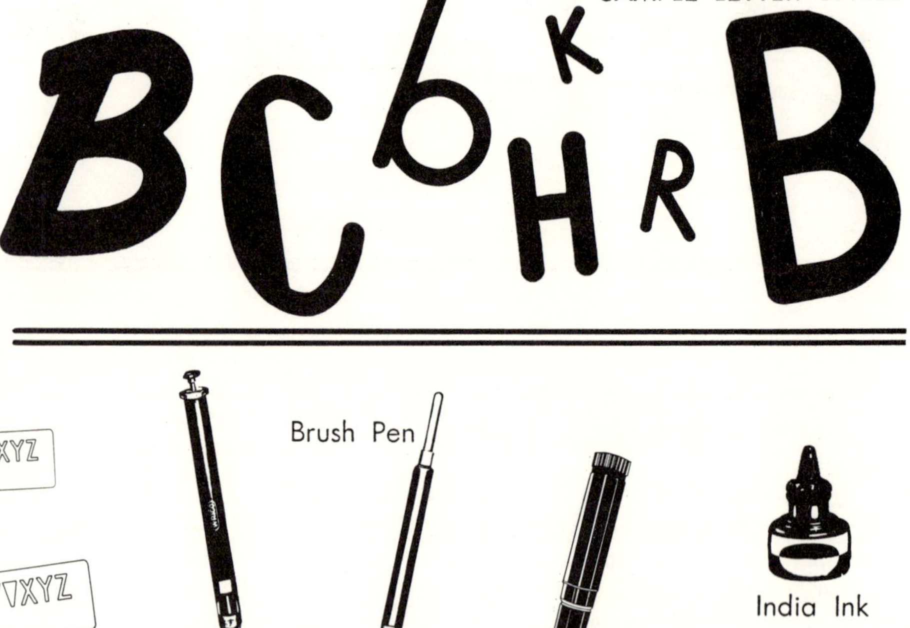

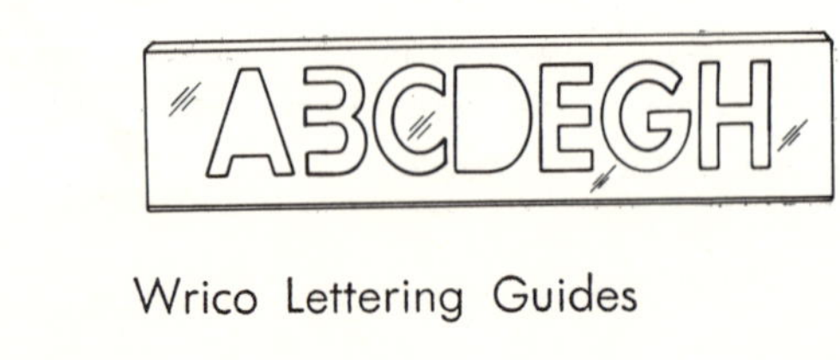

Print Pen

Brush Pen

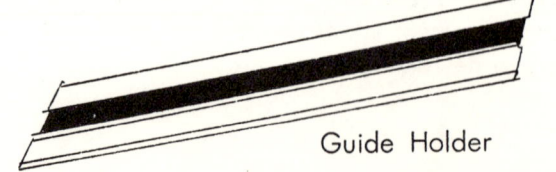

Pen HF

India Ink

Wrico Lettering Guides

Guide Holder

2-36 To 2-40

DIRECTIONS

2-36 FILL BRUSH PEN by dipping pen in ink and working plunger up and down. Adjust as illustrated.

2-37 FILL PRINT PEN by using eye dropper or dropper-stopper of ink bottle. Start with 1½ drops. Work plunger up and down to start ink flowing and to adjust flow.

FILL FELT PENS by using eye dropper and following instructions with pen.

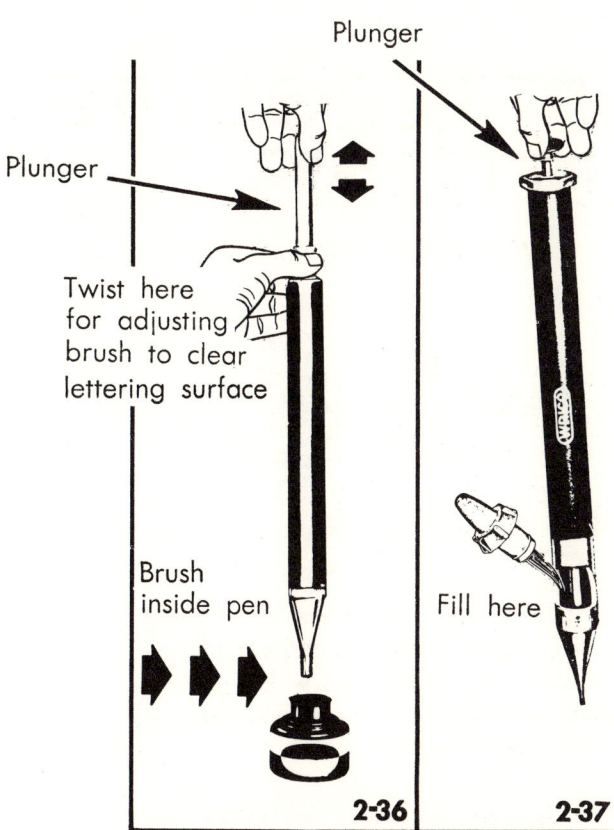

2-38 PLACE GUIDE HOLDER on surface to be lettered. Insert desired guide in channel of holder. This permits the guide to be moved smoothly to left or right without touching the surface to be lettered.

2-39 INSERT PEN IN THE FIRST DESIRED LETTER. Hold it vertically, and glide the pen through the letter form until the complete letter has been formed. Slide guide to next letter and repeat same instructions.

2-40 CLEAN PEN by disassembling the parts and soaking in liquid pen cleaner or in warm water to which a small quantity of liquid soap has been added.

LETTERGUIDE LETTERING
(Mechanical Tracing)

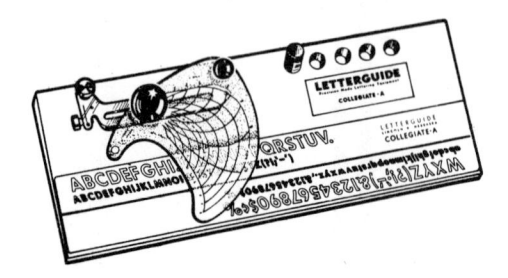

The Letterguide system consists of an adjustable scriber, a variety of templets, and accessories which go together to solve a large number of lettering problems.

The adjustable scriber is calibrated so that with a single adjustment letters can be enlarged, reduced, and slanted from just one templet. The templets (lettering guides) are designed to align horizontally with a T-square or ruler. Many letter styles and sizes are available.

Accessories include India Ink pens, reservoir pens, ball point pens, lead clutch, silk screen knife, and swivel knife, all of which fit into the scriber.

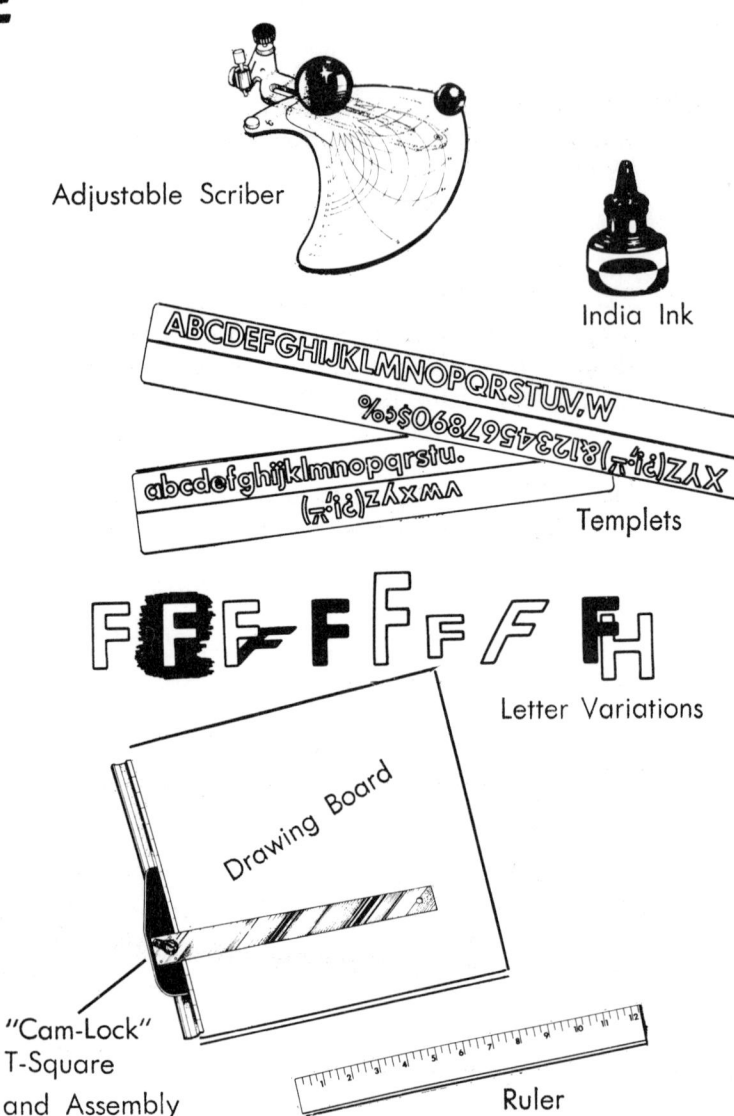

EQUIPMENT AND MATERIALS

Adjustable Scriber

India Ink

Templets

Letter Variations

Drawing Board

"Cam-Lock" T-Square and Assembly

Ruler

FOR PREPARING

Artwork
Charts
Diazo Masters
Displays and Exhibits
Fluid Duplicating Masters
Graphs
Maps

Paper Offset Masters
Posters
Projected Titles
Signs
Silk Screen Lettering
Silkscreen Lettering
Television Titles
Transparencies
Wax Duplicating Stencils

SAMPLE LETTER STYLES

JKD FDE BCFG DECD

2-41 To 2-50

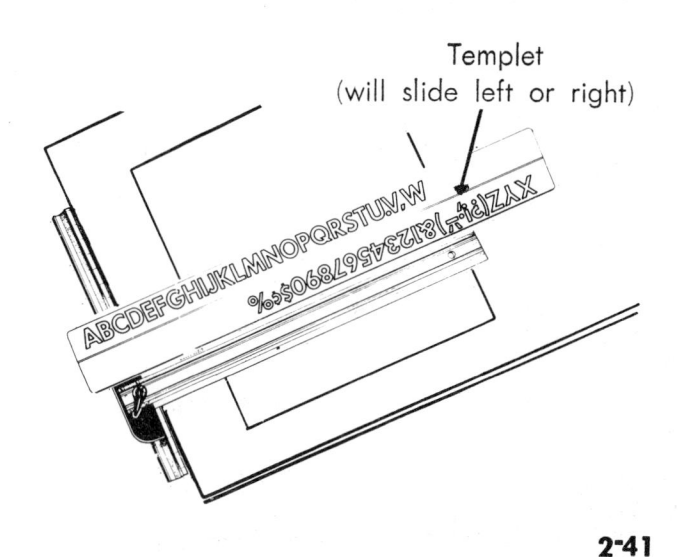

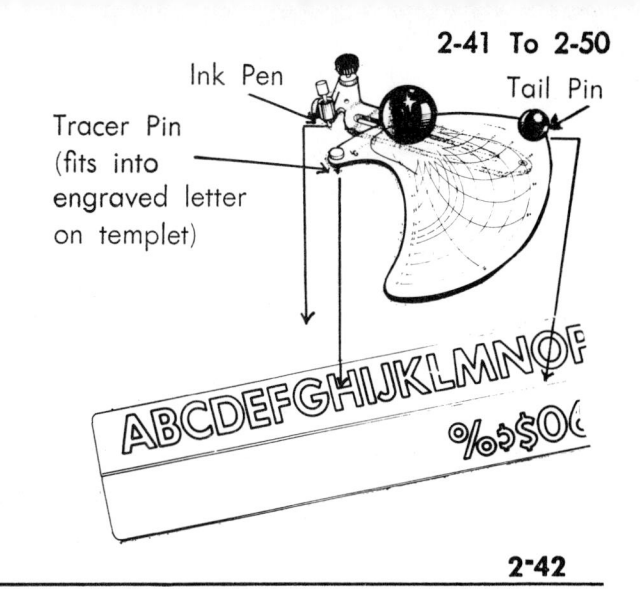

2-41 ALIGN MATERIAL TO BE LETTERED on drawing board or table with T-square or ruler. Fasten with tacks or tape (see 2-51). Secure T-Square with lock. Position templet on T-square.

2-42 PLACE DESIRED POINT IN ADJUSTED SCRIBER and position on templet by placing tail pin in center slot of templet and tracer pin in desired letter groove.

2-43 TO LETTER, hold templet in place with left hand and trace letter with right hand. For next letter, and remaining letters, slightly raise the scriber (leaving the tail pin in the center slot) and slide templet to position next letter and repeat directions for first letter.

2-44 SPACE LETTERS optically rather than mechanically. The open area between letters should appear optically equal.

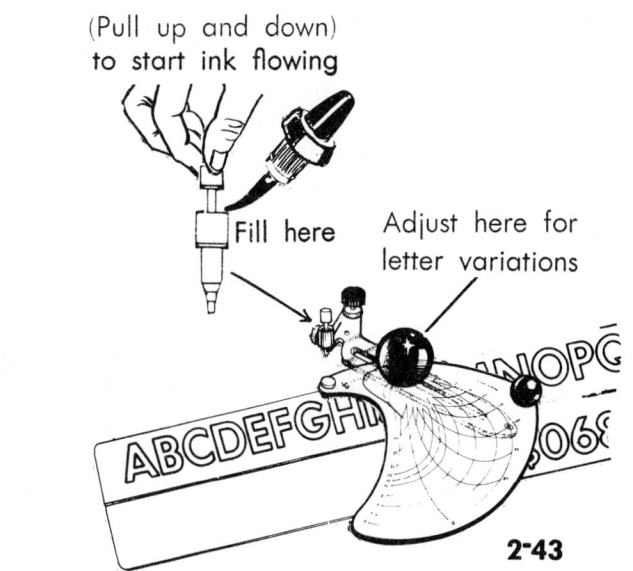

2-44 Mechanical Spacing   Optical Spacing

ACCESSORIES

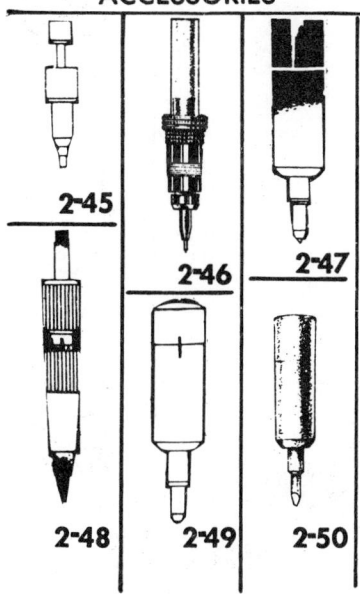

2-45 INK PEN for ink lettering on paper, cardboard, acetate, etc.

2-46 RESERVOIR PEN, a fountain-type pen holding a large supply of ink which will last for several weeks.

2-47 BALL POINT PEN STYLUS for lettering on paper, cardboard, wax stencils, duplicating masters, and paper offset masters with special ink.

2-48 LEAD CLUTCH for pencil lettering and direct lettering on paper offset masters when equipped with reproducing lead.

2-49 SILK SCREEN KNIFE for cutting silk screen film direct from outline templets (open letters).

2-50 SWIVEL KNIFE cuts all types of silk screen films, color and texture adhesive sheets, and thin stencil papers from outline templets.

LEROY LETTERING

LeRoy lettering sets consist of a scriber, template, and pen. Some of the scribers can be adjusted to make a slanted letter.

The Height and Slant Control Scriber can be adjusted to enlarge, reduce, and slant letters from a single template. Templates range in letter size from 1/16-inch to two inches. A variety of lettering and cutting devices can be used in the scriber to meet most lettering needs.

When lettering on paper offset masters use direct offset ink.

EQUIPMENT AND MATERIALS

Template

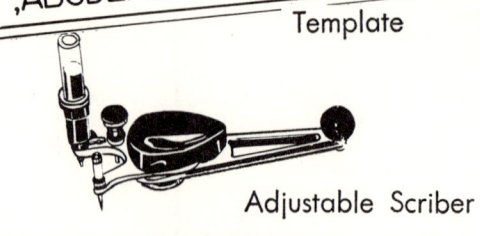

Adjustable Scriber

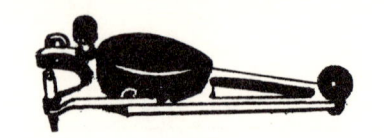

Fixed Scriber

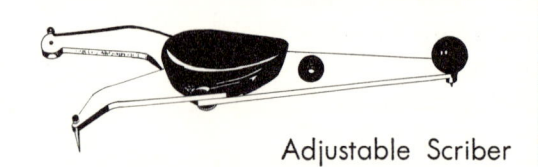

Adjustable Scriber

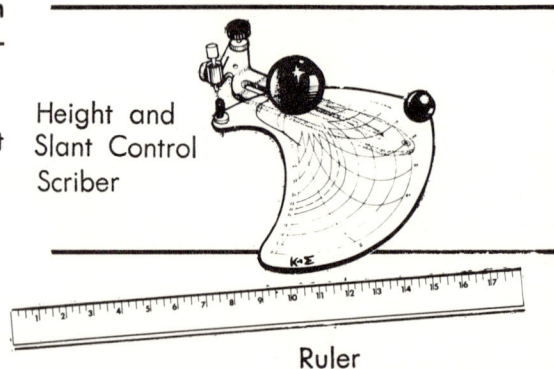

Height and Slant Control Scriber

Ruler

FOR PREPARING

Artwork
Charts
Diazo Masters
Displays
Exhibits
Fluid Duplicating Masters
Graphs
Maps
Paper Offset Masters
Posters
Projected Titles
Signs
Television Titles
Transparencies
Wax Duplicating Stencils

ACCESSORIES

Reservoir Pen

Standard Pen

Ball Point Pen

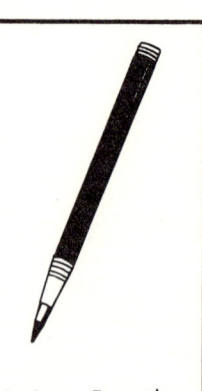

LeRoy Pencil

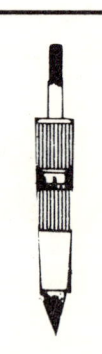

Lead Clutch

India Ink

Tape

SAMPLE LETTER STYLES

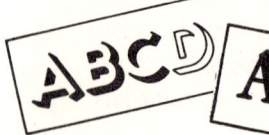

ABCD ABCD ABCD ABCD ABCD ABCD ABCDE
                                    abcde

DIRECTIONS

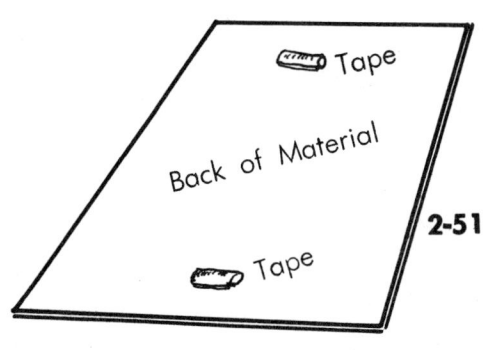

2-51 **FASTEN MATERIAL TO BE LETTERED ON** table or drawing board. Rolled pieces of tape can be used (see 2-52).

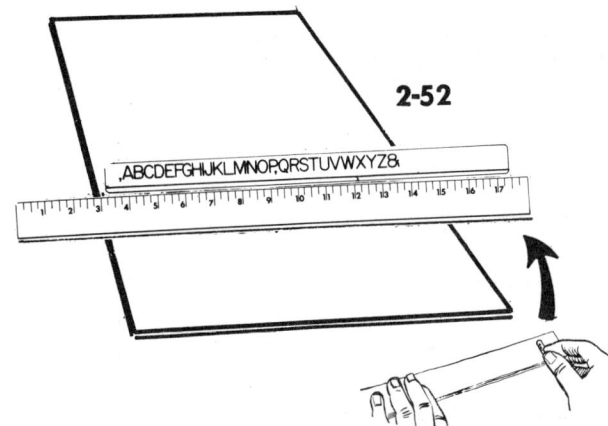

2-52 **FASTEN RULER TO WORKING SURFACE.** Roll one inch pieces of masking tape, "sticky" side out, and stick one piece at each end on back of ruler. Kueffel and Esser sells a LeRoy straightedge that will eliminate the use of tape. Turn ruler over and stick to working surface. **PLACE DESIRED TEMPLATE ON TOP EDGE OF RULER.**

FILL PEN, if Reservoir Pen is not used, with eye-dropper or stopper-dropper (see 2-43).

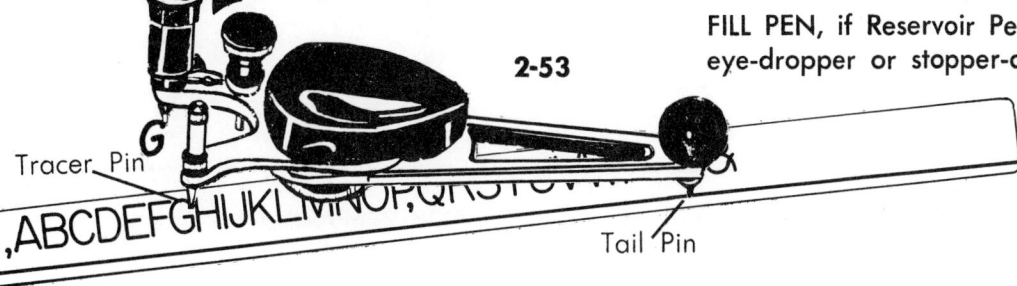

2-53 **MAKE FIRST LETTER** by setting tail pin of scriber in the straight guide groove of the template. With the tracer pin of scriber, simply trace the engraved letter on the template. It is recommended that one hand be used to hold template in place while tracing letter.

2-54 **MAKE REMAINING LETTERS** by slightly raising the scriber and leaving tail pin in groove; then slide template to next letter and repeat step 2-53.

FOR LETTER SPACING, see 2-44.

VARIGRAPH LETTERING

The Varigraph lettering system consists of a lettering instrument (scriber), templet, and a variety of lettering accessories. Two dial controls, one for controlling letter height and one for controlling letter width, make possible infinite variations of the letter traced. The instrument is designed so that it can be used by either a right handed or left handed person.

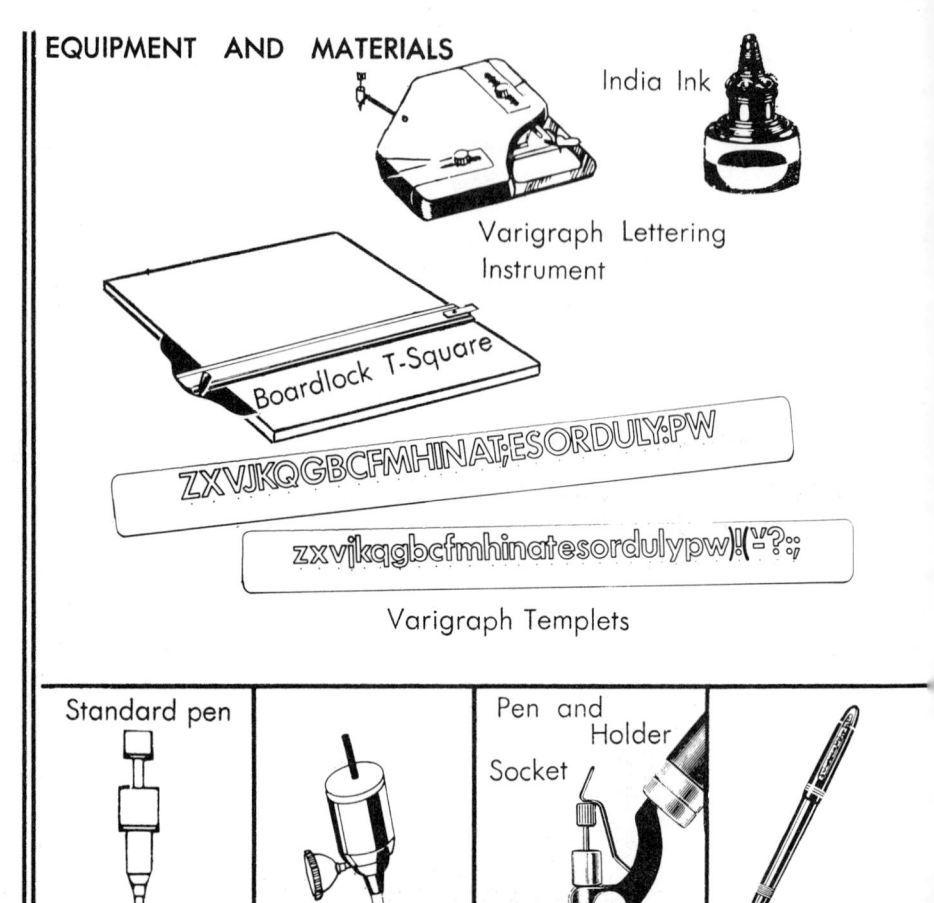

EQUIPMENT AND MATERIALS

- Varigraph Lettering Instrument
- India Ink
- Boardlock T-Square
- Varigraph Templets
- Standard pen
- Pencil Attachment
- Pen and Holder Socket
- Rapidograph Pen

FOR PREPARING

Artwork
Charts
Diazo Masters
Displays
Exhibits
Graphs
Maps
Paper Offset Masters
Posters
Projected Titles
Signs
Television Titles
Transparencies

SAMPLE LETTER STYLES

DIRECTIONS

2-55 FASTEN DOWN SURFACE TO BE LETTERED (see 2-51). Lock or secure T-Square in position. Place Varigraph instrument on upper edge of T-Square. Slide desired templet beneath the instrument which retains it automatically.

SET DIALS controlling height and width to size of desired letter. Scales are graduated in thousandths of an inch; from .150-inch to .750-inch. See 2-57 for three of the many variations from one templet. Select proper pen size and fill with ink.

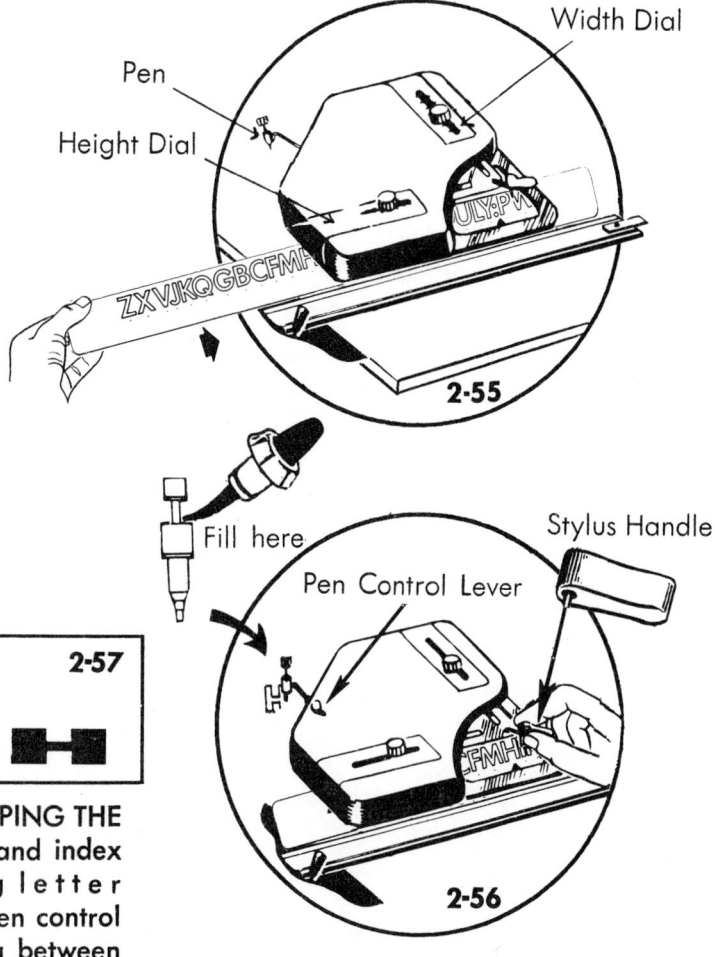

2-56. MAKE FIRST LETTER BY GRASPING THE STYLUS HANDLE between thumb and index finger, and move the stylus along letter groove. To lower pen, move the pen control lever forward. Control the spacing between letters by moving the instrument left or right.

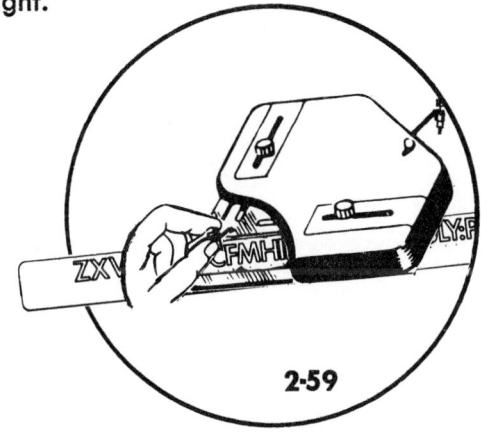

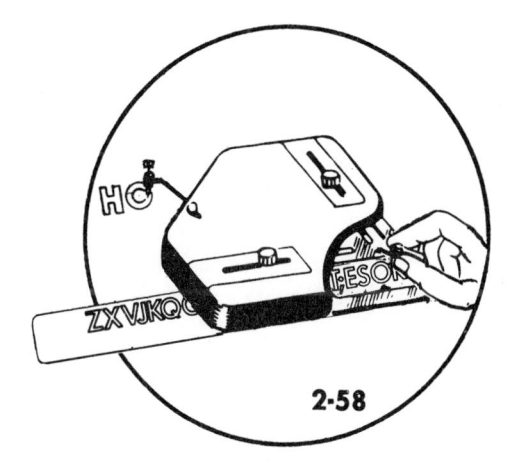

2-58 LEFT HANDED USERS, position instrument so that the stylus handle is on the left.

2-57 MAKE REMAINING LETTERS by sliding instrument and templet so that desired letter is in position. Repeat step 2-56.

51

SECTION 3

VISUAL TECHNIQUES

VISUAL TECHNIQUES

Recognizing that not too many persons can draw visuals (figure, picture, etc.), and that many instructional materials require visuals of one type or another, this section on visual techniques is included.

Posters, bulletin boards, exhibits, etc., usually require visuals for effective communication.

A selected group of visual techniques, designed mainly for the person lacking basic skills in drawing, is illustrated and described on the pages that follow. Also included in this section are a number of drawing and lettering devices, cutting aids, and inks and liquid colors useful in preparing simple visuals.

▶ VISUALS BY PROJECTION

▶ ENLARGING AND REDUCING VISUALS

▶ VISUALS BY TRACING

▶ DRAWING AND LETTERING DEVICES

▶ INKS AND LIQUID COLORS

▶ CUTTING AND DRAWING AIDS

VISUALS BY PROJECTION

Several of the projection devices can be used to make professional looking visuals for posters, murals, large cut-out figures, etc. Commercial artists h a v e used these devices for years to reproduce enlargements of small visuals. The original to be reproduced must be the size of the projection device used. Here are a few such devices recommended for this technique.

FOR PREPARING

Chalk Board Visuals
Charts
Graphs
Large Cut-Out Figures
Large Letters
Large Signs
Maps
Posters

OPAQUE PROJECTOR

DIRECTIONS

3-1 INSERT ORIGINAL IN PROJECTOR. Visual must be small enough to fit into projector.

3-2
POSITION PROJECTOR TO GIVE VISUAL SIZE DESIRED. Turn off room lights and trace visual on material mounted on wall with ordinary pencil or felt point pen.

3-3
ATTACH MATERIAL ON WHICH VISUAL IS TO BE REPRODUCED to wall or bulletin board, (see pages 24 and 25 for mounting materials).

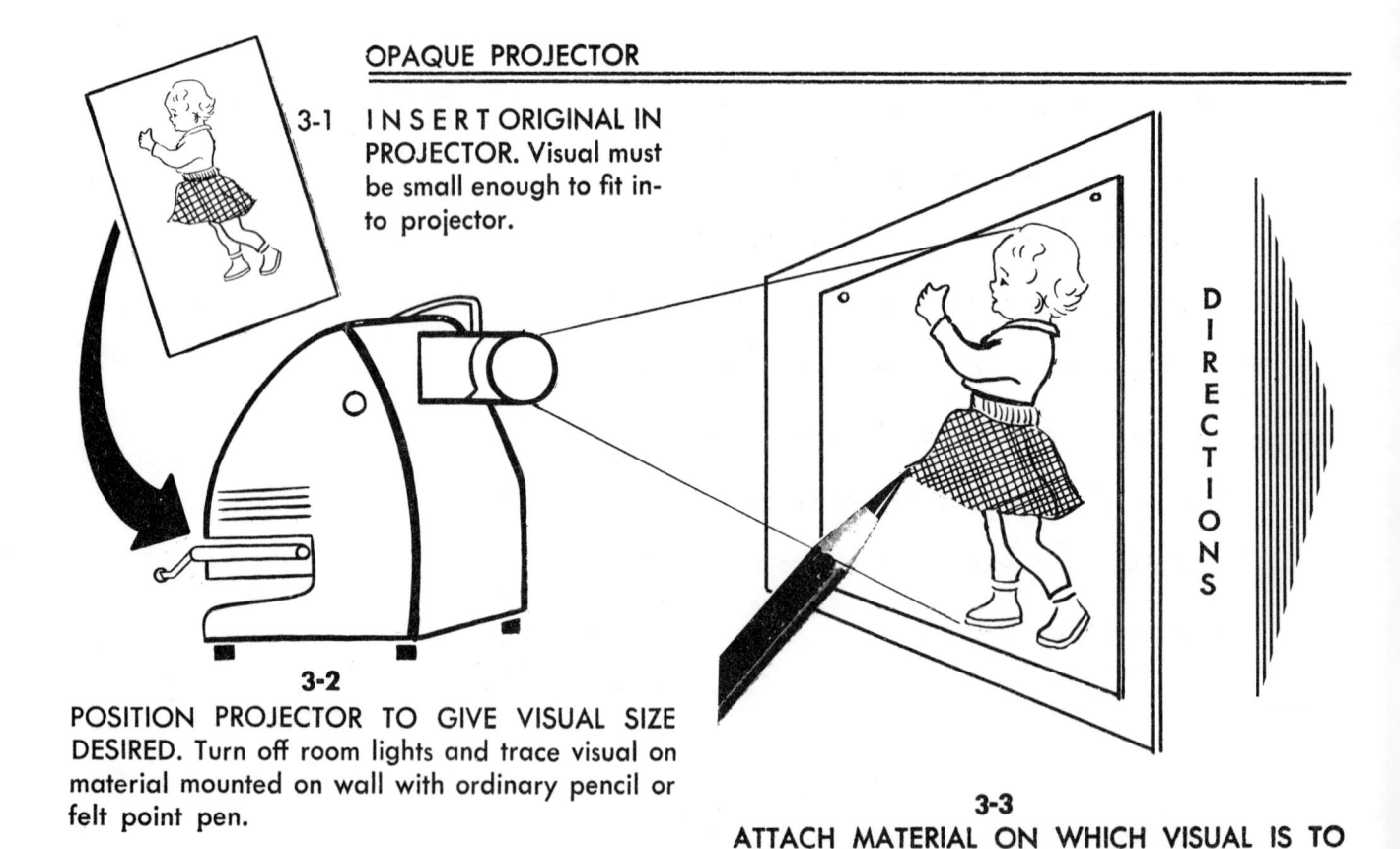

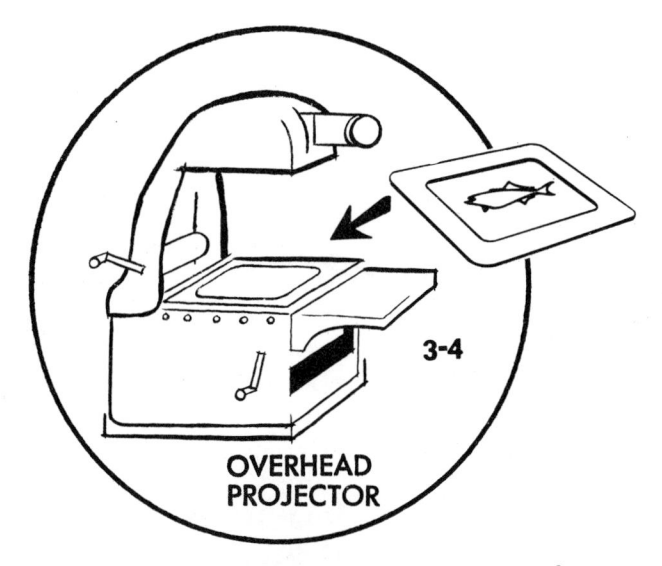

OVERHEAD PROJECTOR

3-4 **OVERHEAD PROJECTOR.** Visual must be transparent and small enough to fit on the projector. Follow instructions in 3-1, 3-2, and 3-3.

3-5 **FILMSTRIP PROJECTOR** can be used to make visuals only if the original visuals on a filmstrip. Follow instructions in 3-2 and 3-3.

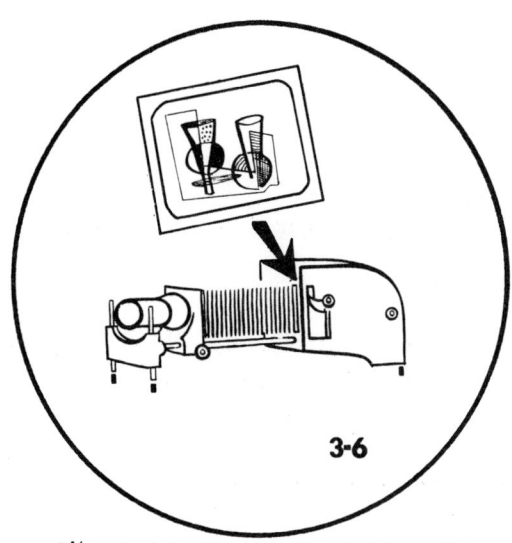

3-6 **3¼-BY 4-INCH SLIDE PROJECTOR.** Original must be transparent and on a 3¼-by 4-inch slide or on acetate or frosted glass the same size. Follow instructions in 3-1, 3-2, and 3-3.

3-7 **2-by 4-INCH SLIDE PROJECTOR.** Original visual must be on a 2-by 4-inch slide or on clear or frosted acetate the same size. Follow instructions in 3-1, 3-2, and 3-3.

3-8 **PHOTOGRAPHIC ENLARGER** can be used if original is transparent and the size accepted by the enlarger. Lay material on which visual is to be reproduced on base of enlarger. Follow instructions in 3-1, 3-2, and 3-3.

PHOTOGRAPHIC ENLARGER

FILMSTRIP PROJECTOR

3¼-BY 4-INCH SLIDE PROJECTOR

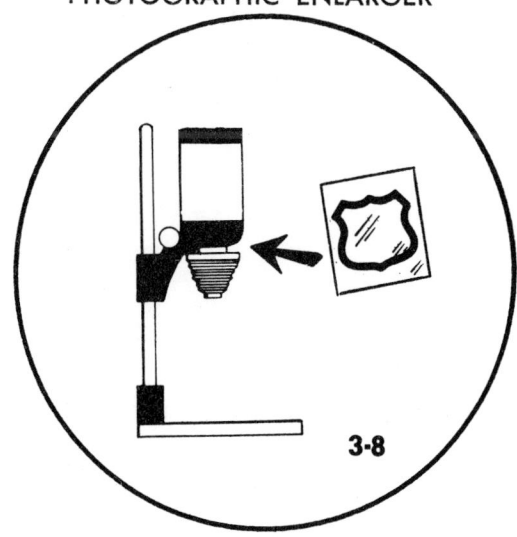

2-BY 2-INCH SLIDE PROJECTOR

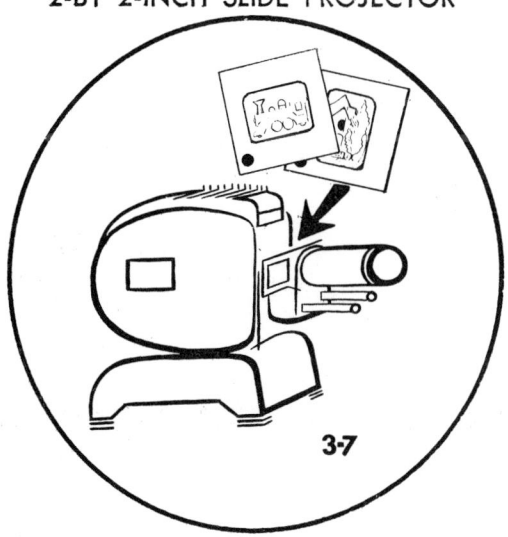

ENLARGING AND REDUCING VISUALS

Existing drawings, symbols, letters, etc., may not be exactly the size needed for a project. Here is an easy way to enlarge or reduce an original so that all parts remain in proportion.

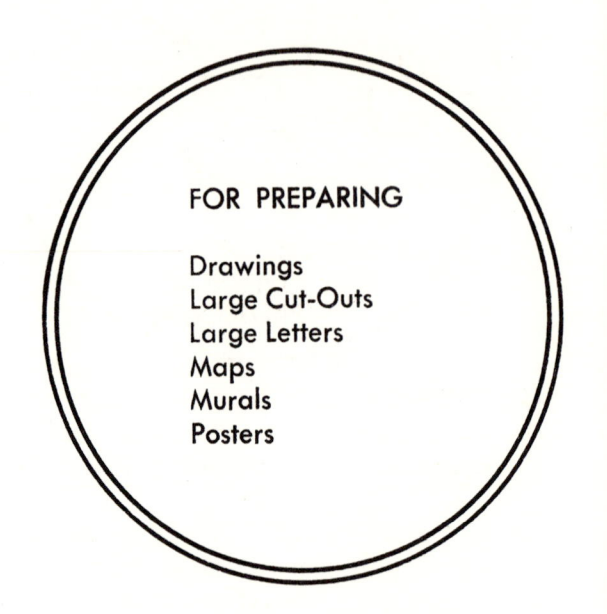

FOR PREPARING

Drawings
Large Cut-Outs
Large Letters
Maps
Murals
Posters

DIRECTIONS

3-9 MAKE A TRACING OF DESIRED VISUAL (see page 59 for instructions).

3-10 MARK OFF THE TRACING with one-quarter inch squares for small tracings, one-half inch or one inch for larger tracings. Number squares as illustrated.

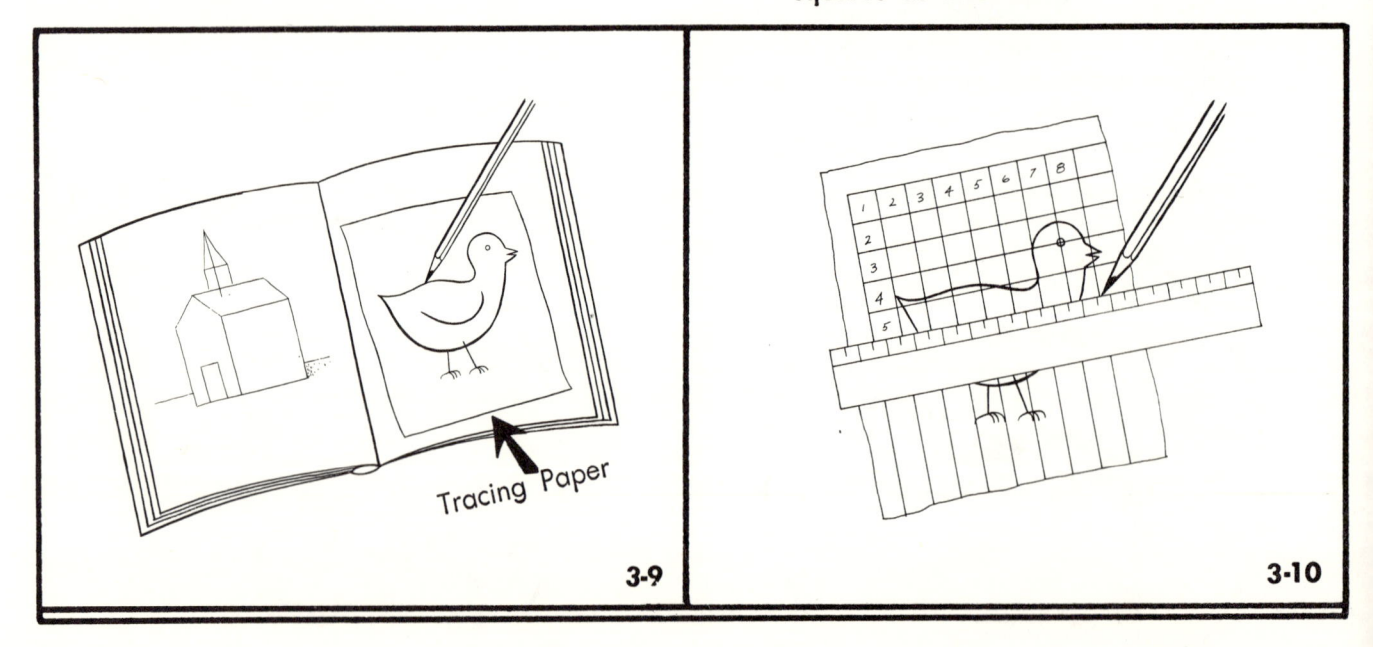

56

3-9 To 3-14

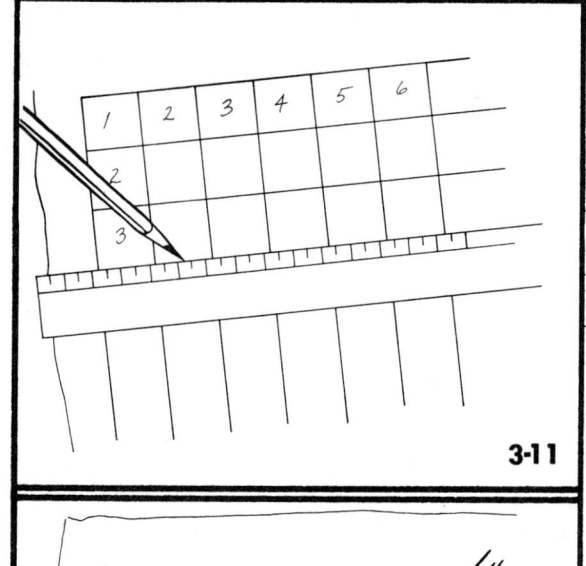

3-11 MARK OFF SECOND SHEET FOR ENLARGEMENT. If enlarged visual is to be twice as large as original, make the same number of squares TWICE AS LARGE. If the original was marked off in one-half inch squares, then on the second sheet mark off one inch squares. Number second set of squares the same way.

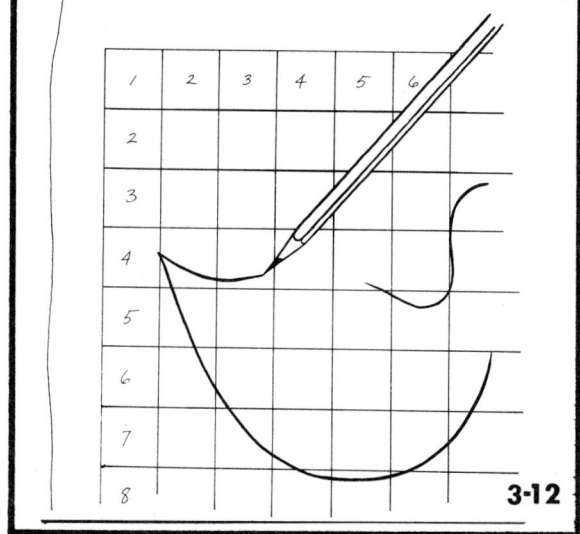

3-12 CAREFULLY DRAW IN THE OUTLINES OF THE ORIGINAL VISUAL in the corresponding larger squares with a pencil. Draw in one square at a time.

3-13 REFINE PENCIL LINE OF COMPLETED VISUAL, and transfer to desired surface (see page 59).

3-14 MAKE A REPRODUCTION SMALLER by reversing the above steps. Start with larger squares for the original visual and smaller squares for the reduced visual.

57

VISUALS BY TRACING

Modern materials, such as clear and special surfaced acetate, frosted glass and acetate, and tracing paper make it possible to trace visuals from books, magazines, newspapers, and other sources.

USING FROSTED ACETATE OR GLASS

3-15 ATTACH FROSTED ACETATE OR GLASS to original to be traced. Check acetate to make certain it will accept drawing device. Masking tape can be used to attach acetate.

3-17 IF TRACING IS TO BE PROJECTED, spray dull side with plastic spray (see 5-9). Spray will make acetate more transparent and will provide a protective coating.

3-16 TRACE ORIGINAL with 3-43, 3-44, or 3-45. TO ADD COLOR (see 3-42 and 3-44).

3-18 IF TRACING IS TO BE MOUNTED FOR PROJECTION (see pages 100 and 101).

USING CLEAR OR SPECIAL-SURFACED ACETATE

3-19 ATTACH ACETATE TO ORIGINAL to be traced with masking tape. Check surface of acetate to see if it will accept drawing device desired.

3-21 ADD COLOR OR TEXTURE (see Section 4). Color and texture should be applied to opposite side of acetate to avoid smearing inked side.
TO ADD LETTERING (see pages 37, 39, 41, 45, 47, 49, and 51).

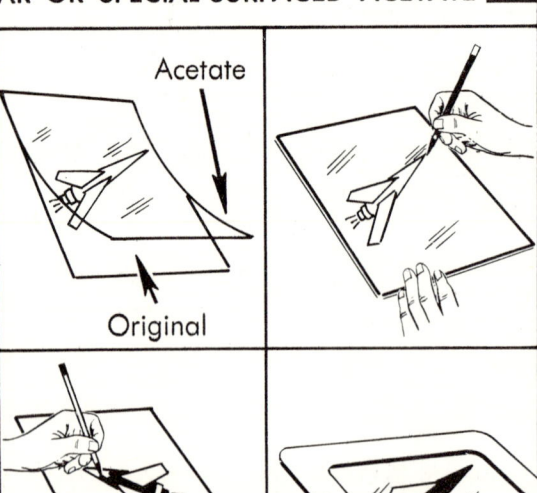

3-20 TRACE ORIGINAL with 3-31, 3-32, 3-33, 3-34, 3-35, 3-37, 3-39 or 3-40.

3-22 IF TRACING IS TO BE MOUNTED FOR PROJECTION (see pages 100 and 101).

where the original visual cannot be removed. Moreover, the preparation of diazo masters, slides, transparencies, posters, etc., may require quality visuals which, for the most part, would require the skills of an artist to reproduce. If the original visual is the exact size needed, the directions that follow will be sufficient. If the original visual is too small or too large, follow the directions for tracing with tracing paper, then refer to pages 56 and 57 for directions on enlarging and reducing visuals.

USING TRACING PAPER

3-23 ATTACH TRACING PAPER TO ORIGINAL to be traced with masking tape.

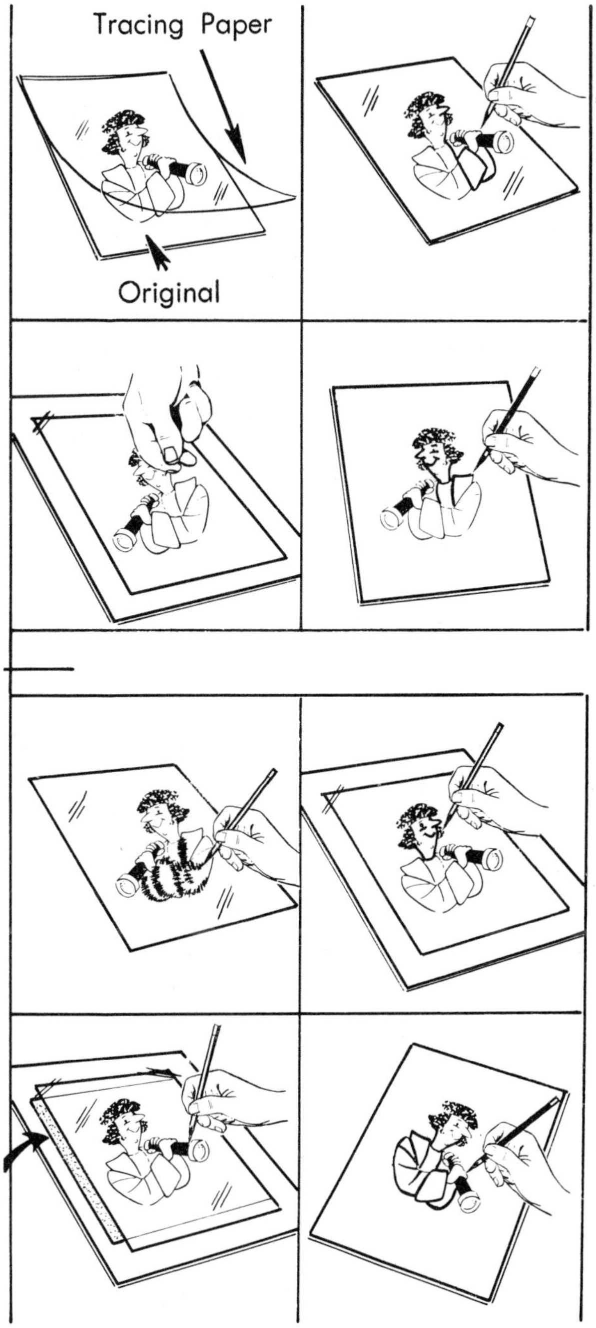

3-24 TRACE ORIGINAL with an ordinary pencil.

3-25 TRANSFER TRACED VISUAL to desired surface by turning the tracing over on the new surface and using the nail of a finger or back of a teaspoon to rub down the pencil lines. The carbon from the pencil will leave a light guide line. Visual will now be facing the opposite direction.

3-26 INK OR COLOR REPRODUCTION as desired (see pages 60 and 61 for drawing and lettering devices).

3-27 IF TRACED VISUAL IS TO FACE SAME DIRECTION as original, turn traced visual over and go over the traced lines with a pencil as illustrated.

3-28 TRANSFER TRACED VISUAL to desired surface. Use masking tape to attach tracing.

3-29 USE TRANSFER TRACING PAPER, available in several colors, to transfer tracing to desired surface.

3-30 INK OR COLOR REPRODUCTION as desired (see pages 60 and 61 for drawing and lettering devices).

DRAWING AND LETTERING DEVICES

Drawing and lettering on opaque and transparent surfaces require a variety of devices to accomplish desired results. Illustrated and briefly described are several devices which should meet most drawing and lettering demands.

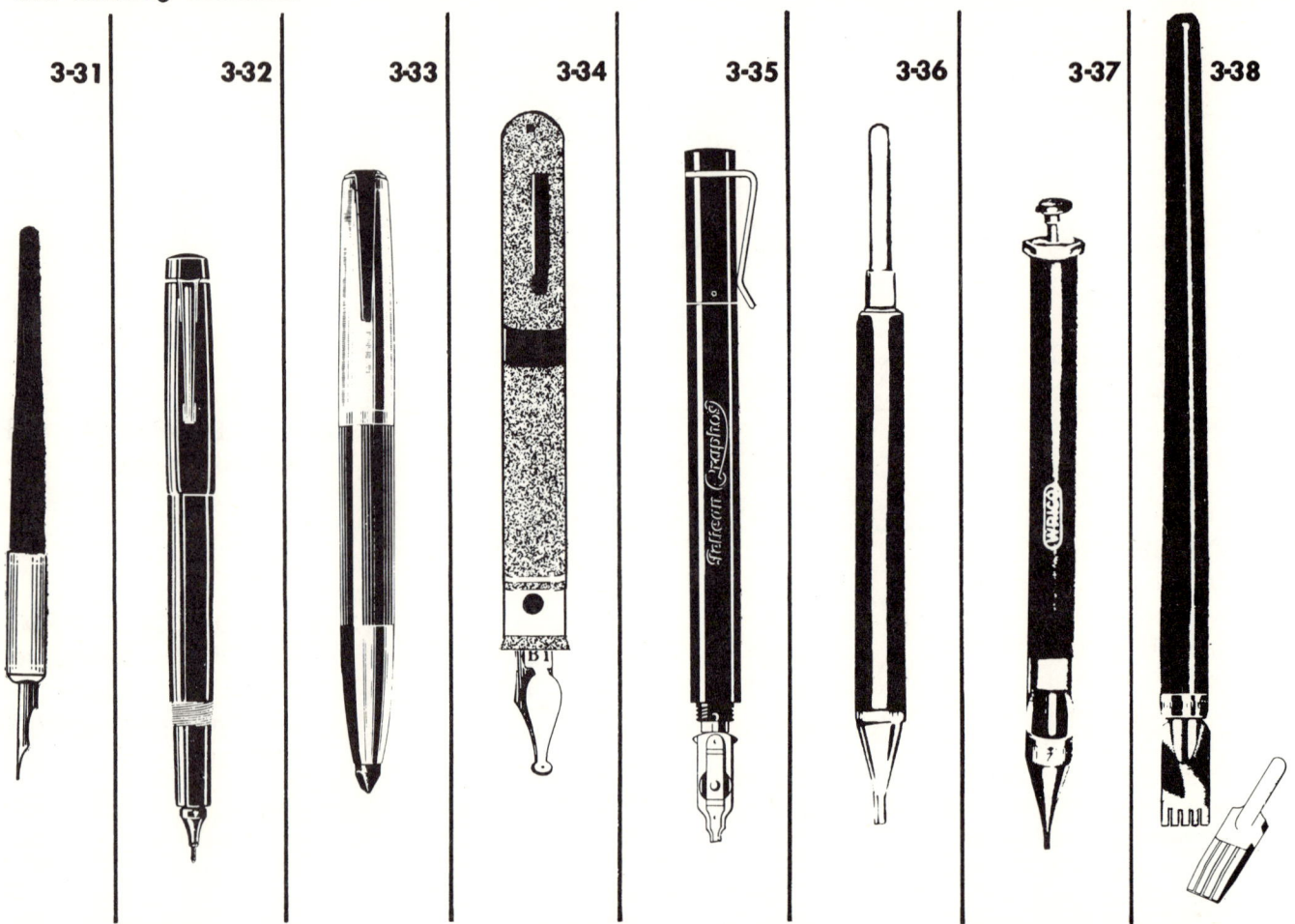

3-31 CROWQUILL PEN
Ideal for drawing and lettering where a fine line is desired.

3-32 TECHNICAL FOUNTAIN PEN
A non-clogging fountain-type pen that uses India or drawing ink. Some models will accept plastic inks. Available in several line widths.

3-33 FELT-POINT PEN
For drawing or lettering on any surface. Assorted nibs (points) available.

3-34 SPEEDBALL AUTO-FEED PEN
Fountain-type pen holder that accepts all Speedball pens.

3-35 PELICAN GRAPHOS PEN
Fountain-type pen for drawing, lettering and stencil work. Sixty interchangeable nibs available. Uses drawing inks.

3-36 WRICO BRUSH PEN
Used with Wrico Sign-Maker guides. Ideal for drawing lines and curves with the aid of a ruler, transparent curves and ellipse guides (See page 63).

3-37 WRICO PRINT PEN
Used with Wrico lettering guides. Ideal for filling in open letters and drawing lines and curves (see page 63).

3-38 METAL BRUSH LETTERING PENS
Works like a brush. Available in widths from 1/16 to 1 inch.

3-39 SOCKET and PENHOLDER
Uses same pens as lettering Scribers (see 2-45). Can be used to draw lines and curves.

3-40 SPEEDBALL PENS
Available in four different point styles. Stlyus available for left-handed users. All points will fit in "Auto-Feed" Pen.

3-41 WRICO BALL PEN
Used with Wrico Manuscript lettering set. Ideal for lettering and drawing on wax duplicating stencils and fluid duplicating masters. Available in red and blue ink.

3-42 KEYSTONE SLIDE CRAYONS
For applying color to frosted glass or acetate. Assorted colors available.

3-43 DRAWING PENCILS
For drawing or lettering on frosted acetate or glass. Available in black and colors.

3-44 LUMACHROM COLOR PENCILS
Transparent color leads; Ideal for applying color letters, and drawings on frosted acetate or glass. Several colors available.

3-45 MARKING PENCIL
Will mark on any surface, rough, smooth, or slick. Available in wax or hard lead. Marks easily removed off smooth surface with a cloth or tissue.

3-46 BALL POINT PEN
Can be used with stencil tracing lettering guides. For drawing and lettering on wax duplicating stencils and fluid duplicating masters. Available with special ink for use on paper offset masters.

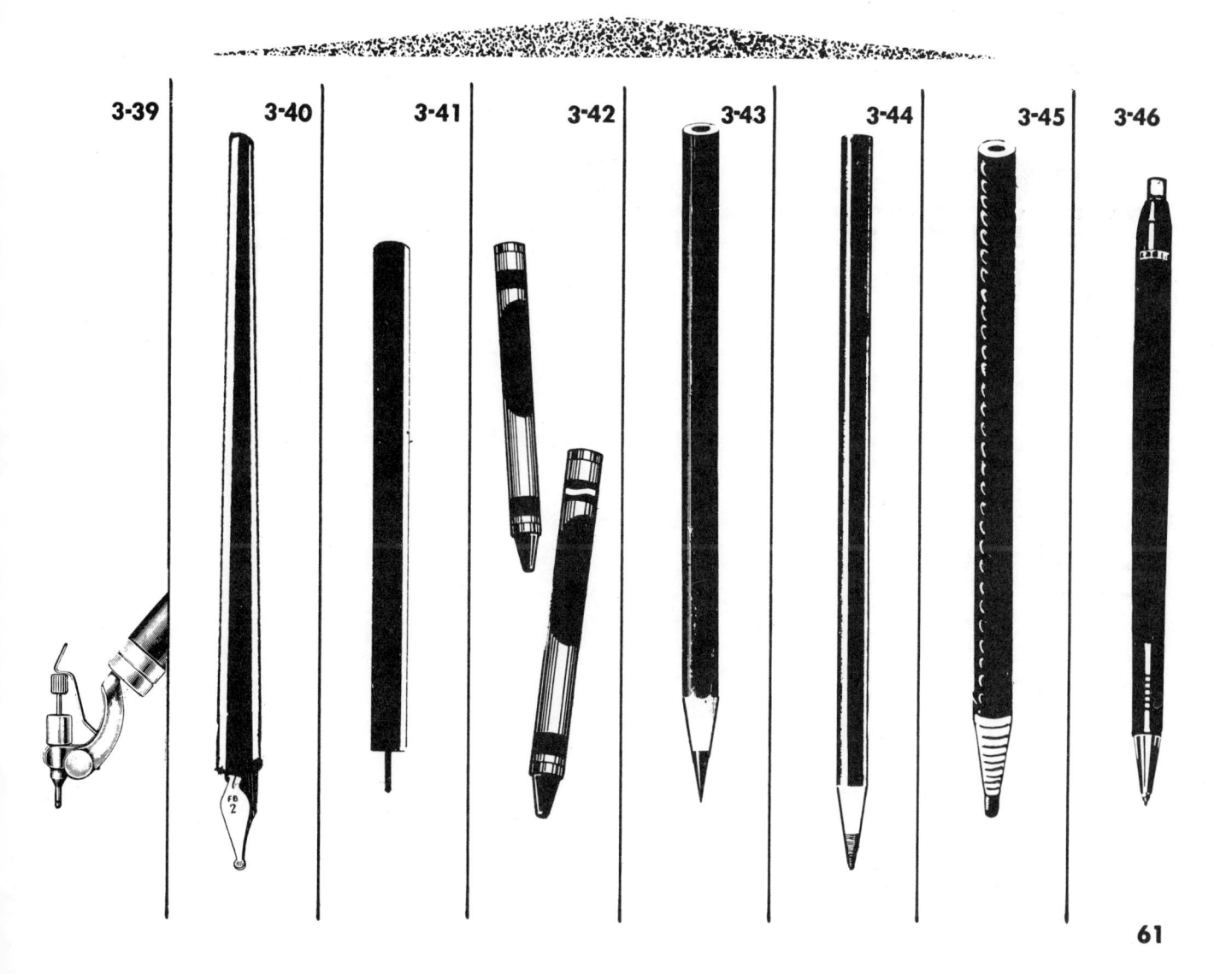

CUTTING AND DRAWING AIDS

Drafting instruments, such as ink compass, pencil compass, dividers, etc., and drawing aids such as flexible rulers, transparent curves, ellipse guides, etc., can be used to cut and draw circles and forms often required for the preparation of visual instructional materials. Here are a few such aids.

CUTTING AIDS

3-47 CIRCLE CUTTER cuts perfect circles from 1/16 inch to 26 inches with some models. Cuts circles out of paper, color or texture adhesive sheets, acetate or plastic, light weight cardboard, etc.

3-48 DRAFTING DIVIDERS can be used to cut perfect circles out of color or texture adhesive sheets, plastic, and acetate. Rotate dividers the same as compass or circle cutter to cut out circles.

3-49 CUTTING NEEDLE (STYLUS AND DRAFTING DIVIDERS can be used to cut perfect ellipse forms out of color or texture adhesive sheets, plastic, and acetate. To use, trace inside desired form with either of the cutting aids.

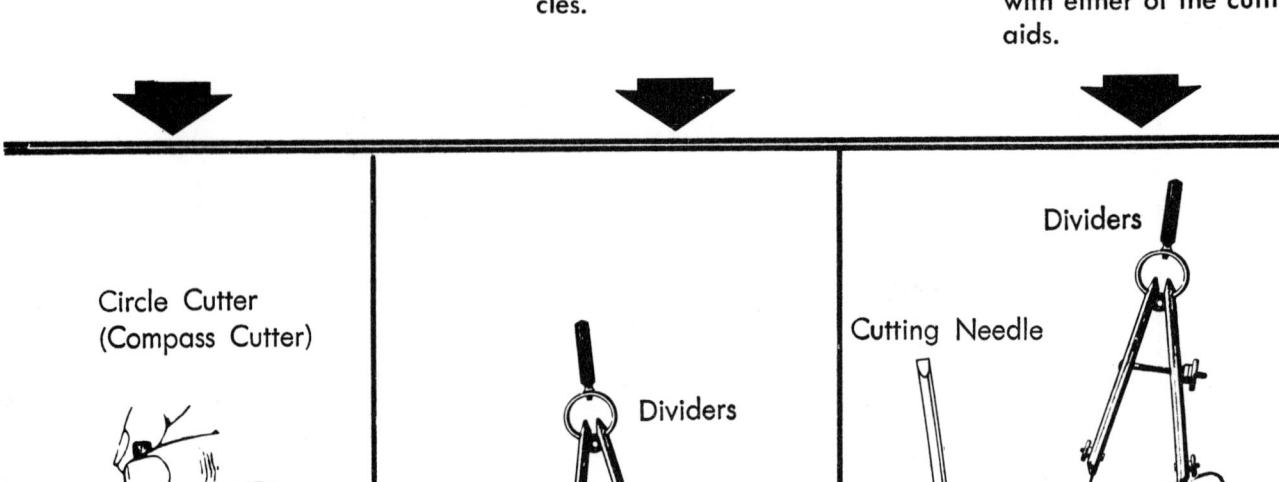

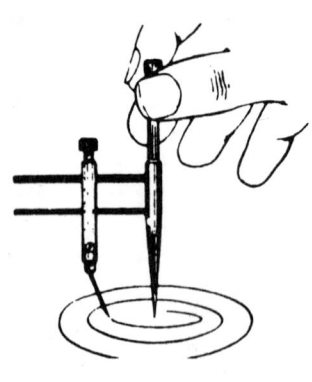

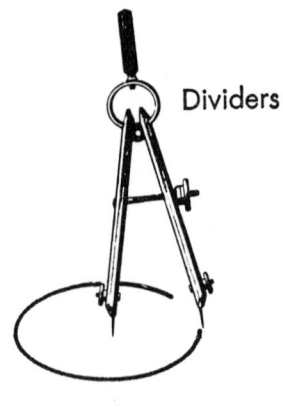

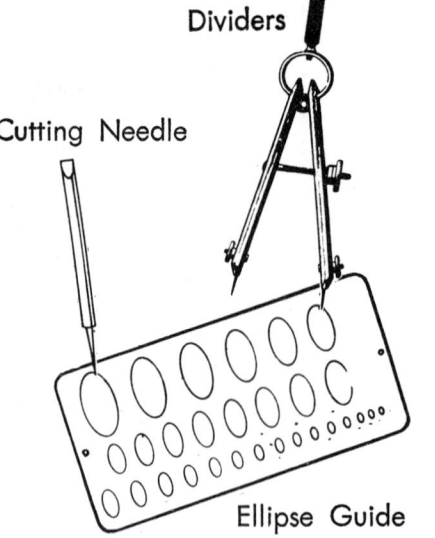

Circle Cutter (Compass Cutter)

Dividers

Dividers

Cutting Needle

Ellipse Guide

3-47 To 3-55

3-50 FOR DRAWING LARGE CIRCLES, cut a strip of cardboard 1-by12-inches with holes punched in it 1-inch apart. Will make circles up to 23-inches.

3-51 PENCIL CIRCLES in black or color can be made with a pencil compass. Circles can be drawn on frosted acetate or on clear acetate when a marking pencil is used.

3-52 INK COMPASS can be used to make ink circles on transparent or on opaque surfaces (see page 64 for inks and liquid colors).

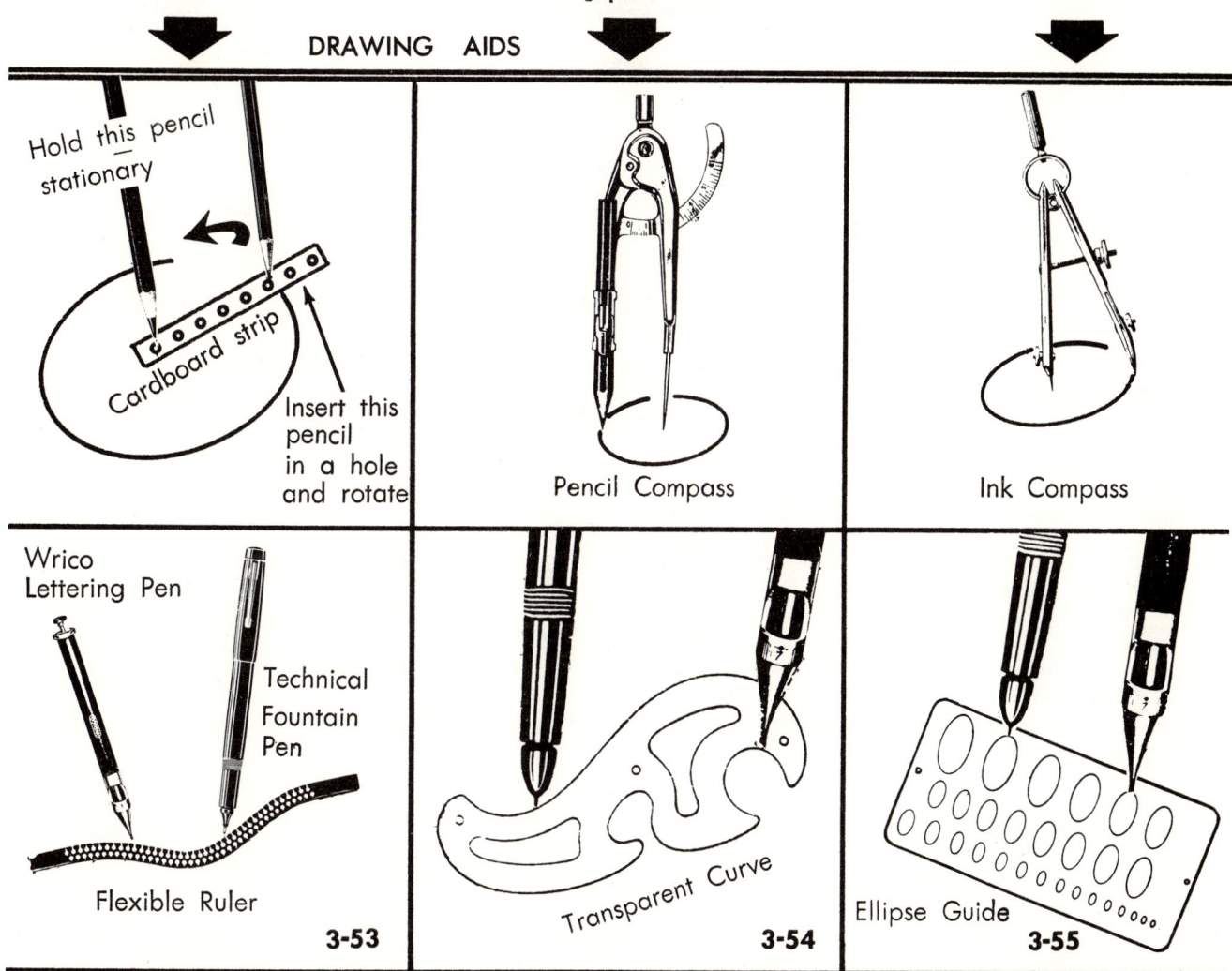

DRAWING AIDS

Hold this pencil stationary
Cardboard strip
Insert this pencil in a hole and rotate

Pencil Compass

Ink Compass

Wrico Lettering Pen
Technical Fountain Pen
Flexible Ruler
3-53

Transparent Curve
3-54

Ellipse Guide
3-55

3-53 FLEXIBLE RULER can be bent in desired shape and used as a guide for drawing a variety of curves and shapes. A Wrico lettering pen and a technical fountain pen are two devices that can be used with the ruler.

3-54 TRANSPARENT CURVES can be used to make a variety of curves and shapes on most surfaces when the appropriate drawing or lettering device is used. If an inking device is used, place curve on top of another curve or a thin piece of cardboard to elevate the curve during the tracing to prevent ink from smearing on the drawing surface.

3-55 ELLIPSE GUIDES are used to draw uniform, well defined, hard to draw ellipses of many sizes. If an inking device is used to trace ellipses, place guide on top of another guide or a thin piece of cardboard to elevate the guide during tracing to prevent ink from smearing on the drawing surface.

INKS AND LIQUID COLORS

Many of the drawing and lettering devices require the use of inks and liquid colors. Those most widely used are described here.

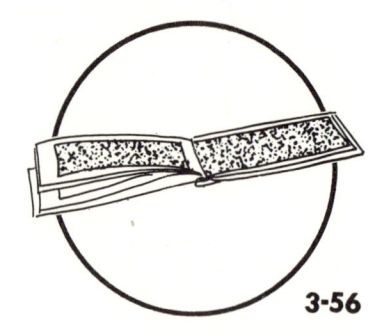

3-56

3-57

3-58

3-59

3-60

3-61

3-62

3-63

3-56 TRANSPARENT WATER COLOR STAMP BOOK
Dry transparent colors in leaflet form. See page 75 for directions.

3-57 FELT POINT PEN INK
Marks on any surface. Dries in a few seconds on porous surfaces; about 30 seconds on non-porous surfaces. Available in about ten colors. Used in 3-33.

3-58 INDIA INK
A dense, black, opaque drawing and lettering ink. Used in 3-31, 3-32, 3-34, 3-35, 3-36, 3-37, 3-38, 3-39, and 3-40.

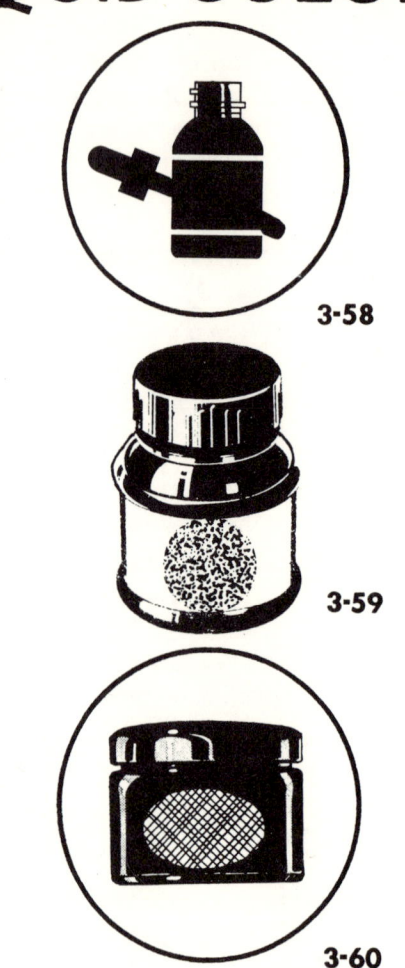

3-59 DRAWING INK
Translucent color inks that can be applied to a transparent and opaque surfaces. Used in 3-31, 3-32, 3-34, 3-35, 3-36, 3-37, 3-38, 3-39, and 3-40.

3-60 DIRECT OFFSET PLATE INK
For drawing and lettering directly on paper offset plates (masters). Used in 3-31, 3-36, 3-37, 3-39, and 3-40.

3-61 PLASTIC INK
Transparent and opaque ink designed for use on acetate or plastic surfaces. Available in several colors.

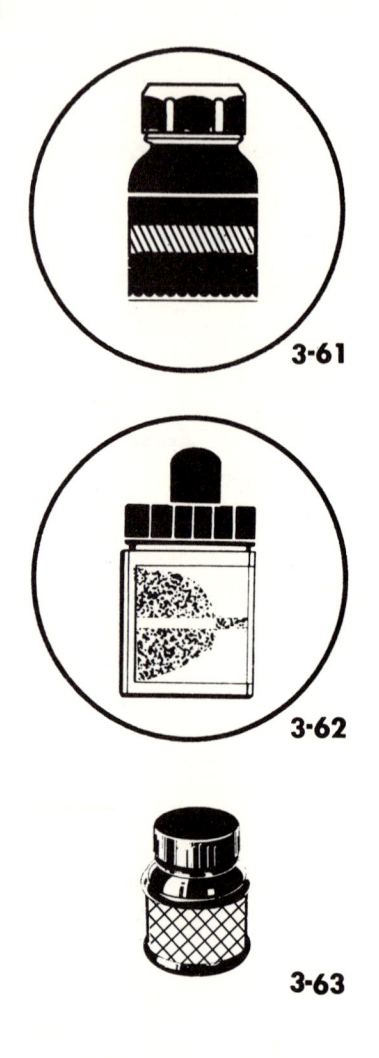

Used in 3-31, 3-32, 3-37, 3-39, and 3-40.

3-62 TRANSPARENT WATER COLORS
Ideal for applying color to transparent and opaque surfaces. Can be applied with pen, brush, or airbrush (see pages 74 and 75).

3-63 METALLIC INK
Gold and silver in ready-to-use ink solution. Can be used in 3-31, 3-35, 3-36, 3-37, 3-38, 3-39, and 3-40.

SECTION 4

COLOR AND TEXTURE TECHNIQUES

► COLOR ADHESIVE SHEETS

► TEXTURE ADHESIVE SHEETS

► CRAFTINT DOUBLETONE SHADING

► COLOR AND PATTERN ADHESIVED-BACKED TAPES

► TRANSPARENT LIQUID COLORS

COLOR AND TEXTURE TECHNIQUES

Color and texture are as important to many instructional materials as they are to an art painting. They do much to add the emphasis and interest that attract and hold attention.

There are many easy-to-use color and texture techniques available today. Of these, easy-to-apply transparent color and texture sheets, tapes and liquid colors are illustrated and discussed in this section.

With just a little practice, one can add quality color and texture to transparent and opaque instructional materials.

COLOR ADHESIVE SHEETS

Transparent and opaque colors printed on thin transparent plastic sheets that have a pressure-sensitive-adhesive backing. The color can be cut out, peeled off the protective sheet and adhered to transparent and opaque surfaces. Transparent colors can be superimposed over each other to obtain additional color values. Available in many colors.

FOR PREPARING

Artwork
Charts
Color Separations
Displays
Exhibits
Graphs
Maps
Photographs
Projected Titles
Slides
Transparencies

4-1

To Loosen Backing Sheet

DIRECTIONS

Backing Sheet
Color Sheet

4-2

4-3

MATERIALS

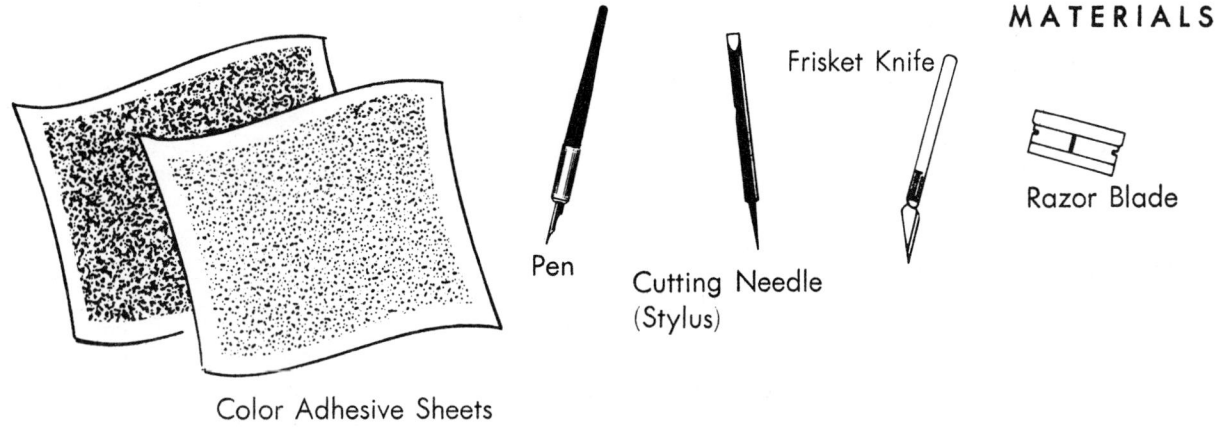

- Color Adhesive Sheets
- Pen
- Cutting Needle (Stylus)
- Frisket Knife
- Razor Blade

DIRECTIONS

4-1 INK LINES AND SOLID AREAS as desired. If color is to be placed on acetate, the inking should be done on the opposite side to avoid contact with color.

4-2 LOOSEN BACKING SHEET by inserting point of cutting tool between layers and peel color sheet away from the backing sheet. Replace loosely.

4-3 CUT AREA OF COLOR SHEET slightly larger than desired, using one of the cutting tools. Cut through the color sheet only.

4-4 POSITION CUT PIECE OF COLOR SHEET on artwork, completely covering the area to which color is to be added. Burnish lightly within this area. CUT ACCURATELY AND LIGHTLY around the area to be colored. Cut through the color sheet only. Lift away the remainder of the color sheet and replace it on the backing sheet. Smooth color on artwork so that it lies evenly. If bubbles appear, make a pin hole and burnish down.

4-5 PRESTO! YOU HAVE COLOR!

TEXTURE ADHESIVE SHEETS

MATERIALS

These opaque patterns are printed on an acetate sheet with a pressure-sensitive adhesive back. For direct use or for reproduction, they are ideal for applying texture or shading to opaque and transparent surfaces. Special and unusual effects may be obtained by combining two or more identical patterns at different angles. More than 200 patterns in black, white and other colors are available.

FOR PREPARING

- **Artwork**
- **Charts**
- **Diazo Masters**
- **Displays**
- **Exhibits**
- **Graphs**
- **Maps**
- **Projected Titles**
- **Television Titles**
- **Transparencies**

Texture Adhesive Sheets

Razor Blade

Cutting Needle (Stylus)

Frisket Knife

DIRECTIONS

Backing Sheet

Texture Sheet

4-6 **LOOSEN BACKING SHEET** by inserting point of cutting tool between layers and peel away from texture sheet. Replace loosely.

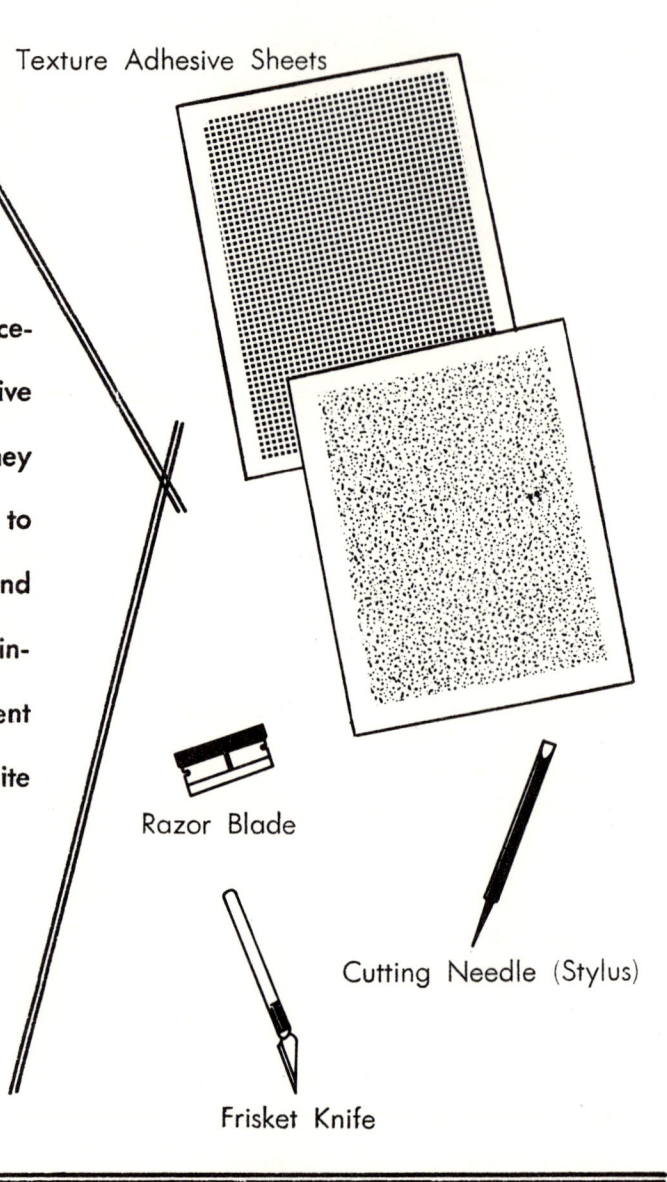

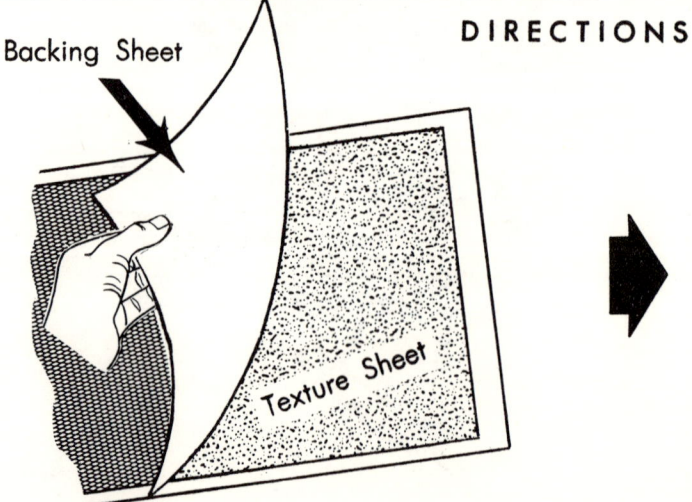

68

INK SOLID LINES AND AREAS as desired.

4-7 CUT AREA OF TEXTURE SHEET slightly larger than desired, using one of the cutting tools. Cut through the texture sheet only.

4-8 SEPARATE CUT PIECE OF TEXTURE SHEET from backing sheet and position on artwork, completely covering area desired. Burnish lightly within the area to be shaded.

4-9 CUT ACCURATELY and **LIGHTLY** with the point of cutting tool around the area to be shaded. Cut through the texture sheet only.

4-10 LIFT AWAY THE REMAINDER of the texture sheet and replace on backing sheet. When shading is complete, use beveled edge of stylus or back of finger nail and burnish firmly until edges become invisible.

CRAFTINT DOUBLETONE SHADING

(Shading)

FOR PREPARING

- Artwork
- Charts
- Graphs
- Maps

Craftint Doubletone drawing papers have the appearance of ordinary high grade drawing board. These papers are processed with two invisible shading screens, one a light tone—the other a darker tone.

The quick application of Craftint Developers, either with a brush or pen, instantly makes these shading screens visible on the drawing itself in only the places desired.

Completed drawing, although having two gray tones plus black and white, will reproduce as straight line artwork.

Doubletone is available in a 3-ply Strathmore board and a tracing vellum.

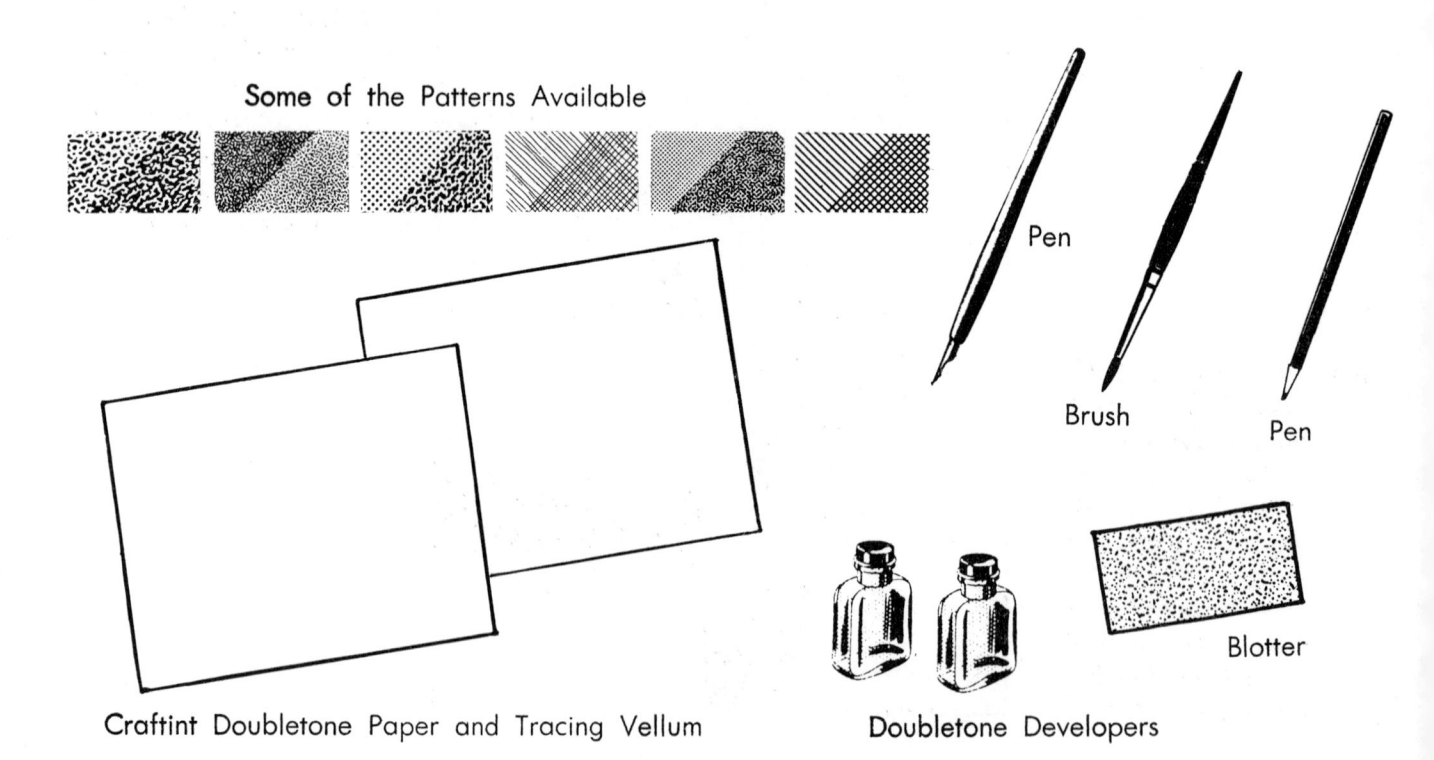

Some of the Patterns Available

Pen

Brush

Pen

Craftint Doubletone Paper and Tracing Vellum

Doubletone Developers

Blotter

DIRECTIONS

4-11 OUTLINE DRAWING on Doubletone paper or tracing vellum. Solid blacks are put in with brush or pen, using waterproof ink. If erasing is necessary, use only art gum.

4-12 APPLY DARK TONE DEVELOPER First, using pen or brush to bring out dark tones where desired. Make certain all dark tones are developed first. BOTH DEVELOPERS MUST BE BLOTTED IMMEDIATELY and not permitted to dry of their own accord.

ENGRAVER OR LITHOGRAPHER then handles completed drawing as line copy.

4-13 APPLY LIGHT TONE DEVELOPER where light tones are desired.

ERASE PENCIL OUTLINES with art gum.

USE DIFFERENT BRUSHES FOR EACH DEVELOPER

COLOR AND PATTERN SELF-ADHERING TAPES

Color and pattern self-adhering tapes take the drudgery out of chart, graph, map, and transparency making. These tapes roll on transparent or opaque colors, patterns, and symbols (from 1/32-inch to 1/4-inch wide). Their pressure-sensitive adhesive backing holds them quickly and firmly in place, yet permits instant removal and replacement when corrections are necessary. A variety of tape accessories greatly enhance this technique.

FOR PREPARING

Artwork
Charts
Diagrams
Diazo Masters
Displays
Exhibits
Graphs
Maps
Slides
Transparencies

Sample Tape Patterns

EQUIPMENT AND MATERIALS

Ruler

Tape Cutter

Chart-Pak Beam Compass Tape-Pen Holder

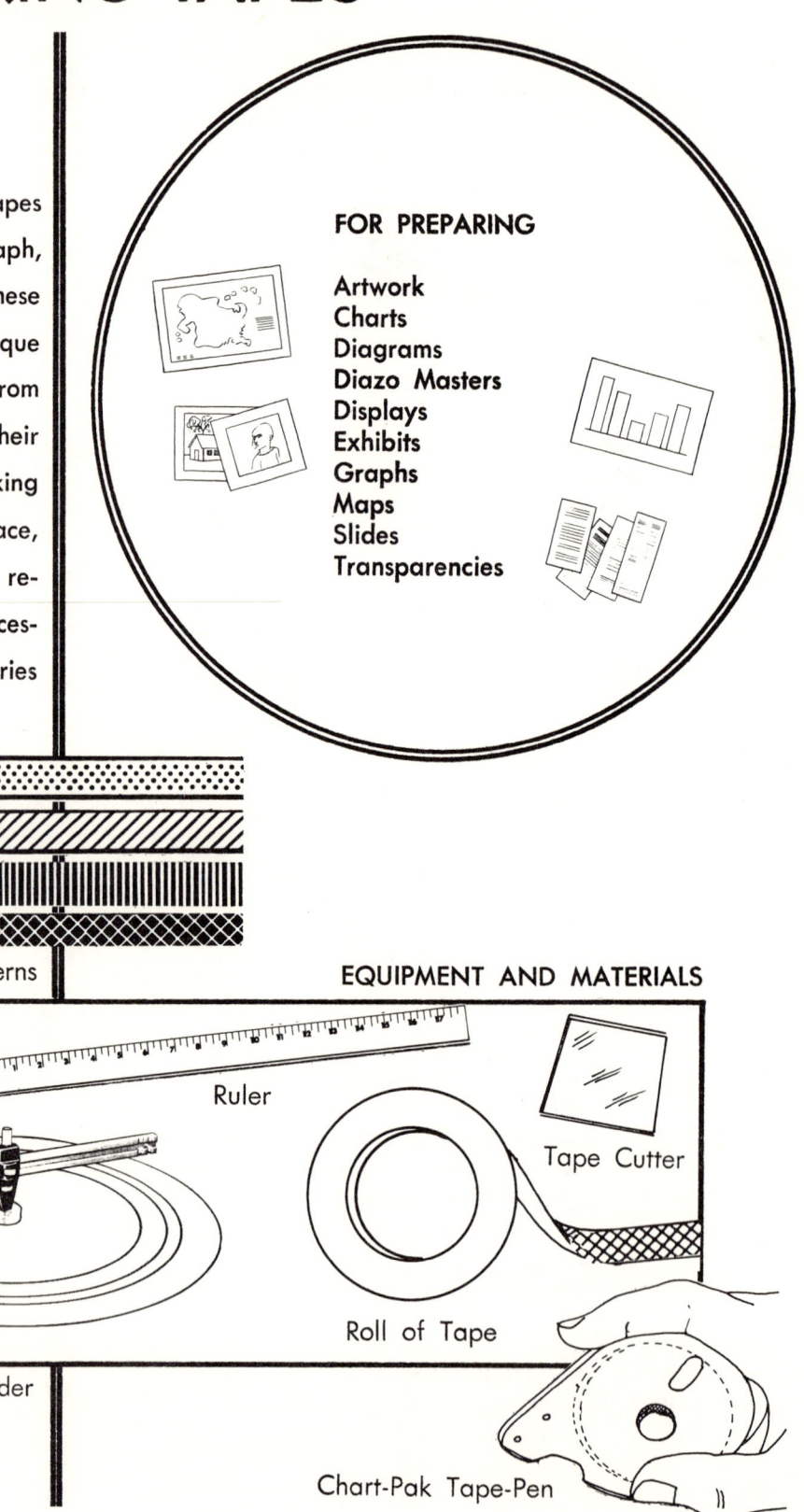

Roll of Tape

Chart-Pak Tape-Pen

72

4-14 To 4-17

D
I
R
E
C
T
I
O
N
S

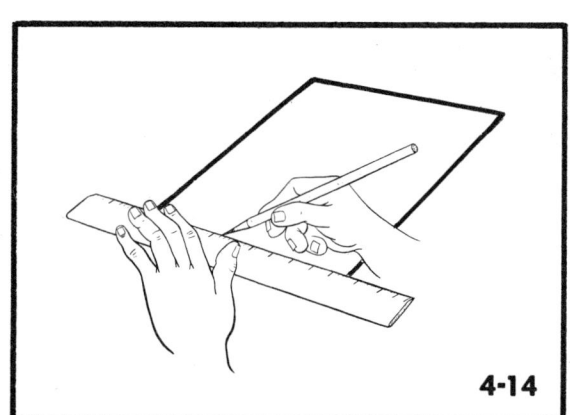

4-14

4-14 **LIGHTLY LINE OFF AREA** to which tape is to be applied. If the surface is transparent, acetate or plastic, line off a plain sheet of paper and attach acetate with masking tape. In some cases lining off a surface may not be necessary.

4-15 **APPLY TAPE** by unrolling short length of the color or pattern desired. Place approximately one inch ahead of the starting point. Continue to lay tape to desired length. To cut tape, place cutter at desired cut-off point and pull roll of tape diagonally against cutting edge of cutter. A razor blade can be used for the cutting. Apply pressure at cutting device to avoid slippage.

OR

4-16 **ROLL ON TAPE WITH TAPE-PEN** which has been loaded with desired tape. A ruler or transparent curve can be used to correctly guide the pen.

4-17 **THE BEAM COMPASS TAPE-PEN HOLDER** can be used to apply tape circles and arcs 2 to 18 inches.

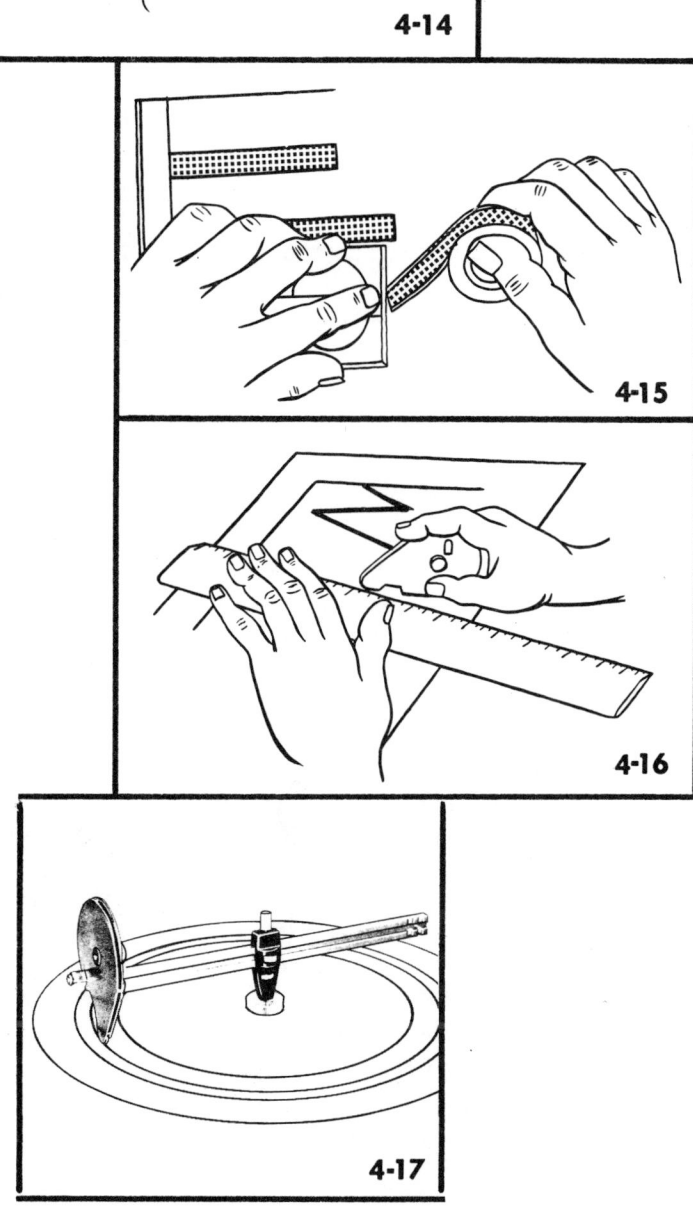

4-15

4-16

4-17

TRANSPARENT COLOR TAPES are especially designed for the preparation of projection transparencies. T h e s e tapes are available in several colors and widths.

TRANSPARENT LIQUID COLORS

Transparent liquid colors are designed for coloring visual materials which require the application of transparent colors. These colors can be applied to transparent and opaque surfaces. Only a few simple devices and materials are required for the proper application of these coloring techniques.

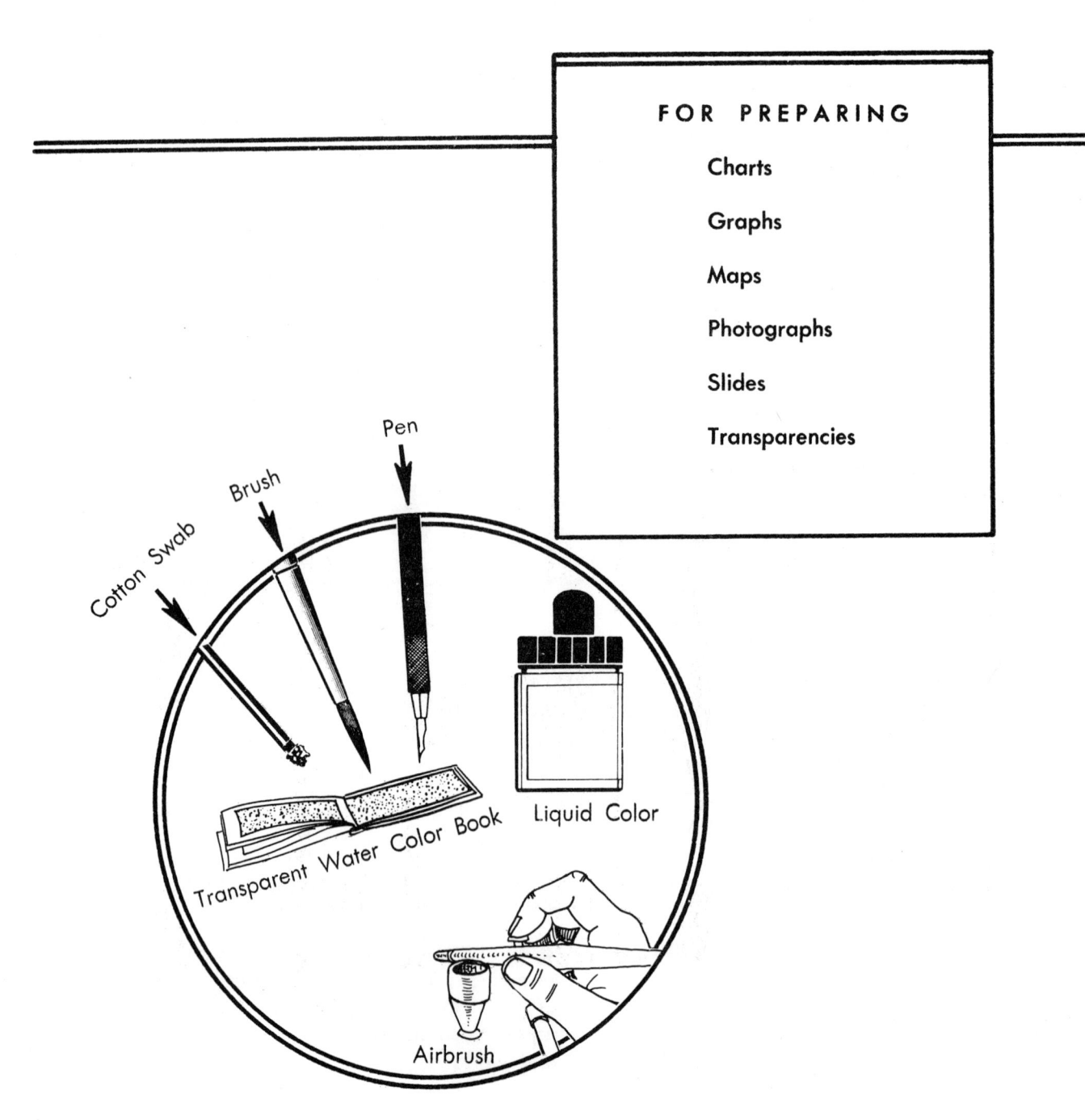

FOR PREPARING

Charts

Graphs

Maps

Photographs

Slides

Transparencies

Cotton Swab

Brush

Pen

Transparent Water Color Book

Liquid Color

Airbrush

DIRECTIONS

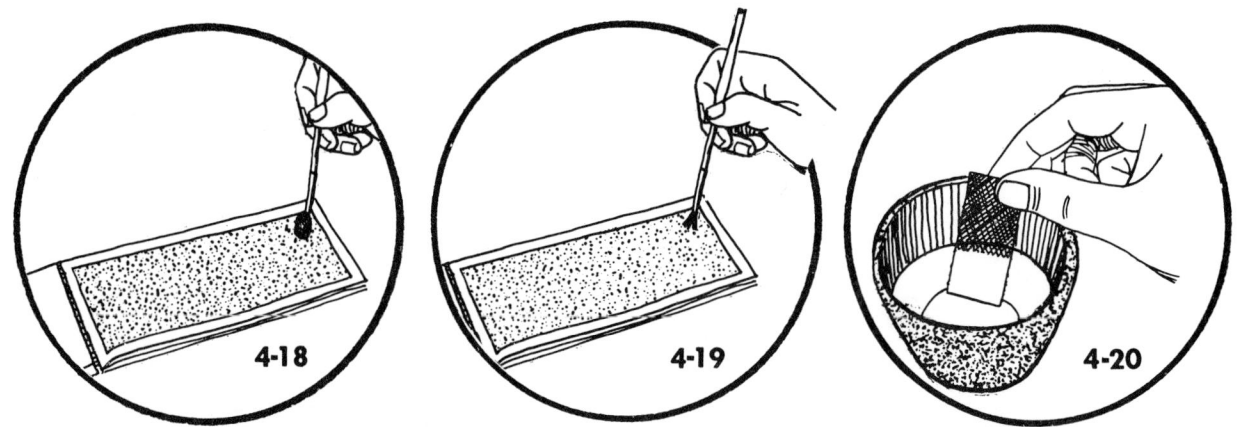

TRANSPARENT WATER COLOR STAMP BOOK represents transparent color in one of the most convenient forms. The book is made up of water soluble leaves (pages) of transparent colors. Described below are three easy ways to use these handy color books.

4-18 COTTON SWAB APPLICATION DIRECTLY FROM BOOK. Rub a wet swab or tuft of cotton lightly over a small section of the color page selected and apply directly to the desired surface. Color should be applied evenly with a circular motion. Immediately remove any excess color with a blotter of cotton. First application of color should be barely noticeable. If deeper color is desired, repeat application.

4-19 BRUSH APPLICATION DIRECTLY FROM BOOK. Rub a wet brush over a small section of the color page selected. Follow directions in 4-18.

4-21 TRANSPARENT INKS AND LIQUID COLORS may be applied to transparent and opaque surfaces with these devices.

4-20 PREPARING COLOR SOLUTION. If a large quantity of color is needed, dissolve a small section of the desired color page in a small glass or paper cup containing enough water to dissolve the color in the paper. Move paper around in water with toothpick or end of brush. This solution may be applied with any of the devices illustrated in 4-21, and in 3-32, 3-34, 3-35, 3-36, 3-37, 3-38, 3-39, and 3-40.

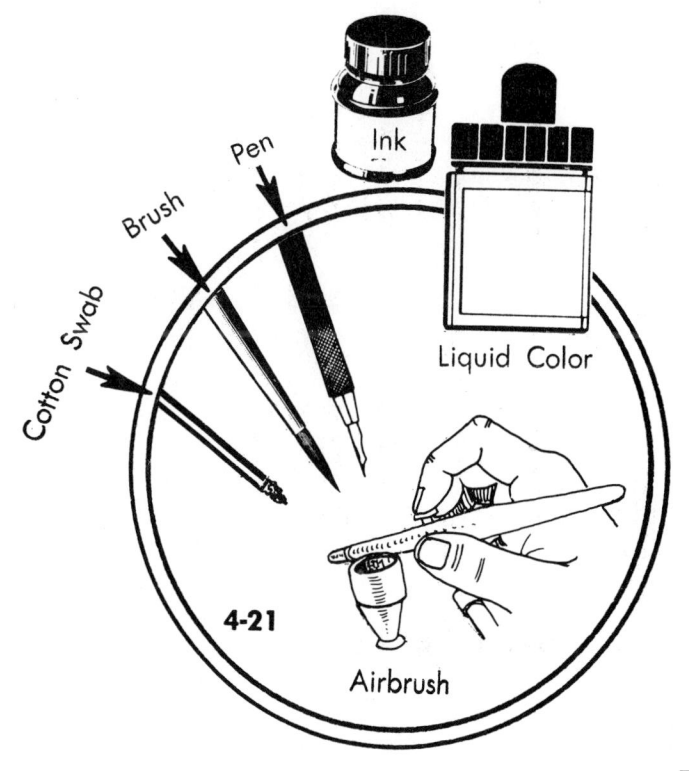

SECTION 5

PHOTOGRAPHIC AND NON-PHOTOGRAPHIC TRANSPARENCIES

PHOTOGRAPHIC AND NON-PHOTOGRAPHIC TRANSPARENCIES

During the past few years, there have been many new developments in the field of photography and related areas. Some of these developments are of direct and immediate benefit to non-professional makers of transparent projection materials; others are relatively technical. Still other new techniques are not feasible at this writing; yet they indicate the trends of thought and research in photography and related areas at this time.

The techniques for preparing transparencies presented in this section have been selected with the simplicity of preparation in mind. These techniques will not, for the most part, require special photographic equipment and darkroom facilities. Not all of the photographic and non-photographic techniques for preparing transparencies are included in this section; however, those presented represent the more practical and more promising techniques available today.

- ▶ PICTURE-TRANSFER—
    - RUBBER CEMENT
    - SEAL PROCESS
    - THERMO-FAX COLOR-LIFT
    - SELF-SEALING ACETATE

- ▶ DIFFUSION-TRANSFER TRANSPARENCIES

- ▶ THERMO-FAX TRANSPARENCIES

- ▶ DIAZO TRANSPARENCIES

- ▶ POLAROID TRANSPARENCIES

- ▶ ELECTRONIC STENCIL TRANSPARENCIES

- ▶ FLUID DUPLICATOR TRANSPARENCIES

- ▶ BESELER SLIDE-O-FILM SLIDES

- ▶ SLIDE BINDING AND MOUNTING

- ▶ LARGE TRANSPARENCIES MASKING AND MOUNTING

PICTURE-TRANSFER RUBBER-CEMENT

Pictures and printed matter from magazines printed on a clay-coated paper (LIFE and LOOK are two) can be transferred to a sheet of acetate with the aid of a few easy-to-obtain materials and projected on the overhead projector or one of the various slide projectors.

DIRECTIONS

5-1 "CLAY-TEST" MAGAZINE to determine suitability for use. Lightly rub a moist finger over an unprinted area. If a white chalky residue appears on the finger, this indicates the paper is clay-coated and is suitable for this process. Carefully remove desired page from magazine.

Cut acetate slightly larger than printed page.

5-6 SOAK IN A CONTAINER OF WATER for about ten minutes. A tablespoon of liquid soap will help speed up the soaking time. Thicker paper will require additional soaking time.

5-7 GENTLY PEEL PAPER FROM ACETATE. "Flick" back one corner to help release the paper. If peeling is difficult, return paper and acetate to the water for additional soaking.

MATERIALS REQUIRED

Clear Acetate Sheets
Comb or Razor Blade
Container of Water
Cotton
Liquid Soap
Magazine Visuals
Paper Towels
Plastic Spray
Protective Paper
Rubber Cement
Rubber Cement Thinner
Steel Wool
Two-Inch Brush
Transparency Mounts

FOR PREPARING

Diazo Masters
Transparencies
Slides

5-2 **LIGHTLY ETCH ONE SIDE OT THE ACETATE** with fine grade steel wool. Move the steel wool lightly over the acetate.

5-3 **APPLY A THIN EVEN COAT OF RUBBER CEMENT** to etched side of acetate and to FACE of printed page. Apply cement with quick even strokes.

5-4 **ATTACH RUBBER CEMENTED SIDE OF ACETATE** to face of printed page (visual). Look through the acetate to accurately position on the visual. Make the first contact at the center.

5-5 **TURN PRINTED PAGE (VISUAL) OVER** and rub down the entire surface with the flat side of a comb or a razor blade held at a slight angle. Use heavy even strokes. Place a protective sheet of paper on top to prevent damage to visual during the rubbing.

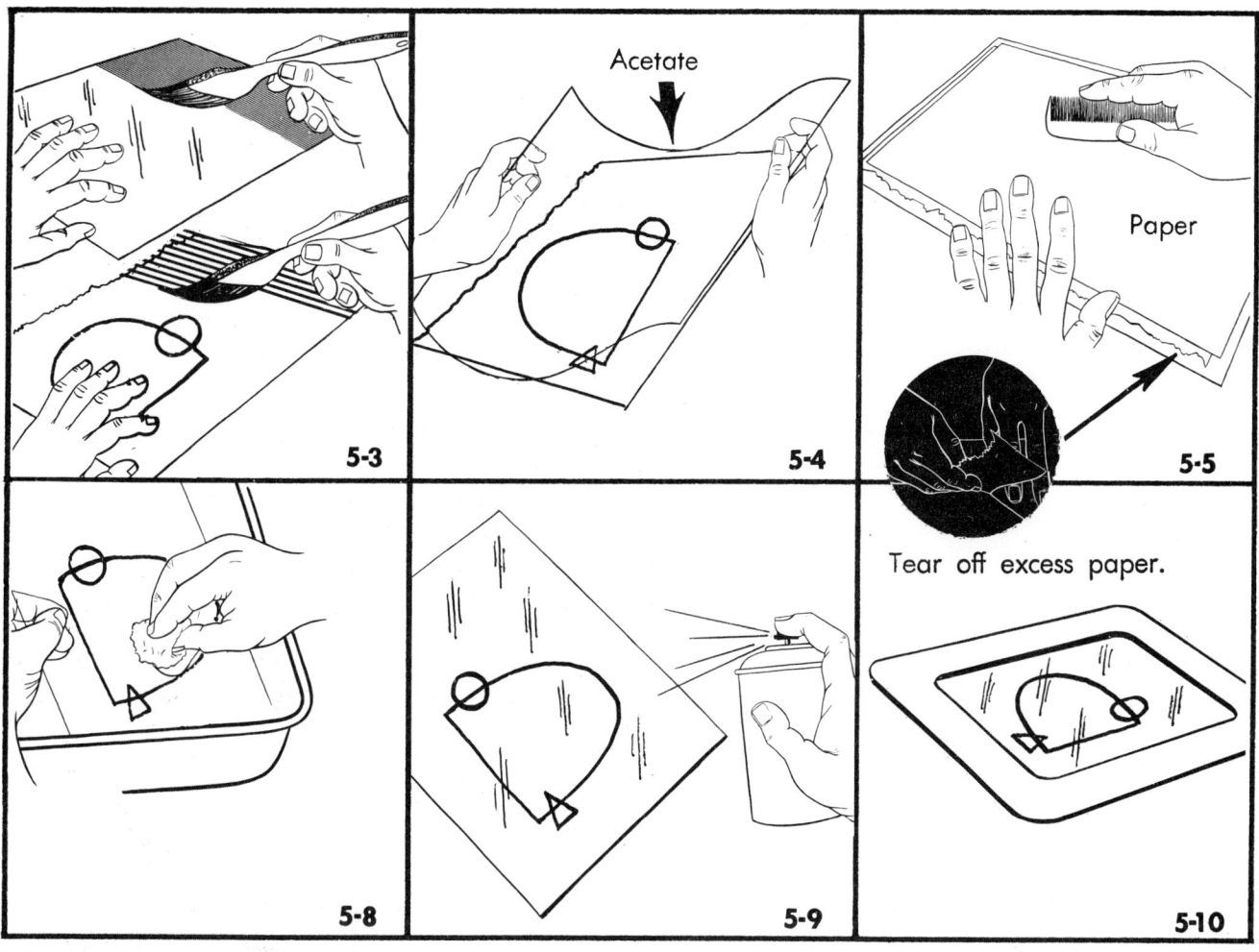

Tear off excess paper.

5-8 **RETURN TRANSPARENCY TO THE WATER** and gently wash off clay residue from transfer side (dull side) with cotton or soft tissue **BLOT TRANSPARENCY DRY** with paper towels or hang to dry. When dry, dull side will have an "ashy" appearance.

5-9 **SPRAY DULL SIDE OF ACETATE** with clear plastic spray. This will make the transparency more transparent and will provide a protective coating for the transfer side. Hold spray can about ten inches above the transparency and spray back and forth to apply an even coating of plastic.

5-10 **MOUNT FOR PROJECTION OR VIEWING** (see pages 100 and 101 for masking and mounting ideas).

HELPFUL HINTS

- Thin rubber cement with rubber cement thinner.
- Use .005-inch thick acetate for best results.
- Select visuals that are without creases or surface flaws.

PICTURE-TRANSFER — SEAL PROCESS

Full color transparencies can be made with Seal Transpara Film and pictures or printed matter printed on a clay-coated paper (LIFE and LOOK are two magazines printed on clay-coated paper). In addition to the Transpara Film and a printed visual, a dry mounting press is necessary to complete the process.

EQUIPMENT AND MATERIALS

Dry Mounting Press — Transpara Film — Paper Towels — Plastic Spray — Seal Tonic

DIRECTIONS

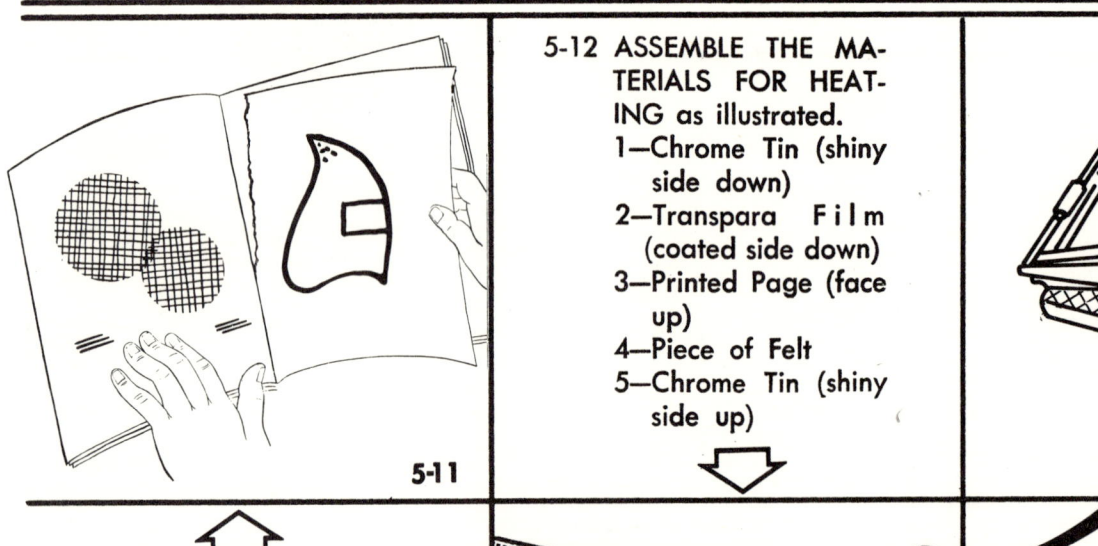

5-11 CAREFULLY REMOVE DESIRED PAGE FROM MAGAZINE after it has been given the "clay-test" (see 5-1).

5-12 ASSEMBLE THE MATERIALS FOR HEATING as illustrated.
1—Chrome Tin (shiny side down)
2—Transpara Film (coated side down)
3—Printed Page (face up)
4—Piece of Felt
5—Chrome Tin (shiny side up)

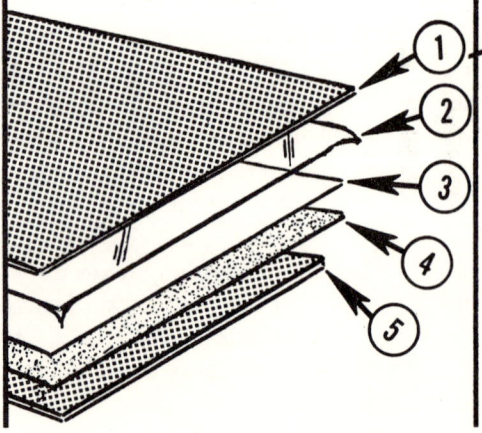

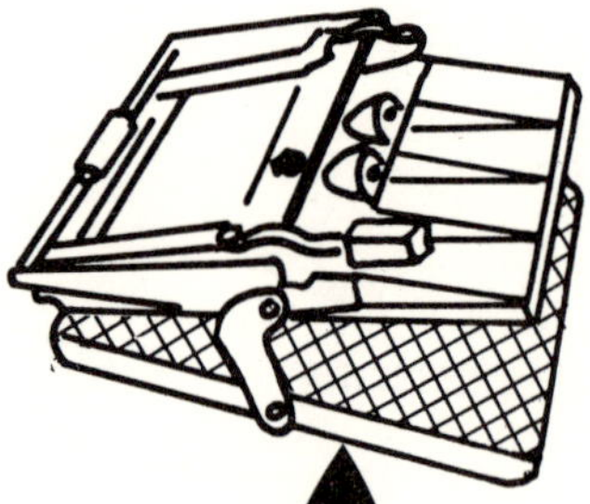

5-13 INSERT ASSEMBLED MATERIALS IN PRESS for 2½-minutes at 270° F. Make certain the press is completely closed during this operation.

FOR PREPARING: Diazo Masters — Transparencies — Slides

5-14 SOAK IN A CONTAINER OF WATER for about one minute. Add Seal tonic to water (1 tablespoon to each gallon of water). Film will have a tendency to curl. This is natural; it will uncurl during the soaking. Thicker paper may require a longer soaking period.

5-15 GENTLY PEEL PAPER FROM FILM. "Flick" back one corner to help release the paper. If peeling is difficult, return paper and film to the water for additional soaking.

5-16 RETURN TRANSPARENCY (FILM) TO THE WATER and gently wash off clay residue from transfer side (dull side) with cotton or soft tissue.
BLOT TRANSPARENCY DRY with paper towels or hang to dry. When dry, dull side will have an "ashy" appearance.

5-17 SPRAY DULL SIDE OF FILM with clear plastic spray. This will make the image on the film more transparent and will provide a protective coating for the transfer side. Hold spray can about ten inches above the film and spray back and forth to apply an even coat of plastic.

5-18 MOUNT FOR PROJECTION OR VIEWING (see pages 100 and 101 for masking and mounting ideas).

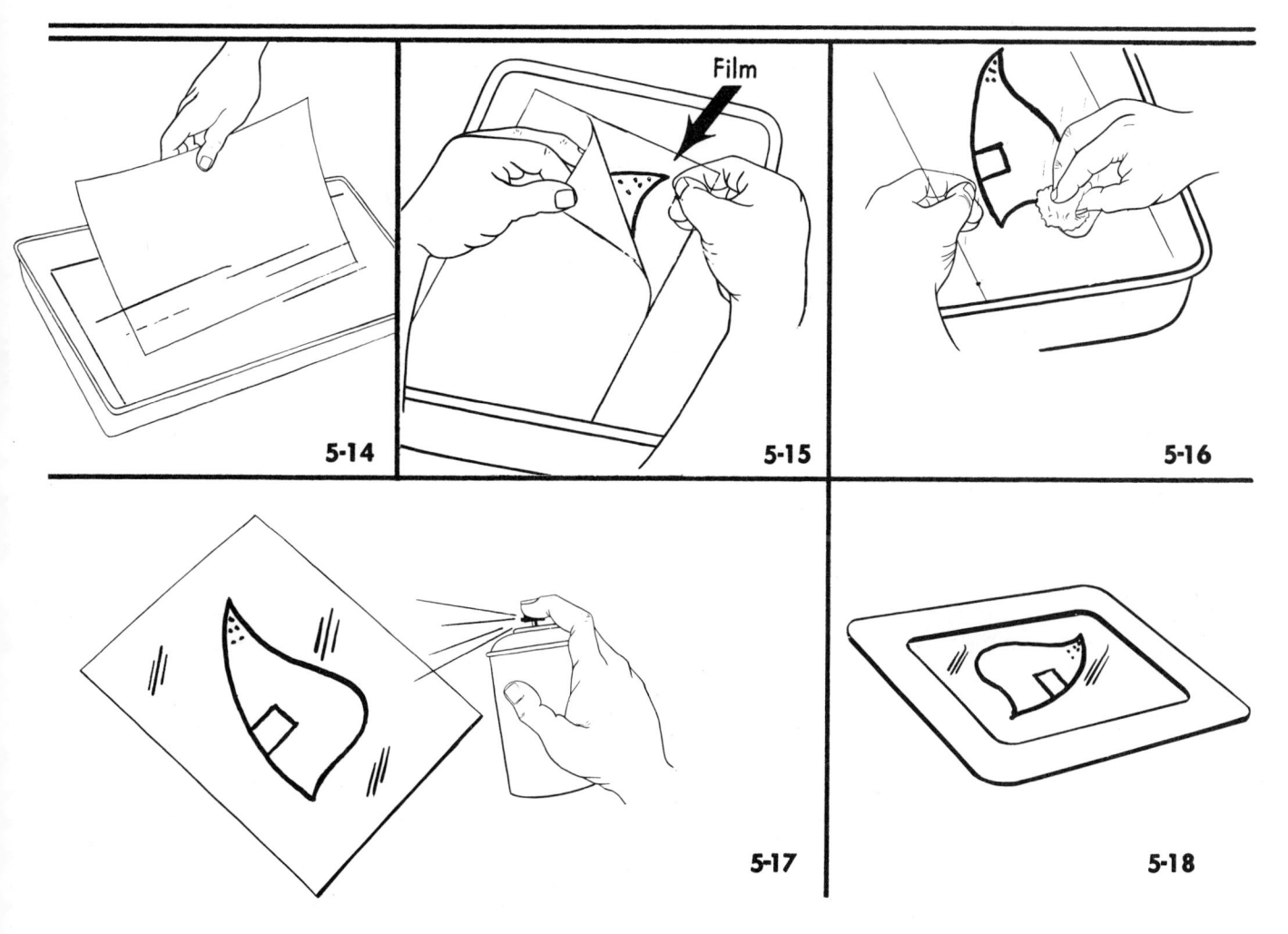

PICTURE-TRANSFER THERMO-FAX COLOR-LIFT

Black and white and full color transparencies can now be made with the Thermo-Fax Copying Machine and Thermo-Fax "Color-Lift" Film. Illustrations from magazines (LIFE, LOOK, and NATIONAL GEOGRAPHIC are three) printed on a clay-coated paper can be used in this process.

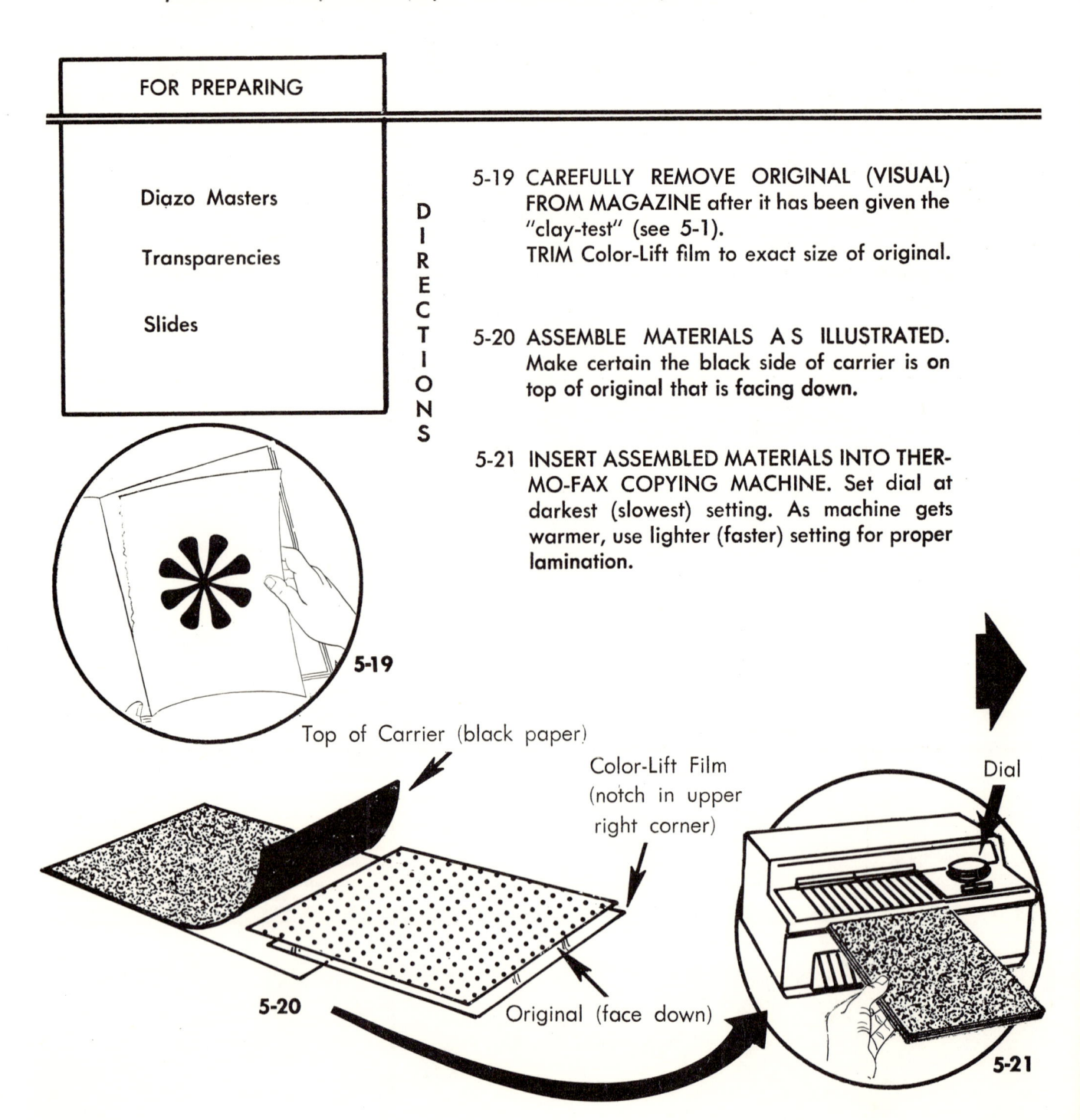

FOR PREPARING

Diazo Masters

Transparencies

Slides

DIRECTIONS

5-19 CAREFULLY REMOVE ORIGINAL (VISUAL) FROM MAGAZINE after it has been given the "clay-test" (see 5-1).
TRIM Color-Lift film to exact size of original.

5-20 ASSEMBLE MATERIALS AS ILLUSTRATED. Make certain the black side of carrier is on top of original that is facing down.

5-21 INSERT ASSEMBLED MATERIALS INTO THERMO-FAX COPYING MACHINE. Set dial at darkest (slowest) setting. As machine gets warmer, use lighter (faster) setting for proper lamination.

Top of Carrier (black paper)

Color-Lift Film (notch in upper right corner)

Original (face down)

Dial

EQUIPMENT AND MATERIALS

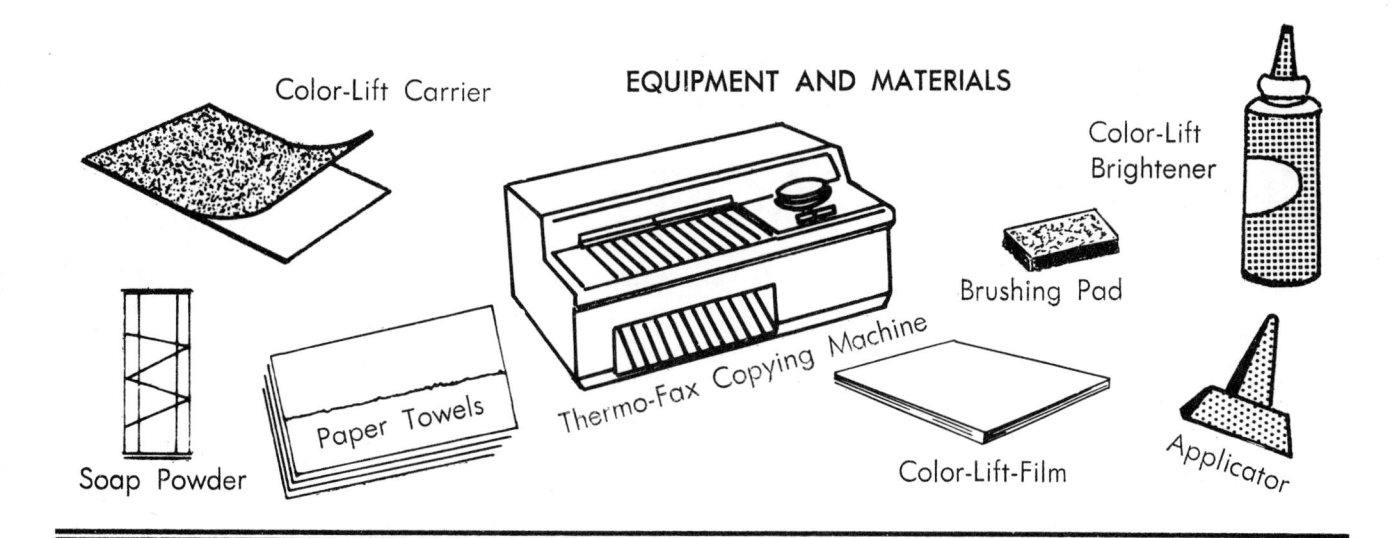

- Color-Lift Carrier
- Soap Powder
- Paper Towels
- Thermo-Fax Copying Machine
- Brushing Pad
- Color-Lift-Film
- Color-Lift Brightener
- Applicator

5-22 REMOVE LAMINATED ORIGINAL (film and paper) from carrier and **SOAK IN CONTAINER OF WATER** to which soap powder has beens added. Allow about two minutes for original to soak.

5-23 PEEL PAPER AWAY FROM FILM. "Flick" back one of the corners to help release the paper. If peeling is difficult, return film to the water for additional soaking.

5-26 MOUNT FOR PROJECTION OR VIEWING if desired (see pages 100 and 101 for masking and mounting ideas).

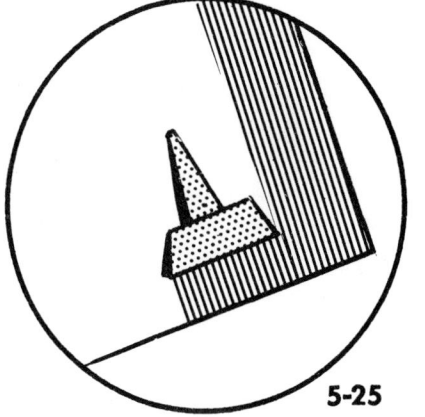

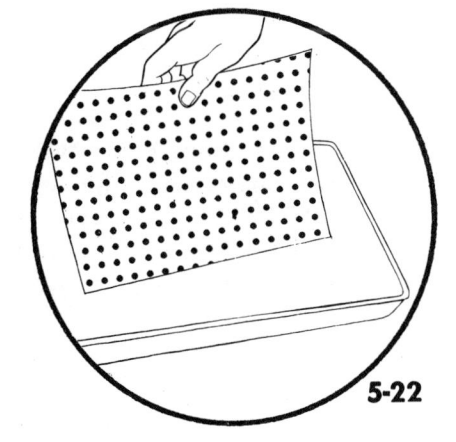

5-24 RETURN FILM TO WATER and brush the image (dull) side with the brushing pad or soft tissue to remove fine deposits of clay. Blot film dry between paper towels or hang to dry.

5-25 APPLY COLOR-LIFT BRIGHTENER to image (dull) side of film. Make certain film is lying on a flat surface. Apply brightener with slow even strokes. Allow about two minutes for drying.

83

PICTURE-TRANSFER SELF-SEALING ACTEATE

DIRECTIONS

Transparencies in full color can be made with self-sealing acetate. This type of acetate is transparent and has a pressure-sensitive adhesive on one side. Printed matter and visuals on clay-coated paper, combined with self-sealing acetate, can be processed to produce quality transparencies for projection or viewing.

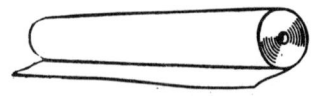

MATERIALS REQUIRED

Self-Sealing Acetate
Comb or Razor Blade
Container of Water
Cotton
Liquid Soap
Magazine Visuals
Paper Towels
Plastic Spray
Protective Paper
Transparency Mounts

Tear off excess paper

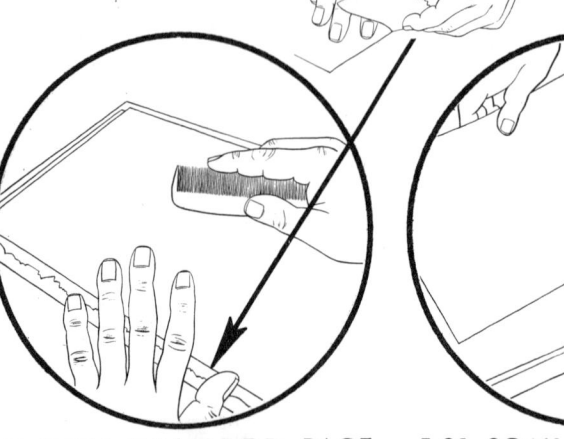

5-30 **TURN PRINTED PAGE (VISUAL) OVER** and rub down the entire surface with the flat side of a comb or a razor blade held at an angle. Use heavy even strokes. Place a protective sheet of paper on top to prevent damage to visual during rubbing.

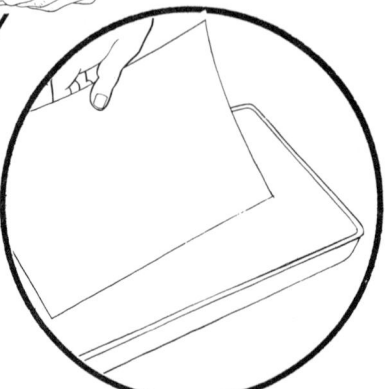

5-31 **SOAK IN CONTAINER OF WATER** for about ten minutes. A tablespoon of liquid soap will help speed up the soaking time. Thicker paper will require additional soaking time.

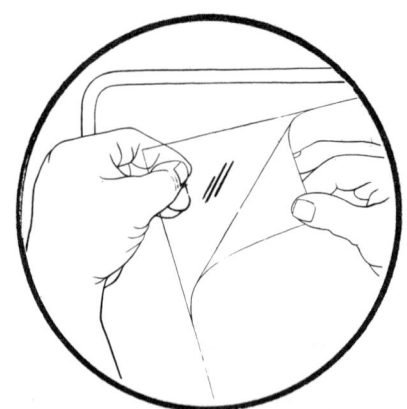

5-32 **GENTLY PEEL PAPER FROM ACETATE.** "Flick" back one corner to help release the paper. If peeling is difficult return paper and acetate to water for additional soaking.

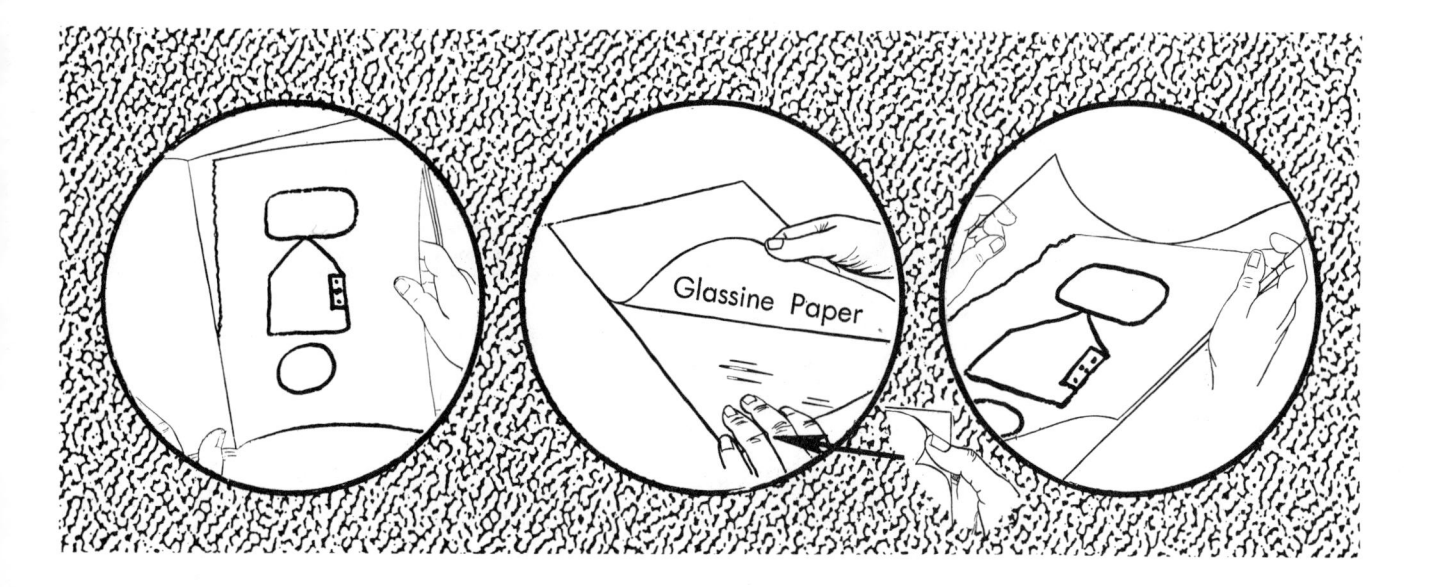

5-27 CAREFULLY REMOVE DESIRED PAGE FROM MAGAZINE after it has been given the "clay-test" (see 5-1).

5-28 CUT ACETATE SLIGHTLY LARGER THAN VISUAL to be transferred. PEEL GLASSINE PAPER FROM ACETATE by first "flicking" back one of the corners. This will help release the paper and allow for easy peeling.

5-29 ATTACH "STICKY" SIDE OF ACETATE to face of visual. Look through the acetate to accurately position on the visual. Make first contact at center.

5-33 RETURN TRANSPARENCY (ACETATE) TO THE WATER and gently wash off clay residue from transfer side (dull side) with cotton or soft tissue.

BLOT TRANSPARENCY DRY with paper towels or hang to dry. When dry, dull side will have an "ashy" appearance.

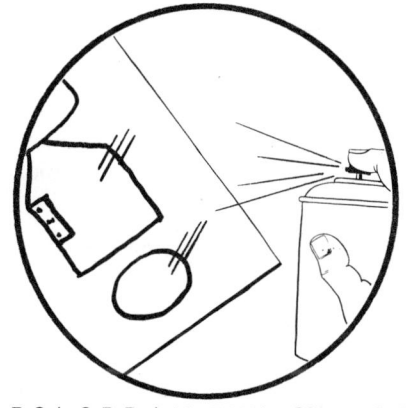

5-34 SPRAY DULL SIDE OF TRANSPARENCY with clear plastic spray. This will provide a protective coating and will make the image more transparent. Hold spray can about ten inches above the transparency and spray back and forth to apply an even coat.

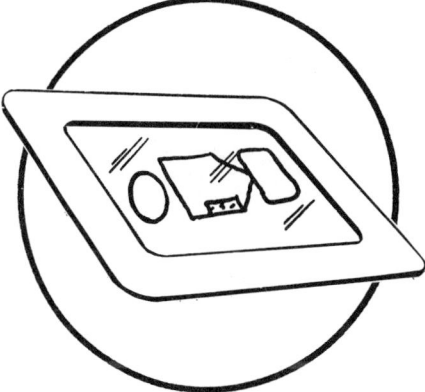

5-35 MOUNT FOR PROJECTION OR VIEWING if desired (see pages 100 and 101 for masking and mounting ideas).

DIFFUSION-TRANSFER TRANSPARENCIES

Diffusion-Transfer is a negative-to-positive photographic reflex process which makes it possible to convert existing ready-made visuals into projection transparencies in a matter of minutes in normal room light. Originals and printed matter may come from books, magazines, newspapers, etc.

To produce a transparency, expose the negative paper to a light source in contact with the original to be copied. A "reflex" exposure takes place. The negative paper, attached to a sheet of transparent positive film, is passed through a liquid developer. The exposed negative image develops; then a positive image also develops and transfers to the transparent positive film.

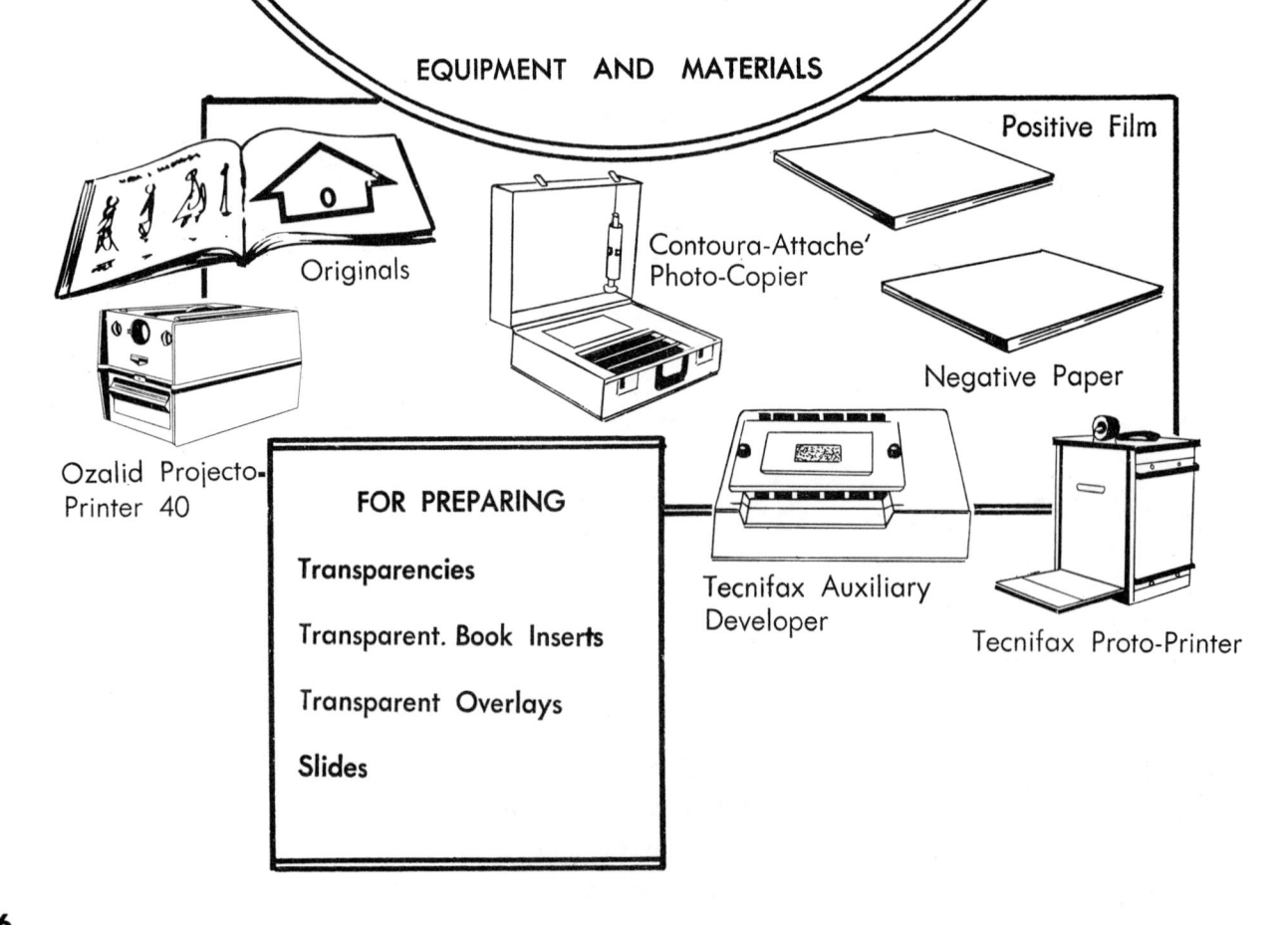

EQUIPMENT AND MATERIALS

Originals

Contoura-Attache' Photo-Copier

Positive Film

Negative Paper

Ozalid Projecto-Printer 40

Tecnifax Auxiliary Developer

Tecnifax Proto-Printer

FOR PREPARING

Transparencies

Transparent. Book Inserts

Transparent Overlays

Slides

5-36 To 5-42

DIRECTIONS

5-36 **EXPOSE SINGLE SHEET ORIGINAL** with negative paper by assembling the materials as illustrated.

5-37 **FEED ORIGINAL AND NEGATIVE PAPER** into Photo-Copier or a similar photo copy machine. Make certain the negative paper is next to the light source. Expose as instructed.

5-38 **EXPOSE BOUND ORIGINAL** with negative paper, using the Contoura-Attaché exposure unit by placing negative paper (sensitive side up) on top of the plastic pillow. Place the page of book, face down, on top of paper. Expose as instructed.

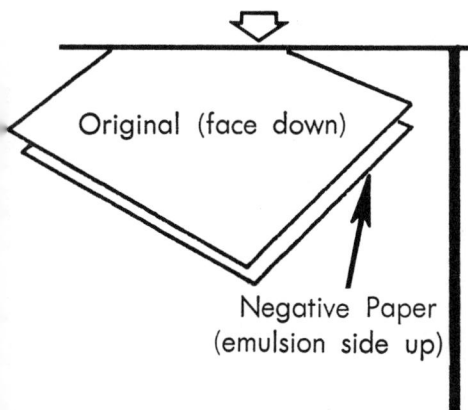

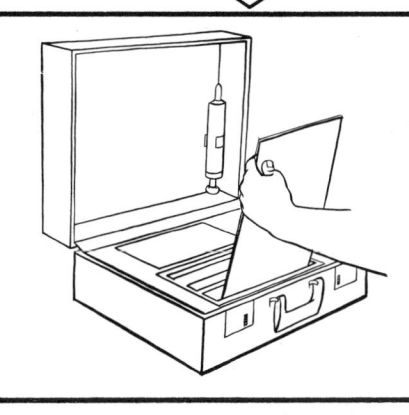

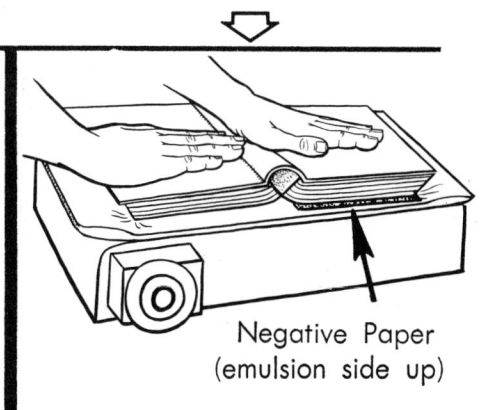

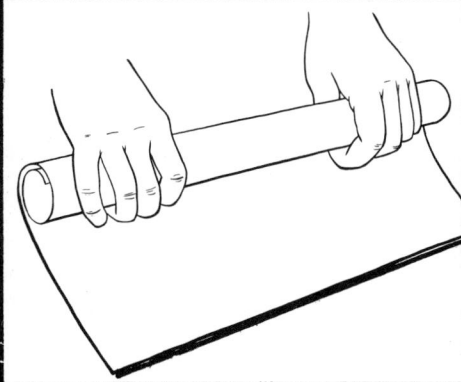

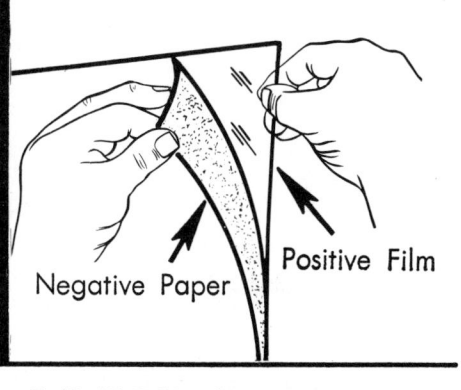

Original (face down)

Negative Paper (emulsion side up)

Negative Paper (emulsion side up)

Auxiliary Developer

Negative Paper

Positive Film

Notched Corner

Negative Paper

Positive Film

5-39 **DEVELOP FOR TRANSPARENCY** by placing exposed negative paper (emulsion side down) on top of positive film (emulsion side up) and feed into a developing unit.

5-40 **INSURE EVEN TRANSFER** by rolling film and paper as illustrated. Make certain the negative paper is on top. Allow a few seconds for developing to complete.

5-41 **UNROLL AND PEEL PAPER FROM THE FILM.** The transferred image will remain on the film.

5-42 **MOUNT FOR PROJECTION OR VIEWING** if desired (see pages 100 and 101 for masking and mounting ideas).

87

THERMO-FAX TRANSPARENCIES

Thermo-Fax, through a dry-heat process, makes possible the preparation of transparencies of nearly any original material in a matter of seconds. Original materials may be opaque or translucent, printed on one or both sides, and should conform to the size and thickness accepted by the Thermo-Fax Copying Machine. Two types of Themro-Fax transparencies are presented here.

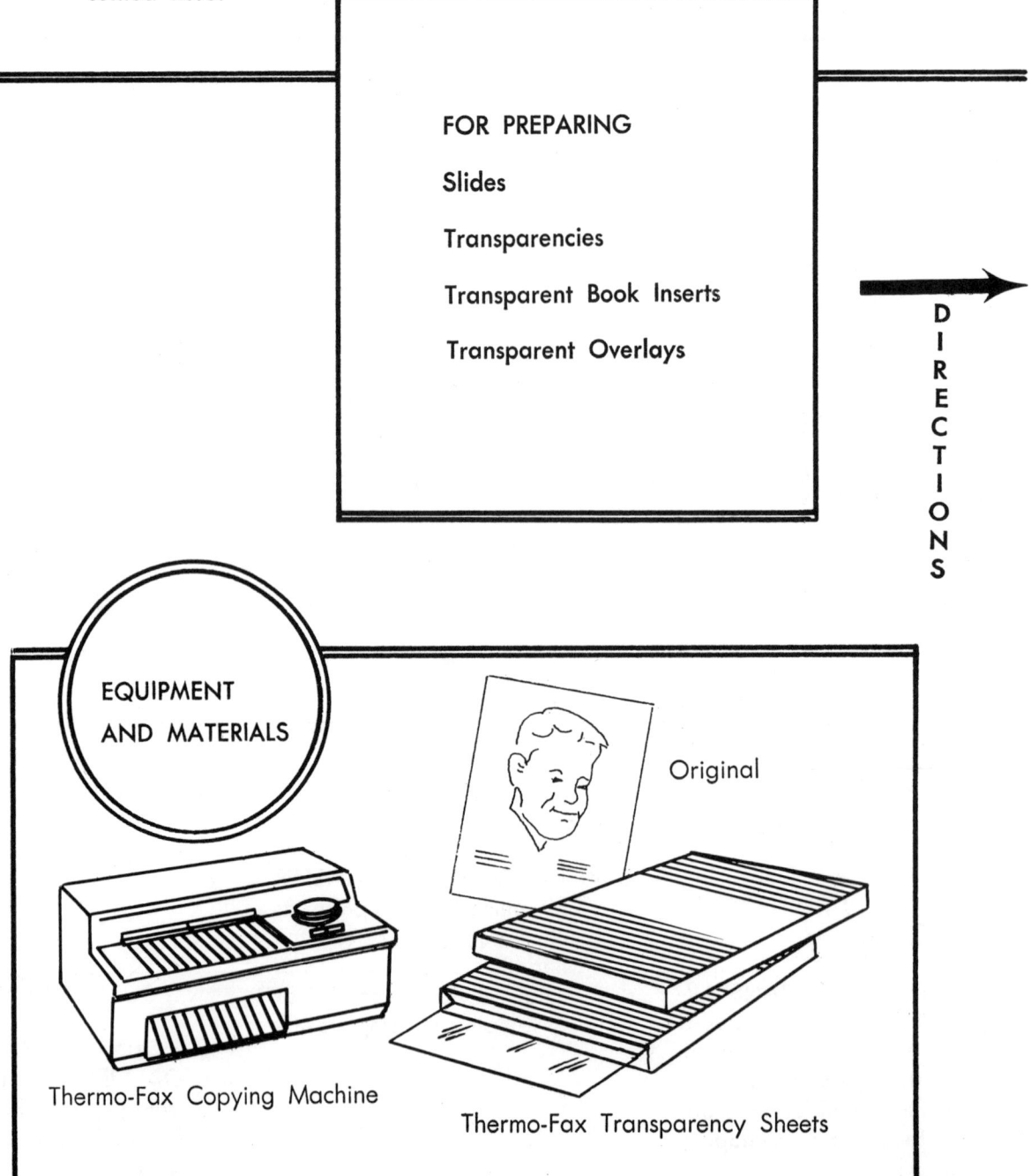

FOR PREPARING

Slides

Transparencies

Transparent Book Inserts

Transparent Overlays

DIRECTIONS

EQUIPMENT AND MATERIALS

Original

Thermo-Fax Copying Machine

Thermo-Fax Transparency Sheets

88

DIRECTIONS

DIRECT READING IMAGE PROJECTION TRANSPARENCY

This type of transparency produces a black image on a clear transparent sheet. The black image on the overhead projector stage makes possible easy reading for the user. Marking pens and pencils (see 3-33 and 3-45) and color and texture materials (see Section 4) can be used with this type of transparency.

5-43 PLACE THE TRANSPARENCY SHEET, with notched corner in the upper right-hand position, on top of the original.

5-44 PASS TRANSPARENCY AND ORIGINAL through a Thermo-Fax Copying Machine for the recommended time.

5-45 PRESTO! A TRANSPARENCY of the original in seconds.

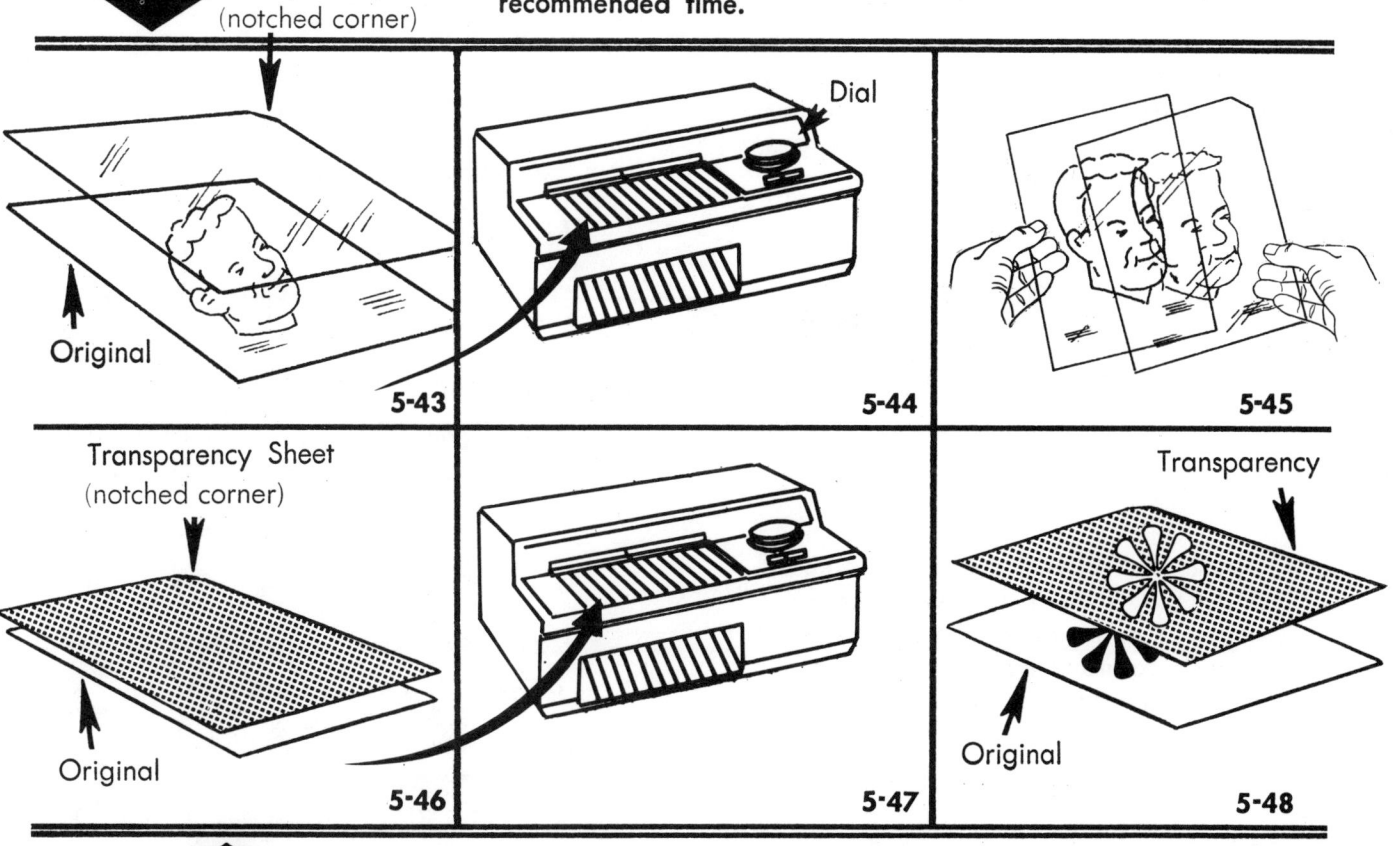

COLOR NEGATIVE TRANSPARENCY

This type of transparency produces a colored image on a dark background. It is available in a variety of colors. A ball point pen (see 3-46) can be used to draw, write, or letter directly on the transparency.

5-46 PLACE THE TRANSPARENCY SHEET, with notched corner, in the upper right-hand position, on top of the original.

5-47 PASS TRANSPARENCY AND ORIGINAL through a Thermo-Fax Machine for the recommended time.

5-48 PRESTO! A COLOR TRANSPARENCY of the original in seconds.

89

DIAZO TRANSPARENCIES

Diazo transparencies are made from acetate films sensitized with a diazo coating. These films (foils) are exposed with a transparent or translucent master to ultra-violet light in one of several types of diazo machines, or other recommended light sources. The exposed films are then developed by ammonia vapor. Transparencies may be mounted or unmounted for projection.

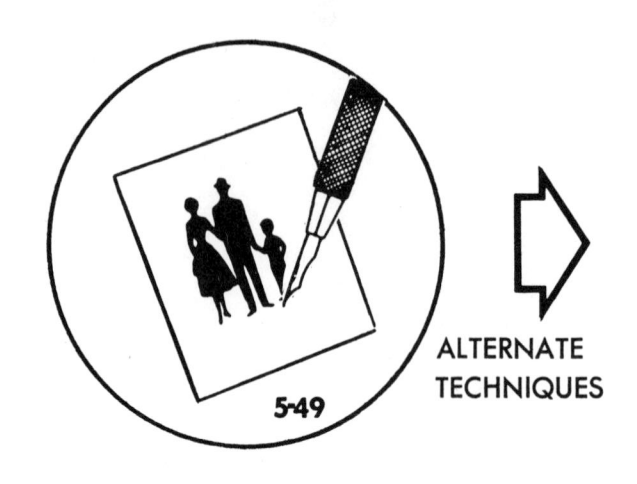

5-49 PREPARE A TRANSPARENT OR TRANSLUCENT MASTER. Drawing directly on a sheet of clear or frosted acetate, tracing paper or cloth is one way (see page 58).

Master (face down)
Diazo Film (sensitized side up)

5-50 ASSEMBLE MATERIALS FOR EXPOSURE AS ILLUSTRATED. INSERT IN TECNIFAX PROTO-PRINTER and expose for the recommended time. Exposure will vary according to the type of master and equipment used.

5-51 DEVELOP EXPOSED FILM IN TECNIFAX PROTO-COUPLER. This unit is designed to develop materials exposed in the Tecnifax Proto-Printer. Usually, exposure and developing times are approximately equal.

5-52 MOUNT TRANSPARENCY FOR PROJECTION (see pages 100 and 101 for masking and mounting suggestions). Transparencies may be projected unmounted.

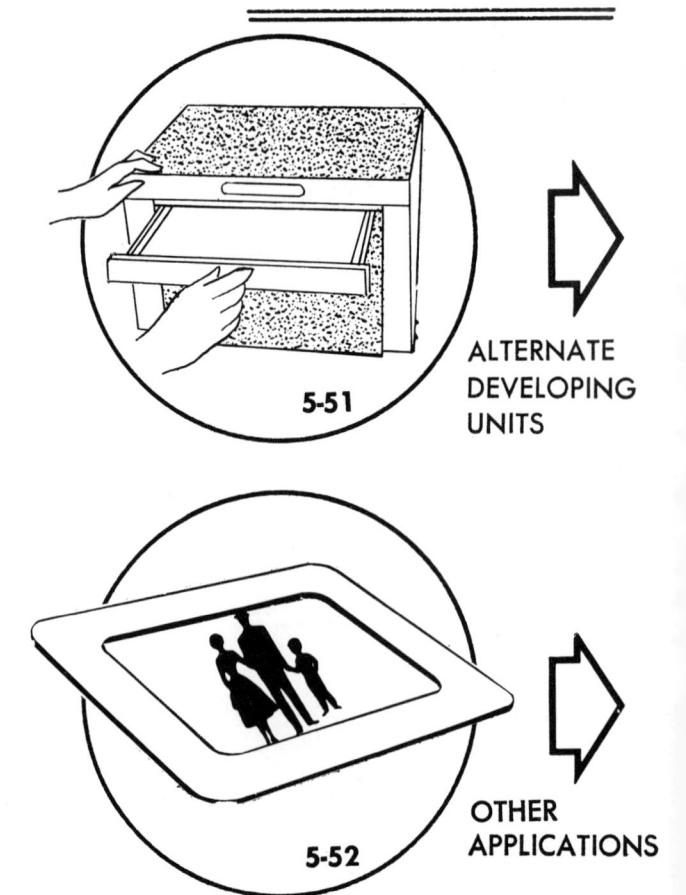

5-49 ⇨ ALTERNATE TECHNIQUES

5-50 ⇨ ALTERNATE EXPOSURE UNITS

5-51 ⇨ ALTERNATE DEVELOPING UNITS

5-52 ⇨ OTHER APPLICATIONS

5-70 To 5-76

5-53 Contoura-Attaché A Diffusion-Transfer Unit (see page 87).

5-54 Ozalid Projecto-Printer 40

5-55 Diffusion-Transfer Transparency (see pages 86 and 87).

5-56 Xerox Transparency

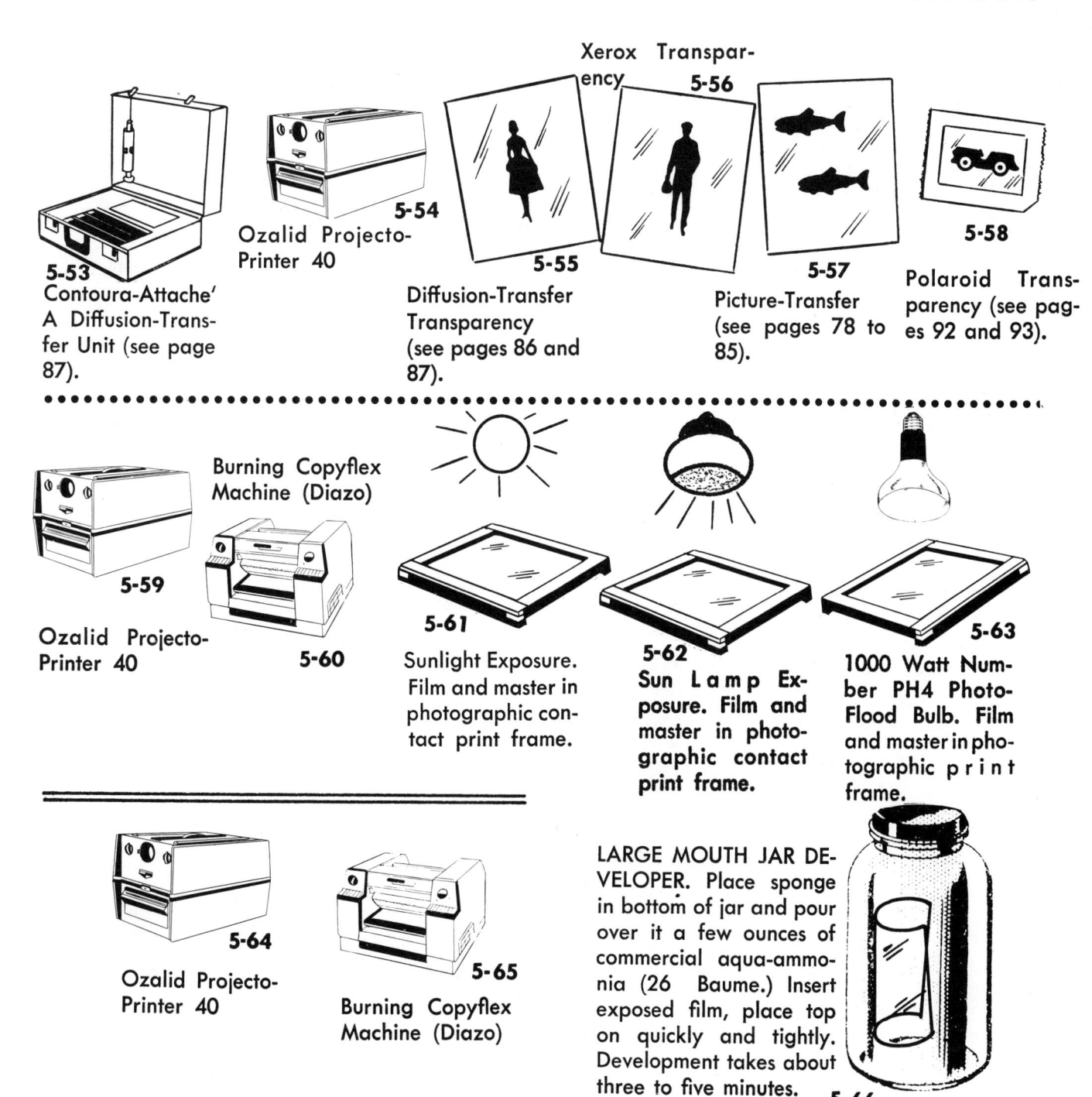

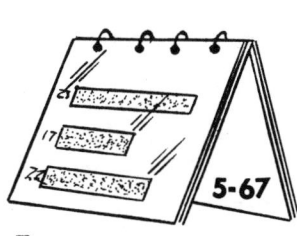

5-57 Picture-Transfer (see pages 78 to 85).

5-58 Polaroid Transparency (see pages 92 and 93).

5-59 Ozalid Projecto-Printer 40

5-60 Burning Copyflex Machine (Diazo)

5-61 Sunlight Exposure. Film and master in photographic contact print frame.

5-62 Sun Lamp Exposure. Film and master in photographic contact print frame.

5-63 1000 Watt Number PH4 Photo-Flood Bulb. Film and master in photographic print frame.

5-64 Ozalid Projecto-Printer 40

5-65 Burning Copyflex Machine (Diazo)

5-66 LARGE MOUTH JAR DEVELOPER. Place sponge in bottom of jar and pour over it a few ounces of commercial aqua-ammonia (26 Baume.) Insert exposed film, place top on quickly and tightly. Development takes about three to five minutes.

Lighted Displays Exhibits

5-67 Transparent Overlays

5-68

5-69 Transparent Inserts for Books

91

POLAROID TRANSPARENCIES

The Polaroid Corporation, makers of the Polaroid Land Camera, has developed a transparency (slide) making process which requires less than two minutes of total production time, and at about one-third the cost of commercially prepared transparencies. When transparencies are desired (3¼- by 4-inch or 2¼- by 2¼-inch), Polaroid Projection Films are used in place of the regular Polaroid film. The Projection Film produces a black and white image on a transparent film base, ready for immediate projection. At present, there are two types of Polaroid Projection Film, 146-L for line copy and 46-L for continuous tone.

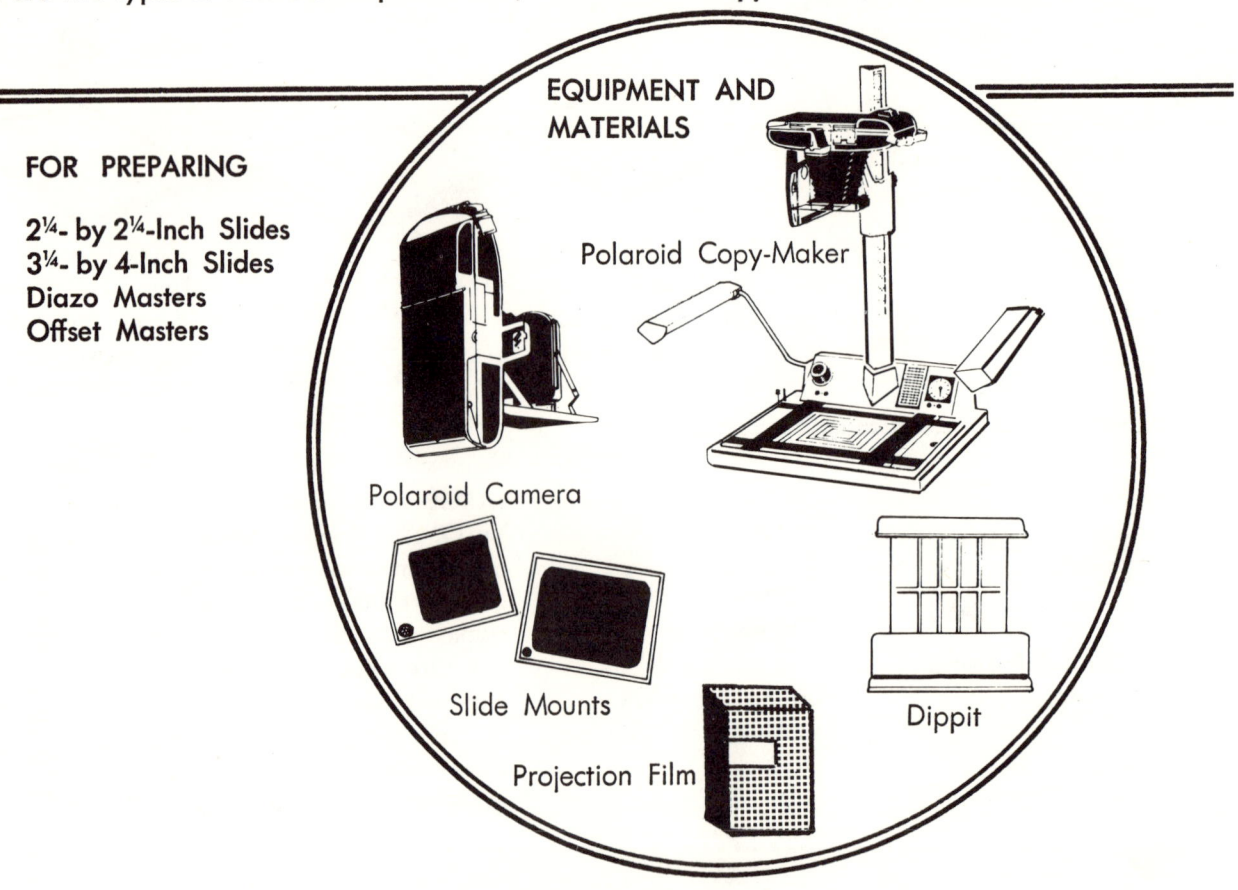

FOR PREPARING

2¼- by 2¼-Inch Slides
3¼- by 4-Inch Slides
Diazo Masters
Offset Masters

EQUIPMENT AND MATERIALS

- Polaroid Copy-Maker
- Polaroid Camera
- Slide Mounts
- Projection Film
- Dippit

POLAROID PROJECTION FILMS

TYPE 146-L FOR LINE COPY (Polaroid PolaLine Land Projection Film)

A very high contrast film designed to make 3¼- by 4-inch slides from line copy. Development time is 10 seconds; ASA equivalent speed is 120.

TYPE 46-L FOR CONTINUOUS TONE TRANSPARENCIES

Designed for continuous tone reproduction. Type 46-L is for 3¼- by 4-inch slides, Type 46 is for 2¼- by 2¼-inch slides. Development time is two minutes; ASA equivalent speed is 800.

DIRECTIONS

5-70 "SNAP" THE PICTURE TO EXPOSE FILM. Follow directions, enclosed with film, for recommended exposure time. The Polaroid Copy-Maker provides everything necessary to photograph sheets or objects up to 11- by 14-inches in size. TAKE PICTURES HORIZONTALLY ONLY.

5-71 PULL TAB TO START DEVELOPMENT. Use a quick single motion in pulling tab. Type 146L film (PolaLine) requires only 10 seconds for development; type 46, two minutes.

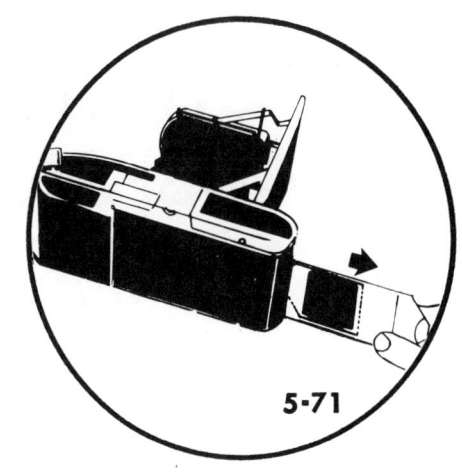

5-72 LIFT OUT FILM in a single motion. Handle by the edge, as the surface of film is soft and extremely delicate.

AFTER REMOVING TRANSPARENCY, FROM CAMERA, allow to air dry (about three minutes). Harden and stabilize in DIPPIT no longer than one hour after removal from camera. Hand-waving the film in the air will help reduce drying time.

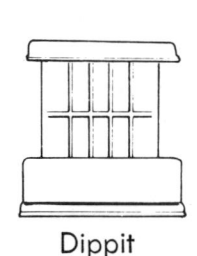

Dippit

5-73 OPEN METAL COVER hinged to the Dippit and carefully slide the film in as far as it will go. Hold film by the tab. Squeeze sides of Dippit to allow film to enter without touching lips of Dippit.

5-74 CLOSE METAL COVER TIGHTLY. Make certain film tab comes out through the slot in the cover. TURN DIPPIT UPSIDE DOWN. Agitate for about 20 seconds ("rock" back and forth).

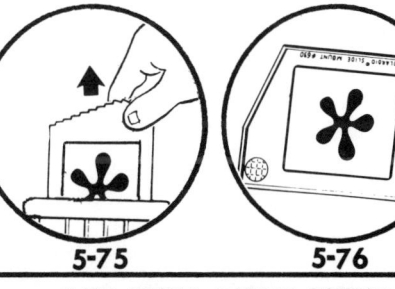

5-75 TURN DIPPIT RIGHT SIDE UP. With cover still closed pull the film out with a rapid motion. The lips of the Dippit will squeegee excess liquid from the film.

5-76 MOUNT FOR PROJECTION (see 5-98 and 5-99 for directions).

ELECTRONIC STENCIL TRANSPARENCIES

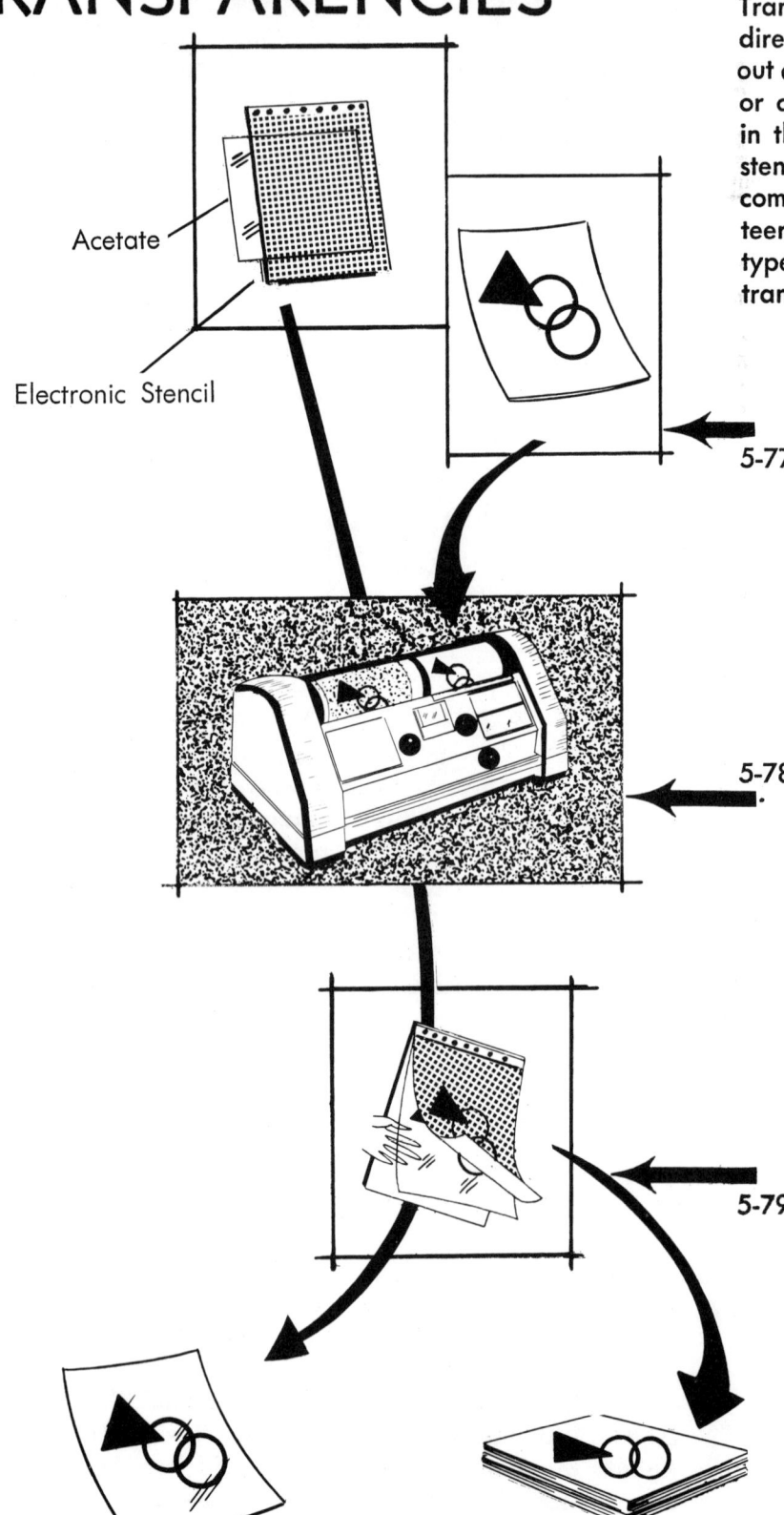

Transparencies can now be prepared, direct from original art or copy, without a photographic camera, darkroom, or chemicals. At the same time, and, in the same operation, a duplicating stencil is being electronically cut. The complete operation takes less than fifteen minutes. Dealers handling this type of equipment usually offer the transparency making service.

Acetate

Electronic Stencil

DIRECTIONS

5-77 INSERT THIN SHEET OF CLEAR ACETATE between electronic stencil and backing sheet. This can be done by slipping a ruler between s t e n c i l and backing sheet, near the top, and moving ruler downward to create a "pocket" for the acetate. Insert acetate in "pocket."

5-78 A T T A C H ORIGINAL ART OR COPY AND STENCIL TO MACHINE, with the stencil going on one drum (cylinder) and the original on the other. Both drums are set in motion, revolving at the same speed. A photo-electric eye scans the original; at the same time a recording stylus traces the original image on the stencil and acetate.

5-79 R E M O V E ACETATE F R O M STENCIL. Acetate can be mounted for projection (see pages 100 and 101). Stencil can be used on an ink duplicating machine to make as many paper copies as desired.

FLUID DUPLICATOR TRANSPARENCIES

A fluid duplicating machine can be used to make excellent color slides and transparencies for projection or display. The simple steps for preparing transparencies are similar to those required for preparing regular fluid paper copies, except that frosted acetate is used in place of paper. Several colors can be applied to a single transparency in one operation.

Color Carbon Sheet

Frosted Acetate (dull side up)

DIRECTIONS

5-80 **PREPARE MASTER FOR PROCESSING.** Follow the same steps used in making a master for paper duplications. Several colors can be placed on a single master by inserting the desired color carbon sheet under the master during the preparation. A stylus, ball point pen, or hard lead pencil can be used to draw or letter on the master. SEVERAL LETTERING DEVICES can be used to make attractive letters on the master (see 2-47, 3-41, and 3-46). SHADING CAN BE APPLIED with plastic shading plates.

5-81 **INSERT FINISHED MASTER IN FLUID DUPLICATOR AND FEED FROSTED ACETATE INTO THE MACHINE.** Several sheets of fluid duplicating paper should be fed into the machine before running the frosted acetate. HAND FEEDING THE ACETATE is recommended.

5-82 **SPRAY FROSTED (DULL) SIDE OF ACETATE** with clear plastic spray. Lay acetate on a flat surface, with a protective sheet of paper under acetate to prevent spray from adhering to working surface. Hold spray can about ten inches above the acetate and spray back and forth to place an even coat of spray on the printed surface.

5-83 **MOUNT FOR PROJECTION OR VIEWING.** (See pages 100 and 101 for masking and mounting ideas).

BESELER SLIDE-O-FILM SLIDES

Beseler Slide-O-Film is a new photographic film that requires no darkroom or chemical processing. This film has unusual adaptions. It makes black and white negatives from color slides, projection positives from negatives, negatives from Polaroid transparency positives (see page 92), negatives from positive motion picture film, etc.

Slide-O-Film operates on a principle involving exposure to light and development through the application of heat. Easy-to-understand steps are presented here.

EQUIPMENT AND MATERIALS

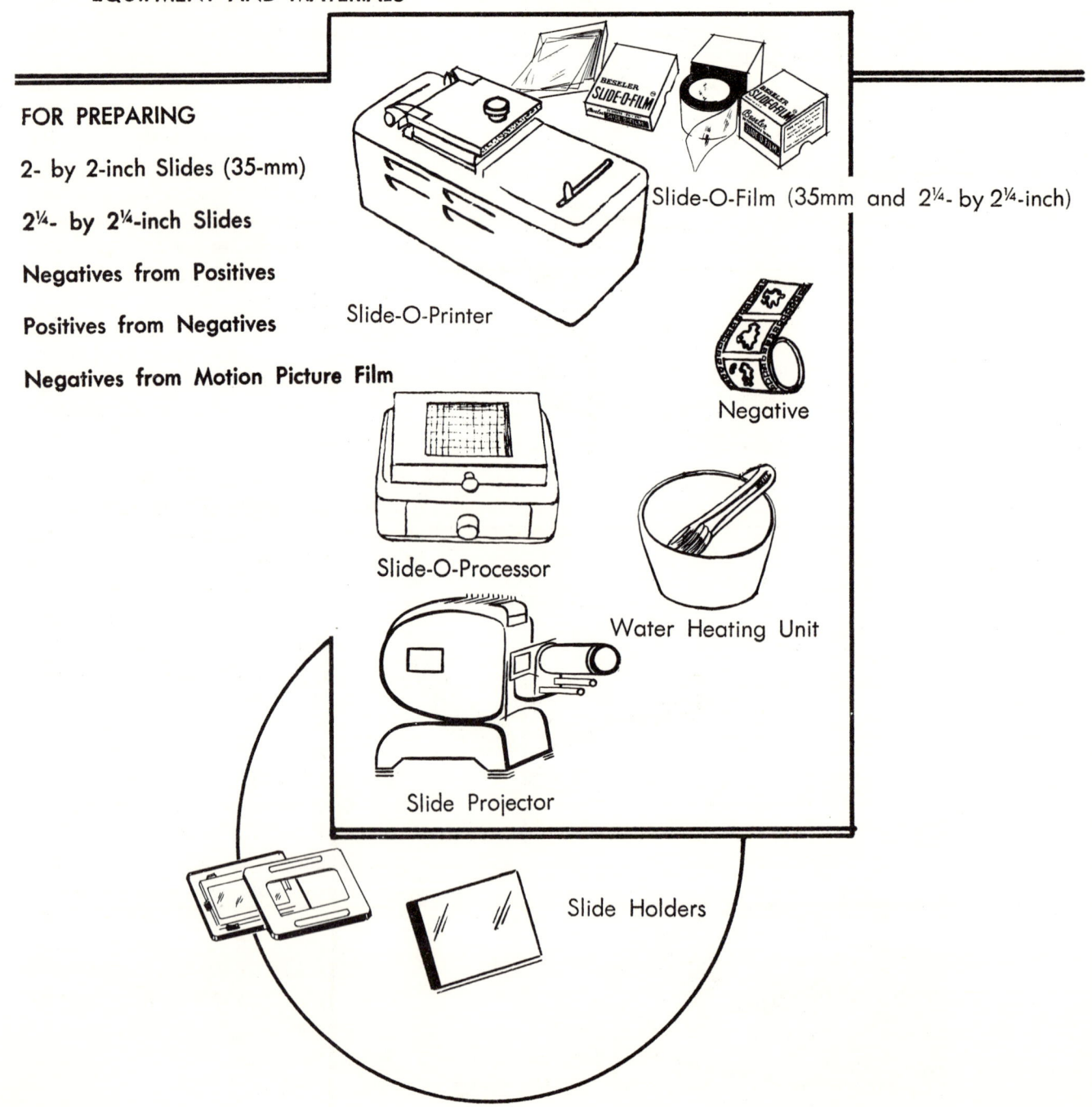

FOR PREPARING

2- by 2-inch Slides (35-mm)

2¼- by 2¼-inch Slides

Negatives from Positives

Positives from Negatives

Negatives from Motion Picture Film

Slide-O-Printer

Slide-O-Film (35mm and 2¼- by 2¼-inch)

Negative

Slide-O-Processor

Water Heating Unit

Slide Projector

Slide Holders

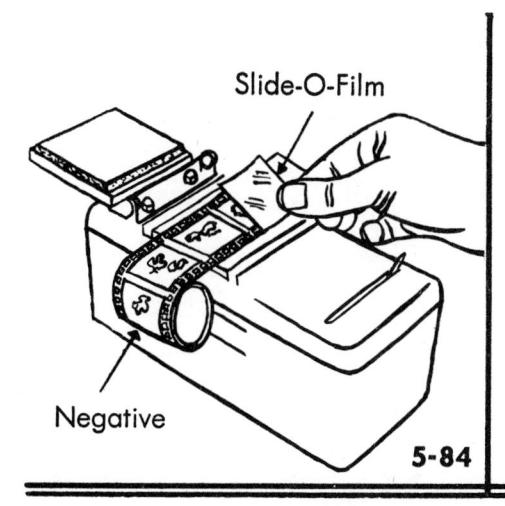

5-84 To 5-90

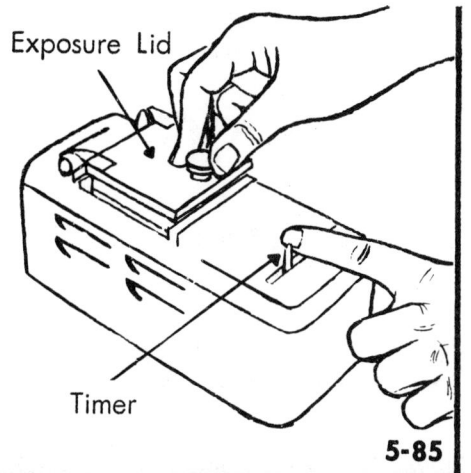

Figure 5-84: Slide-O-Film, Negative
Figure 5-85: Exposure Lid, Timer
Figure 5-86: Exposed Slide-O-Film

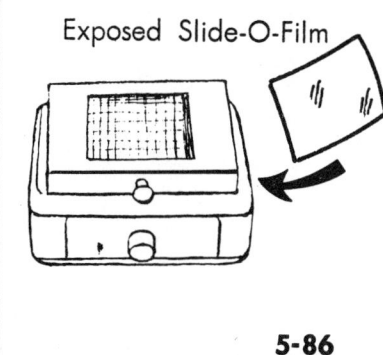

PROCESSING WITH BESELER EQUIPMENT

5-84 PLACE NEGATIVE OR POSITIVE on glass exposure aperature (emulsion or dull side up). Position Slide-O-Film, dull side down, on top of film.

5-85 CLOSE EXPOSURE LID, exerting a little pressure after closing, and set the timer for the time recommended.

5-86 PLACE EXPOSED FILM IN HEATED PROCESSOR, dull side up, for a few seconds. The developed image will be opaque, white, and clear instead of black and clear associated with conventional film.

PROCESSING WITH SLIDE PROJECTOR AND HEAT

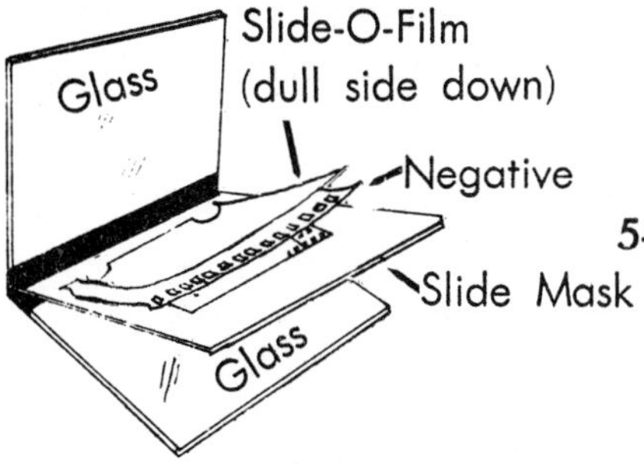

Figure 5-87: Glass, Slide-O-Film (dull side down), Negative, Slide Mask, Glass

5-87 ASSEMBLE MATERIALS FOR EXPOSURE as illustrated. Slide mask is used to assure correct film alignment in holder.

5-88 INSERT IN SLIDE PROJECTOR. Make certain the negative is facing projector's light source. Consult Exposure Table for recommended time.

5-89 DEVELOP by immersing in boiling water for about two seconds. Wipe off moisture with clean soft cloth.

5-90 MOUNT FOR PROJECTION (see pages 98 and 99).

EXPOSURE TABLE

Negative Type	Average 300-Watt Projector	Average 500-Watt Projector
Light Density	5-10 seconds	2-5 seconds
Medium Density	15-40 seconds	7-20 seconds
Heavy Density	50 sec. & up	25 sec. & up

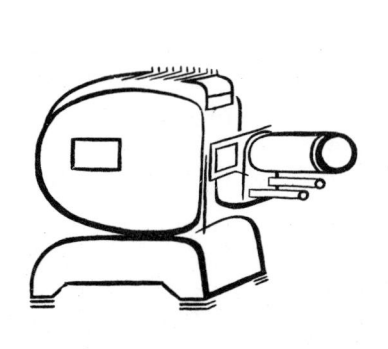

Figure 5-88,  5-89,  5-90

SLIDE BINDING AND MOUNTING

Slides, 2-by 2-inch and 2¼-by 2¼-inch, are normally returned from the photofinisher in cardboard mounts. These mounts do not provide permanent protection from dust, finger prints, and heat buckling. Several of the techniques presented here are designed to give slides permanent protection.

5-92 LIGHTWEIGHT PLASTIC BINDER. The film is placed between two pieces of thin glass and locked in place with the upper half of mount. "Linda" and OPTA-Mounts are two brands.

5-93 INTERLOCKING METAL MOUNT To use, place film between two pieces of thin glass and lock in place with the two sections of the mount.

5-94 SELF-LOCKING WHITE PLASTIC MOUNT. A one-piece self-locking mount. To use, place film in mount and snap close. Mr-E-Enterprises and Sonark Industries distribute these mounts.

5-91 THUMB SPOT is a guide for accurate projection of slides. Thumb spot, usually made of gummed-paper, is placed in the lower left corner of the slide after it has been mounted (turn slide to read right). To project, turn slide so that the thumb spot is in the upper right corner (facing the projector operator). Some thumb spots are numbered to offer the added advantage of indexing slides (Numbatabs and Slide Indexers are two).

5-95 ALUMINUM BINDER. To use, insert film in mask and place between two pieces of glass. Slide film and mask into aluminum frame and close open end.

Open end folds over to lock film and glass in.

5-99 POLAROID SLIDE MOUNT NO. 633 (3¼-by 4-Inch Slide) White plastic mount designed for type 46L and 146L Polaroid Transparency Film (see pages 92 and 93). The film is placed between the two sections which snap together. No glass is needed.

5-98 POLAROID SLIDE MOUNT NO. 630 (2¼-by 2¼-Inch Slide) White plastic mount designed for type 46 Polaroid Transparency Film (see pages 92 and 93). The film is placed between the two sections which snap together. No glass is needed.

5-97 KODAK READY MOUNT. A one-piece cardboard mount designed for 35-mm slides. The inside of the mount has an adhesive that seals with heat. To use, insert film in mount and seal with tacking iron (see page 5) or a hand iron.

5-96 GLASS AND TAPE MOUNT. Here is an economical technique for the permanent protection of slides (all sizes). To use, insert film or acetate into mask; sandwich between two pieces of cover glass and bind together by running a strip of slide binding tape completely around the outer edges.

Mask

LARGE TRANSPARENCIES MASKING AND MOUNTING

Unlimited imagination can be employed for the masking and mounting of transparencies for the overhead projector. Here are a few simple techniques for adding versatility to projection transparencies.

Draw or letter directly on mount

5-100 STAPLED MOUNT. Staple transparency to the under side of mount.

5-101 SELF-CONTAINED ALL PLASTIC MOUNT. No mounting or masking is necessary.

5-102 GEMINI TRANSPARENCY MOUNT. A pressure-sensitive self-sealing mount.

5-103 TAPED MOUNT. Tape all four edges to the underside of mount with plastic or masking tape.

MOUNTS ARE EASY TO MAKE. They can be cut out of most sturdy opaque materials, such as cardboard, poster board, or even file folders.

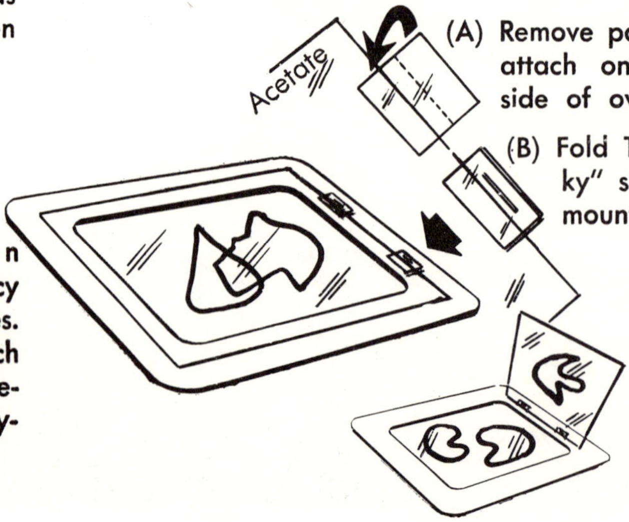

How to Use Techinges.

(A) Remove paper backing and attach one-third to under side of overlay.

(B) Fold Techinge in half ("sticky" sides in) and staple to mount as illustrated.

5-104 SINGLE OVERLAYS can be hinged to transparency with Tecnifax Techinges. These hinges are 1¼-inch square strips of pressure-sensitive metallized "Mylar."

100

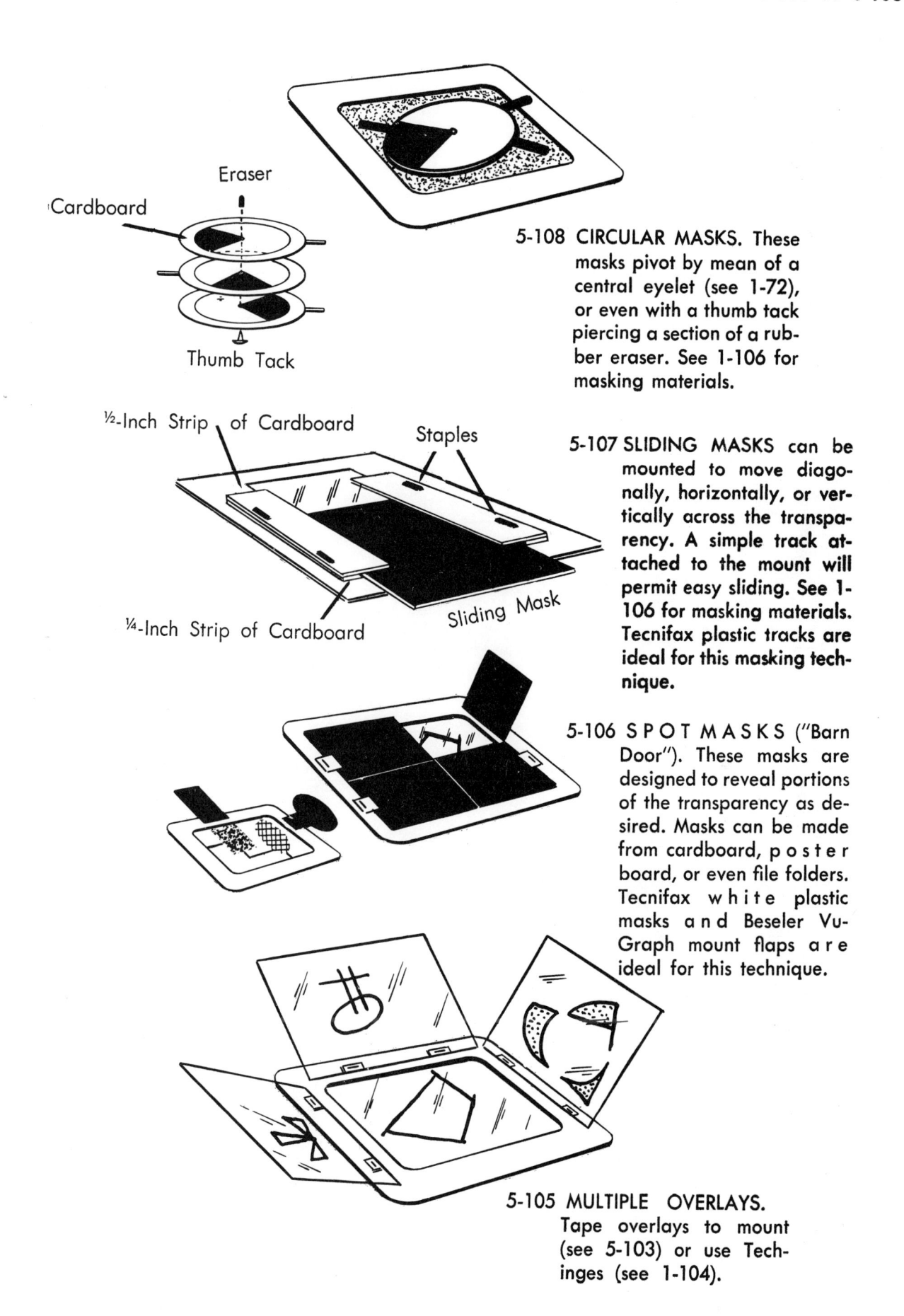

5-108 CIRCULAR MASKS. These masks pivot by mean of a central eyelet (see 1-72), or even with a thumb tack piercing a section of a rubber eraser. See 1-106 for masking materials.

5-107 SLIDING MASKS can be mounted to move diagonally, horizontally, or vertically across the transparency. A simple track attached to the mount will permit easy sliding. See 1-106 for masking materials. Tecnifax plastic tracks are ideal for this masking technique.

5-106 SPOT MASKS ("Barn Door"). These masks are designed to reveal portions of the transparency as desired. Masks can be made from cardboard, poster board, or even file folders. Tecnifax white plastic masks and Beseler Vu-Graph mount flaps are ideal for this technique.

5-105 MULTIPLE OVERLAYS. Tape overlays to mount (see 5-103) or use Tech-inges (see 1-104).

REFERENCE A

PUBLICATIONS

This listing of publications makes no claim to completeness, but merely suggests certain starting points for further reading related to the techniques presented in this manual. The techniques treated by each reference are indicated in brackets following the reference with "M" referring to mounting, "L" to lettering, "V" to visual, "CT" to color texture, and "T" to transparencies. It should be pointed out here that the extent to which each reference treats a technique may range from partial to extensive coverage. Complete addresses may be found in Reference D.

AV MATERIALS HANDBOOK, Audio-Visual Center, Indiana University, Bloomington, 1960, (M-L-V-CT-T).

Benson, John H., and Arthur G. Carey: THE ELEMENTS OF LETTERING, McGraw Hill Book Company, Inc., New York, 1950, (L).

Berg, Esther L., and Florence B. Freedman: AUDIO-VISUAL EDUCATION, Chilton Company, Philadelphia, 1961, (T).

BETTER MOUNTING BY THE DRY MOUNTING METHOD, Seal, Incorporated, Shelton, Connecticut, 1961, (M).

BETTER BULLETIN BOARD DISPLAYS, Visual Instruction Bureau, University of Texas, Austin, (L-V).

Bissex, Henry S.: FOR INSTANCE NUMBER I, Tecnifax Corp., Holyoke, Mass., 1958, (T).

Brown, J. W., and Richard B. Lewis (eds): AV INSTRUCTIONAL MATERIALS MANUAL, McGraw-Hill Book Company, Inc., New York, 1959, (M-L-V-T).

Brown, J. W., R. B. Lewis, and F. F. Harcleroad: AV INSTRUCTION MATERIALS AND METHODS, McGraw-Hill Book Company, Inc., New York, 1959, (M-L-V-T).

Cardamone, Tom: ADVERTISING AGENCY & STUDIO SKILLS, Watson-Guptill Publications, Inc., New York, 1959, (M-L-V-CT).

Coffman, Joe W.: TECHNOLOGY OF THE DIAZOTYPE PROCESSES, Tecnifax Corporation, Holyoke, Mass., 1957, (T).

Cross, A. J. Foy, and Irene F. Cypher: AUDIO-VISUAL EDUCATION, Thomas Y. Crowell Company, New York, 1961, (T).

Dale, Edgar: AUDIO-VISUAL METHODS IN TEACHING, Holt, Rinehart and Winston, Inc., New York, 1954, (CT-T).

De Kieffer, Robert, and Lee W. Cochran: MANUAL OF AUDIO-VISUAL TECHNIQUES, Prentice-Hall, Inc., Englewood Cliffs, N. J., 1958, (V-T).

Denno, Raymond: USING THE OPAQUE PROJECTOR, Squibb-Taylor, Inc., Dallas, (M-V).

DIAZOCHROME SLIDES FOR VISUAL COMMUNICATION, Tecnifax Corporation, Holyoke, Mass, 1956, (T).

Dunavan, Carl C., and Emma Fantone: TEACHERS MAKE: SLIDES, TRANPARENCIES, OPAQUES, TAPE RECORDINGS, Audio-Visual Office, New Jersey State Department of Education, Trenton, (V-T).

East, Marjorie, and Edgar Dale: DISPLAY FOR LEARNING, MAKING AND USING VISUAL MATERIALS, Holt, Rinehart and Winston, Inc., New York, 1952, (M-L-V-CT-T).

Eboch, Sidney C.: OPERATING AUDIO-VISUAL EQUIPMENT, Chandler Publishing Company, San Francisco, 1960, (T).

Finstad, Charles: VU-GRAPHICS, A MANUAL ON VU-GRAPH PROJECTION, Charles Beseler Company, Newark, N. J., 1952, (V-CT-T).

Frye, R. A.: GRAPHIC TOOLS, Graphic Tools, Roswell, New Mexico, 1960, (M-L-V-CT-T).

Gnaedinger, William G., and Sheldon Osborne: HANDMADE LANTERN SLIDE MANUAL, Community College Service, State College of Washington, Pullman, 1952, (T).

Hamilton, G. E.: HOW TO MAKE HANDMADE LANTERN SLIDES, Keystone View Company, Meadville, Pa., 1956, (T).

HANDMADE LANTERN SLIDES, Teaching Aids Laboratory, The Ohio State University, Columbus, (T).

HANDMADE MATERIALS, International Cooperative Administration, Washington, D. C., 1960, (M-L-V).

Hartsell, H. C., and W. L. Veenendall: OVERHEAD PROJECTION, Henry Stewart, Inc., Buffalo, N. Y., 1960 (T).

Hass, Kenneth B., and Harry Q. Packer: PREPARATION AND USE OF AUDIO-VISUAL AIDS, Prentice-Hall, Inc., Englewood Cliffs, N. J., 1955, (M-L-V).

Holland, Ben F., and others: AUDIO-VISUAL MATERIALS AND DEVICES, Rogers Litho, Lubbock, Texas, 1958, (M-T).

Jones, B. A.: MAKE SLIDES WORTH WHILE, Ethyl Corporation, Detroit, Michigan, 1952, (T).

———SLIDES: CONFUSING OR CLEAR, Ethyl, Corporation, Detroit, Michigan, 1952, (T).

Kinder, James S.: AUDIO-VISUAL MATERIALS AND TECHNIQUES, American Book Company, New York, 1959, (M-V-T).

LANTERN SLIDES AND HOW TO MAKE THEM, Bausch and Lomb Optical Company, Rochester N. Y., 1949, (T).

Maurello, S. Ralph: HOW TO DO PASTE-UPS AND MECHANICALS, Tudor Publishing Company, New York, 1960, (M-L-V-CT).

McCALL'S GOLDEN DO-IT-BOOK, Golden Press, Inc., New York, 1960, (L-V).

Meeks, Martha F.: LETTERING TECHNIQUES, Visual Instruction Bureau, University of Texas, Austin, (L).

Memott, E. J., and L. R. Linderman: SIGHT AND SOUND IN TEACHING, Audio-Visual Center, Brigham Young University, Provo, Utah, (M-L-V-CT-T).

Nelson, Leslie W.: INSTRUCTIONAL AIDS, HOW TO MAKE AND USE THEM, William C. Brown Company, Dubuque, Iowa, 3rd ed., 1961, (M-L-V-T).

OPAQUE PROJECTOR, Visual Instruction Bureau, University of Texas, Austin, (M-V).

Orr, W. N.: EFFECTIVE SLIDE PREPARATION, Reproduction Dept., Lockheed Aircraft Corp., Georgia Division, Marietta, (T).

PICTURE POWER, Charles Beseler Company, East Orange, New Jersey, (T).

PRODUCTION OF 2-by 2-inch SLIDES, Visual Instruction Bureau, University of Texas, Austin, (T).

Randall, Reino W., and Edward C. Haines: BULLETIN BOARDS AND DISPLAYS, Davis Publication, Worcester, Massachusetts, 1961, (M-L-V).

Sands, Lester B.: AUDIO-VISUAL PROCEDURES IN TEACHING, The Ronald Press Company, New York, 1956, (M-V-T).

Shores, Louis: INSTRUCTIONAL MATERIALS, The Ronald Press, New York, 1960, (M-L-T).

TEAR SHEET FOR TEACHING, Visual Instruction Bureau, University of Texas, Austin, 1954, (M-V).

THEY SEE WHAT YOU MEAN, Ozalid, Johnson City, New York, 1959, (L-V-CT-T).

TRANSPARENCY PREPARATION METHODS, Central Film and Equipment Exchange, Fort McPherson, Ga., (T).

VARIGRAPH INSTRUCTION MANUAL, Varigraph Company, Madison, Wisconsin, (L).

Weaver, Gilbert, and Elroy W. Bollinger: VISUAL AIDS: THEIR CONSTRUCTION AND USE, D. Van Nostrand Company, Inc., New York, 1949, (M-L-V-T).

Wittich, Walter A., and Charles F. Schuller: AUDIOVISUAL MATERIALS: THEIR NATURE AND USE, Harper and Brothers, New York, 3rd ed., 1962, (M-V-T).

REFERENCE B

VISUAL AIDS

The visual aids listed below and on the following pages may be used to supplement the material in this manual. The aids have been grouped under the technique with which the aid is related. Some of the aids can be used to supplement reference to other techniques. It should be pointed out here that the extent to which a motion picture or filmstrip treats a technique may range from partial to extensive coverage. It is also recommended that they be viewed before use in order to determine their suitability for a particular group.

Titles of motion pictures (marked "MP") and filmstrips (marked "FS") are included in the following list. Each title is followed by the name of the producer or distributor. Abbreviations are used for the name of the producers or distributors, and these abbreviations are identified at the end of this reference. In many instances, the films can be borrowed or rented from local or state 16-mm-film libraries. (A nationwide list of these sources is given in A DIRECTORY OF 3660 16-mm FILM LIBRARIES, available for 35 cents from the Superintendent of Documents, Washington 25, D. C.). THE AV INDEX, published by Audio-Visual Research Institute, 1346 Broadway, Detroit, Michigan is another recommended reference. Unless otherwise indicated, the motion pictures are 16-mm sound black-and-white films and the filmstrips are 35-mm black-and-white and silent. The length of motion pictures is given in minutes (min), that of filmstrips in frames (fr). Complete addresses may be found in Reference D.

MOUNTING TECHNIQUES

BETTER BULLETIN BOARDS (MP, IndU, 13 min color) Presents a variety of bulletin boards; how they are constructed and how they can be used. Demonstrates the use of golf tees, hangers, and strings on peg boards. Illustrates how to attach pictures and objects through the use of thumb tacks, pins, special wax, and holders.

DRY MOUNT YOUR TEACHING PICTURES (MP, McGraw, 10 min) Illustrates the use of dry mount tissue and an ordinary iron to enable a teacher to mount, for classroom use, a variety of valuable teaching pictures collected from many sources.

MOUNTING PICTURES (FS, UTex, 58 fr color) Presents methods of mounting pictures for a variety of purposes. Describes materials used, steps in mounting, and ways of protecting pictures. Shows basic steps in mounting with rubber cement and dry mounting tissue.

PASSE PARTOUT FRAMING (MP, IndU, 12 min color) Shows how to mount materials for display by making a sandwich of backing, material, mat and glass or plastic. Demonstrates variations of this technique for mounting three-dimensional materials.

LETTERING TECHNIQUE

BULLETIN BOARDS: AN EFFECTIVE TEACHING DEVICE (MP, Bailey, 11 min color) Presents a graphic picturization of how bulletin boards can be made to function as a most effective instructional tool. Discusses a wealth of background materials, lettering tools, fastening devices, and illustrations.

BULLETIN BOARDS FOR EFFECTIVE TEACHING (MP, IowaU, 10 min color) Illustrates basic principles. Shows the differences between good and poor bulletin boards. Suggests mounting materials, types of lettering; use of color.

LETTERING INSTRUCTIONAL MATERIALS (MP, IndU, 22 min color) Shows many types of letters and lettering devices which may be used to produce effective printing on such materials as charts, posters, signs, maps, bulletin boards, etc. Illustrates the use of rubber stamps, cut-out letters, 3-D letters, stencil letters, transparent letters, and double-faced letters and pictures mechanical scribers and engraved templates.

POSTER MAKING: PRINTING BY SILK SCREEN (MP, Bailey, 15 min color) Presents the process involved in silk screen printing. Demonstrates preparation of the stencil from design to printing and briefly describes the photographic technique for lettering.

VISUAL TECHNIQUES

FELT PEN SKETCHING (MP, YA, 11 min) Shows how the felt-point pen can be used in sketching; the nature and function of the pen; its variety of interchangeable tips; and some of its uses.

LEARNING TO DRAW (MP, Beseler, 10 min) Presents the fundamentals of perspective. Shows the fundamentals of surfaces, size, surface lines, overlapping circles, and shading. Points out that

105

both instructors and students can learn to draw with a little practice.

OPAQUE PROJECTOR: ITS PURPOSE AND USE (MP, IowaU, 6 min) Demonstrates various uses of the opaque projector. Shows how to operate the projector.

THE OPAQUE PROJECTOR (FS, OSU, 46 fr color) Presents a pictorial analysis of the instructional use of the opaque projector together with suggestions on operation and the preparation of materials to be projected.

POSTER MAKING: DESIGN AND TECHNIQUE (MP, Bailey, 10 min color) Shows a variety of materials and tools for poster making. Illustrates the use of cut paper letters, ruling pen, compass, lettering pen points, and poster paints. Includes steps for complete poster making.

COLOR AND TEXTURE TECHNIQUES

CHARTS FOR CREATIVE LEARNING (MP, Bailey, 10 min color) Shows that charts can be made from a variety of materials; can be hung or supported by a number of devices; and can be prepared with many kinds of inks, paints, crayons, color and texture tapes, lettering sets, and pictures. Also shows the methods of planning and making charts.

TRANSPARENCIES

HANDMADE LANTERN SLIDES (FS, OSU, 46 fr color) Shows simple techniques for preparing 3¼-by 4-inch slides. Includes supplementary information on making and using glass and cellophane slides.

HANDMADE MATERIALS FOR PROJECTION (MP, IndU, 19 min color) Demonstrates various methods of preparing materials to be used with different types of still projectors—overhead, opaque, 3¼-by 4-inch and 2-by 2-inch. Shows the use of carbon film, clear and special-surfaced acetate, shading, and coloring adhesive sheets for preparing slides and large transparencies. Also includes a demonstration of preparing transparencies using the picture-transfer technique.

HIGH CONTRAST PHOTOGRAPHY FOR INSTRUCTION (MP, IndU, 12 min color) Demonstrates the use of high contrast photography for the preparation of 2-by 2-inch and 3¼-by 4-inch negative and positive slides, transparencies, and overlays for overhead projectors and for printing on paper for use in opaque projectors. Shows the basic steps of setting up to photograph materials on high contrast film as well as processing the film. Illustrates the application of this type of photography in the preparation of instructional materials in a variety of subject-matter areas.

HOW TO MAKE HANDMADE LANTERN SLIDES (MP, IndU, 21 min color) Demonstrates the preparation and utilization of seven types of 3¼-by 4-inch handmade slides by the teachers and pupils in various school situations. Shows sources of picture material and special production techniques, such as placement of copy, its size, the use of margin guide, and binding techniques.

MAGAZINES TO TRANPARENCIES (MP, FlaStU, 12 min color) Shows step by step the simple method by which pictures and other printed matter may be transferred from a magazine to acetate for transparency projection.

OVERHEAD PROJECTOR (MP, IowaU, 17 min) Shows a variety of materials that can be used and different techniques for preparing transparencies, including drawing and writing on transparent materials, and using carbon-backed film, and cut-outs. Demonstrates the preparation of diazo transparencies (diazo process) and the use of autopositive paper.

PHOTOGRAPHIC SLIDES FOR INSTRUCTION (MP, IndU, 11 min color) Shows the preparation and use of photographic slides in instruction. Suggests various sources of pictures and shows how they can be photographed by the instructor or copied from other printed matter. Includes an introduction to the Polaroid camera transparency system that can produce positive slides in three minutes. Also includes a discussion on the use of tape narration with slides.

TRAINING AIDS: SLIDES, LARGE DRAWING, AND TRANSPARENCIES (MP, UW, 18 min color) Urges instructors to make their own 3¼-by 4-inch lantern slides, large transparencies for use with the overhead projector. Explains the nature of the equipment and materials which are needed and the opportunity for preparing and using such aids by Naval instructors. (U. S. Department of the Navy production.).

Abbreviations	Producer and Distributor
Bailey	Bailey Films, Inc.
Beseler	Charles Beseler Company
FlaStU	Florida State University
IndU	Indiana University
IowaU	University of Iowa
McGraw	McGraw-Hill Book Company, Inc., Text-Film Dept.
OSU	Ohio State University
UW	United World Films, Inc.
YA	Young American Series, see McGraw

REFERENCE C

MATERIALS AND EQUIPMENT GLOSSARY AND SOURCES

The following is an alphabetical listing and description of materials and equipment presented in this manual. Information following the source consist of either material or equipment trade names or identification. Many of the items included here can be purchased from local sources, such as art supply, hardware, hobby, office supply, paint, and photographic stores. Catalogues and descriptive literature are available from most of the listed sources, and usually at no cost to those who request them on official stationary. Complete addresses may be found in Reference D.

ACETATE, CLEAR. A non-inflammable transparent cellulose acetate, available in rolls and sheets (see pages 58, 78, and 94)..
    American Optical Co.
    Dick Blick Co.
    Robert J. Brady Co. (clear plastic)
    Arthur Brown & Bro., Inc.
    Bee Paper Co.
    Charles Beseler Co.
    Buhl Optical Co. (film)
    Craftint Mfg. Co.
    H. T. Herbert Co. (Clear-Vu)
    Lewis Artist Supply Co.
    Major Services
    National Card, Mat & Board Co.
    Ozalid
    Rosco Laboratories
    Steiner Paper Co.
    Tecnifax Corporation
    Morilla Co., The

ACETATE, DOUBLE COATED. Thin transparent mounting acetate with pressure-sensitive adhesive on both sides (see page 6).
    Lewis Artist Supply Co. (Cold-Mount Tissue)

ACETATE, FROSTED (Matte). A non-inflammable cellulose acetate with frosted (matte) surface on one side. Available in rolls and sheets (see pages 58 and 95).
    Bee Paper Co.
    Charles Beseler Co.
    Dick Blick Co.
    Arthur Brown & Bro., Inc.
    Chart-Pak, Inc. (Matte-Tak)
    Crafting Mfg. Co.
    H. T. Herbert Co. (Clear-Vu)
    Keystone View Co. (frosted glass)
    Lewis Artist Supply Co.
    Major Services
    Morilla Co., The (Supersee)
    National Card Co, Mat & Board Co.
    Ozalid (Duratrace and Drafton)
    Radio-Mat Slide Co., Inc. (for 2-by 2-inch and 3¼-by 4-inch slides)
    Rosco Laboratories
    Slidecraft Co. (for 2-by 2-inch and 3¼-by 4-inch slides)
    Steiner Paper Co.

ACETATE, LAMINATING. A thin transparent cellulose acetate film designed for laminating with the aid of heat and pressure (see pages 10 and 12).
    Dick Blick Co. (Sealamin)
    Arthur Brown & Bro., Inc. (Sealamin)
    Lewis Artist Supply Co. (Sealamin)
    Seal, Inc., (Sealamin)
    Three-M Company (3-M laminating film)

ACETATE, SELF-SEALING (FOR LAMINATING). A thin laminating transparent cellulose acetate with a pressure-sensitive adhesive on one side, seals itself with just a slight hand pressure (see page 8).
    Dick Blick Co. (Permafilm)
    Arthur Brown & Bro., Inc. (Presto-Seal)
    Carr Plastic Corp.
    Chart-Pak, Inc. (Clear Tak)
    Dot & Co. (Permafilm)
    Gaylord Bros., Inc. (Laminate)
    Morilla Co., The (Dura-Seal)
    Para-Tone, Inc. (Blue-Zip Clear Frisket)
    Penn Products Co. (Seal-It)

ACETATE, SELF-SEALING (FOR TRANSPARENCIES). Transparent acetate with pressure-sensitive adhesive on one side (see page 84).
    Best Plastic Corp.
    Carr Plastic Corp.
    Major Services (Clear-Adhere)
    McManus & Morgan, Inc. (size x)
    Stenso Lettering Co. (Clear Seal)

ACETATE, SPECIAL SURFACE. A transparent acetate specially prepared to take all type of ink and liquid colors. (see page 58).
    Dick Blick Co. (G. H. and Kleerkote)
    Bourges, Inc. (Kleerkote)
    Arthur Brown & Bro., Inc. (Prefixed)
    Craftint Mfg. Co., (Draw-Kleer)
    H. T. Herbert Co. (E-Z Cel Prepared)
    Lewis Artist Supply Co. (Art-Stoke Prepared)
    Morilla Co., The (prepared acetate)
    Ozalid (Duratrace—has a matte finish)
    Para-Tone, Inc. (Copy-Zip—has a matte finish)
    Steiner Paper Corp. (prepared acetate)
    Tecnifax Corp. (acetate sheets)
    Winsor & Newton, Inc. (Kleerkote)

ADHESIVE, WAX DISKS AND STICKS (STYX). Adhesive mounting wax in disks and stick form. The disks have adhesive on both sides (see 1-79 and 1-80).
    ABC School Supply (Bulletin Board Styx)
    Beckley-Cardy Co. (Stick-Tack Disk)
    Demco Library Supplies (bulletin board wax sticks)

Kurt Bros. (Bulletin Board Styx and Stick-Tack Disks)
Lae A-V Service (Bulletin Board Styx)

ADHESIVE, LIQUID PLASTIC. A fast-setting white or transparent all-purpose adhesive that holds on wood, paper, cloth, glass, and all porous and semi-porous materials (see 1-84).

 Beckley-Cardy Co. (Elmer's Glue-All and Pliobond)
 Dick Blick Co. (Duco Cement and Elmer's Glue-All)
 Arthur Brown & Bro., Inc., (Duco Cement, Elmer's Glue-All, and Pliobond)
 Demco Library Supplies (liquid plastic glue)
 Gaylords Bros., Inc., (liquid plastic glue)
 Hernard Mfg. Co. (cement for plastic or tile letters)
 Kurtz Bros. (Delkote Book-Saver and LePage's White Glue)
 Mitten's Display Letters (cement for tile letters)
 Morilla Co., The (Elmer's Glue-All and Krylon All-purpose Glue)

ADHESIVE, LIQUID (WET-MOUNTING). A liquid adhesive additive for wheat-paste flour (see 1-34).

 Most hardware and paint stores carry this item.

ADHESIVE, PLIABLE PLASTIC. A white pliable mounting adhesive that will stick to any clean dry surface (see 1-81).

 ABC School Supply, Inc. (Plasti-Tak)
 Brooks Mfg. Co. (Plasti-Tak)
 Gaylord Bros., Inc.
 Kurtz Bros. (Plasti-Tak)

ADHESIVE, SPRAY. Liquid adhesive in spray-can form. Will bind paper to any smooth surface, (see 1-83).

 Dick Blick Co. (Quick-Stick)
 Bradywine Photo Chemical Co. (Spray Mount and Dry-Stick)
 Arthur Brown & Bro., Inc. (Marshall Photo Mount)
 Grand Central Artist's Materials, Inc. (Krylon)
 Krylon, Inc. (Krylon)
 Lewis Artist Supply Co. (Quick-Stick)
 Maker Products, Inc. (Quick-Stick)
 John G. Marshall Mfg. Co., Inc. (Photo-Mount)

AIRBRUSH. A pen-like device used to spray on color with the aid of pressured-air. For photographic retouching, preparing commercial art; for reproduction and artwork requiring a third dimension (see 4-21).

 Dick Blick Co., (Paasche, Thayer & Chandler, and Wold)
 Arthur Brown & Bro., Inc. (Paasche, Thayer & Chandler, and Wold)
 Concord Artists' Materials (Paasche, Thayer & Chandler, and Wold)
 A. I. Friedman, Inc.
 Morilla Co., The (Wold)
 Paasche Airbrush Co. (Paasche)
 Tecnifax Corp.
 Thayer & Chandler
 Wold Air Brush Mfg. Co.

BRUSH, WATER. Small water brushes used to apply liquid color and adhesives (see 4-21).

 Alvin & Co., Inc.
 Dick Blick Co.
 Arthur Brown & Bro., Inc.
 Concord Artists' Materials
 Craftint Mfg. Co.
 Duro Art Supply Co.
 A. I. Friedman, Inc.
 F. Weber Co.

CHROME TINS (FERROTYPE PLATES). Flat metal sheets, usually copper, with a chrome plated finish. (see 5-12).

 Burke & James, Inc.
 Montgomery Ward, Inc.
 Seal, Inc.
 Sears, Roebuck & Company

CIRCLE CUTTER. A metal device for cutting perfect circles out of paper, acetate, thin cardboard, etc. (see 3-47).

 Dick Blick Co.
 Arthur Brown & Bro., Inc. (Craftsman, Compass Cutter, and X-Acto)
 Burke & James, Inc.
 Concord Artists' Materials
 Crane-Callo Artist Supplies
 Gestetner Duplicator Corp. (Compass Pen—for wax duplicating stencils)

COLOR, ADHESIVE SHEETS. Transparent color printed on the underside of a pressure-sensitive clear acetate sheet. Color can be transferred to most surfaces (see page 66).

 Artype, Inc.
 Dick Blick Co. (Colortone Adhesive Sheets)
 Arthur Brown & Bro., Inc. (Colortone Adhesive Sheets, Add-A-Color, and Craft-Color)
 Bourges, Inc. (Cutocolor)
 Cello-Tak Lettering Corp. (Cello-Tak)
 Charles Beseler Co. (Color Stik)
 Chart-Pak, Inc.
 Color Stik (transparent color sheets)
 Concord Artists' Materials (Colortone Adhesive Sheets, Add-A-Color, and Craft-Color)
 Craftint Mfg. Co. (Craft-Color)
 A. I. Friedman, Inc. (Cello-Tak)
 H. T. Herbert Co. (Cello-Tak)
 Lewis Artist Supply Co. (Colortone Adhesive Sheets, Contak, and Craft-Color)
 Jay G. Lissner
 Winsor & Newton, Inc. (Bourges)

CUTTING NEEDLE (STYLUS). A small cutting tool used to cut on color, texture, shading, and paste-up letter sheets (see 2-20, 2-29, 3-49, and 4-9).

 Artype, Inc.
 Dick Blick Co. (Grifhold and Artype)
 Arthur Brown & Bro., Inc. (No. 903)
 Craftint Mfg. Co. (Pin Vise)
 A. I. Friedman, Inc. (Pin Vise No. 44)
 Para-Tone, Inc.

DIAZO EQUIPMENT AND MATERIALS. Equipment and materials necessary to expose and process diazo-sensitized materials such as paper, film, cloth, etc. (see page 90).

 Charles Beseler Co.
 Charles Burning Co., Inc. (Copyflex)

Keuffel & Esser Co. (Saturn Transparency Processor and UHS film).

DIFFUSION-TRANSFER EQUIPMENT AND MATERIALS (PHOTO-COPY). A negative-to-positive photographic process which requires no camera and darkroom. Ideal for preparing transparencies from opaque originals (see page 86).

American Photocopy Equip. Co.
Ampto, Inc.
Charles Beseler Co.
A. B. Dick Co. (Photocopier)
Eastman Kodak Co. (Verifax)
F. G. Ludwig, Inc. (Contura-Attache')
Keuffel & Esser Co. (Saturn Transparency Processor)
Ozalid (Transferon)
Photorapid Corp. (Photorapid)
Tecnifax Corp. (Contoura-Attache')

DOWEL RODS. Round wood rods used to hang maps, charts, etc. (see 1-71).

Hardware stores, hobby shops, and lumber companies may carry this item.

DRY MOUNTING CLOTH. An adhesive-backed cloth used to back maps, charts, etc. Requires heat and pressure for mounting. Available in rolls and sheets (see page 14).

Arthur Brown & Bro., Inc. (Chartex)
Charles Bruning Co. (Chartex)
Burke & James, Inc. (Chartex)
Concord Artists' Materials (Chartex)
Holliston Mills, Inc. (Photo Cloth)
Lewis Artist Supply Co. (Chartex)
Seal, Inc. (Chartex)

DRY MOUNTING PRESS & TACKING IRON (WELDER). Automatic electric mounting devices used to mount prints and other similar materials on mounting board or dry mounting cloth; also used for laminating when "Sealamin" laminating acetate is used (see page 4, 10, and 80).

Dick Blick Co. (Seal)
Arthur Brown & Bro., Inc. (Seal)
Burke & James, Inc. (Seal)
Concord Artists' Materials (Seal)
A. I. Friedman, Inc. (Seal)
International Sales Co., Inc. (Seal)
Lewis Artist Supply Co. (Seal)
Seal, Inc.

DRY MOUNTING TISSUE. A thin sheet of tissue coated on both sides with a special adhesive or wax. Requires heat and pressure for mounting (see page 4).

Dick Blick Co. (Seal)
Arthur Brown & Bro., Inc. (Seal)
Burke & James, Inc. (Seal)
Concord Artists' Materials (Seal)
Eastman Kodak Co.
A. I. Friedman, Inc. (Seal)
International Sales Co., Inc. (Seal)
Lewis Artist Supply Co. (Seal)
Seal, Inc.

ELLIPSE GUIDES (TEMPLATES). Transparent plastic guides used to draw or cut perfect forms and shapes (see 3-49 and 3-55).

Alvin & Co., Inc.
Arthur Brown & Bro., Inc.
Charles Bruning Co., Inc. (Rapidesign)
Concord Artists' Materials
Crane-Gallo Artist Supplies
Lewis Artist Supply
Morilla Co., The (Rapidesign)

ELECTRONIC STENCIL EQUIPMENT AND MATERIALS. Electronic machine cuts stencil and transparency at same time, from almost any type of artwork, using an electronic scanning system (see page 94).

Gestetner Duplicator Corp. (Gestefax)
Milo Harding Co. (Tempotronic)

EYELETS, METAL OR PLASTIC (GROMMETS). Metal or plastic reinforcement eyelets for leather, cardboard, cloth, paper, plastic, etc. An eyelette punch or tool is usually required to attach eyelets to desired material (see 1-72)

Beckley-Cardy Co. (Triumph)
Dick Blick Co.
Arthur Brown & Bro., Inc. (No. 7630-31)
E-Z Buckle Co., Inc.
Kurtz Bros. (Triumph)

FILMSTRIP PROJECTORS. Projection device for projecting filmstrips; also used for preparing large visuals (see 3-5).

American Optical Co.
Argus, Inc.
Bausch & Lomb Optical Co.
Bell & Howell Co.
Arthur Brown & Bro., Inc.
Burke & James, Inc.
Eastman Kodak Co.
Graflex, Inc.
Standard Projector & Equipment Co., Inc.
Victor Animatograph Corp.
Viewlex Co.

FLUID DUPLICATING EQUIPMENT (SPIRIT). A fluid process which will duplicate typing, writing, and drawings in up to five colors, in one operation, on paper or frosted acetate sheets. (see page 95).

A. B. Dick Co.
Ditto, Inc.
General Binding Corp.
Goldsmith Bros. (spirit duplicator)

FLEXIBLE RULER. Plastic or metal ruler that is easily bent to any desired curve or shape (see 3-53).

Dick Blick Co. (adjustable curve)
Arthur Brown & Bro., Inc. (adjustable curve ruler)
Charles Bruning Co.
Concord Artists' Materials
Morilla Co., The (Flexicurve)
F. Weber Co.

FRISKET KNIFE (STENCIL OR ETCHING KNIFE). A small-bladed cutting device with a plastic or wood handle especially designed for cutting film, color and texture adhesive sheets, transparent paste-up letters, etc. (see pages 40, 67, and 68).

Dick Blick Co.
Arthur Brown & Bro., Inc.

Chart-Pak, Inc.
Concord Artists' Materials
Craftint Mfg. Co. (etching knife)
Lewis Artist Supply Co. (Grifhold)
X-Acto, Inc.

HINGES, TRANSPARENCY. Pressure-sensitive backed matallized plastic hinges for transparency overlays (see 5-104).
Tecnifax Corp. (Techinges)

HOOK N' LOOP BOARD. A visual presentation or display board made with a Loop-Pile fabric having many times the holding power of a flannel board (see page 20).
Charles Mayer Studios, Inc.

INK, DIRECT OFFSET MASTER. For direct drawing, lettering, etc. on paper offset masters (see 3-60).
Addressograph-Multigraph Corp. (Ducroclear Writing Fluid)
Letterguide Co. (Di-Rect Plate Ink)
Varigraph Co. (Di-Rect Plate Ink)

INK, DRAWING AND INDIA. Colored inks that can be applied to opaque and transparent surfaces (see 3-58 and 3-59).
Alvin & Co., Inc.
Dick Blick Co.
Arthur Brown & Bro., Inc.
Charles Bruning Co., Inc.
Concord Artists' Materials
Craftint Mfg. Co.
Crane-Gallo Artist Supplies
Duro Art Supply Co.
A. I. Friedman, Inc.
Goldsmith Bros.
Higging Ink Co.
Lewis Artist Supply Co.
Morilla Co., The
Sanford Ink Co.
F. Weber Co.
Winsor & Newton, Inc.

INK, FELT-POINT PEN. A special ink designed for use in felt-point pens; writes on most surfaces; available in several colors (see 3-57).
ABC School Supply, Inc. (Marsh)
Alvin & Co. (Marsh)
Dick Blick Co. (Marsh)
Arthur Brown & Bro., Inc.
Concord Artists' Materials
A. I. Friedman, Inc.
Krutz Bros.
Lewis Artist Supply Co. (Marsh)
Marsh Stencil Machine Co.
Sanford Ink Co.
Speedry Products, Inc.
Tecnifax Corp.
Winsor & Newton, Inc.

INK, METALLIC. Gold and silver in ready-to-use ink solution for lettering, drawing, etc. (see 3-63).
Arthur Brown & Bro., Inc.
Concord Artists' Materials
A. I. Friedman, Inc. (Nonpariel gold and silver water color)
Lewis Artist Supply Co.
Morilla Co., The (Talens)
Sanford Ink Co.
F. Weber Co.
Winsor & Newton, Inc. (gold and silver ink)

INK, PLASTIC (ACETATE). Opaque and transparent black and colored inks designed for use on plastic or acetate surfaces (see 3-61).
Charles Beseler Co. (Vu-Graph)
Dick Blick Co. (Pelikan)
Charles J. Brady Co. (transparent removable)
Arthur Brown & Bro., Inc. (Artone)
Buhl Optical Co.
Crane-Gallo Artist Supplies
Koh-I-Noor, Inc. (Acetograph Ink)
Lewis Artist Supply Co. (Art-Strokes)
Morilla Co., The (Artone)
Tecnifax Corp. (Keystone and Koh-I-Noor)
Varigraph Co. (Pelikan)
F. Weber Co.
Winsor & Newton, Inc. (Higgins)

LETTERS, MECHANICAL TRACING. A lettering system consisting of a scriber, templet (template), and pen (see pages 46, 48, and 50).
Alvin & Co., Inc. (Tech-Graph)
Dick Blick Co. (Letterguide)
Arthur Brown & Bro. Inc. (Wrico Scriber and Zephur)
Charles Bruning Co., Inc. (Wrico Scriber)
A. I. Friedman, Inc. (Doric)
Keuffel & Esser Co. (LeRoy and Doric)
Letterguide Co. (Letterguide)
Lewis Artist Supply Co. (Wrico Scriber and Zephyr)
Tecnifax Corporation (Letterguide)
Varigraph Co. (Varigraph)
Wood-Regan Instrument Co. (Wrico Scriber)

LETTERS, PASTE-UP (PAPER TYPE). Opaque letters, symbols, numerals, etc. printed on tabs or sheets of lightweight cardboard or paper. Can be used when precision hand typesetting is required. Available in many styles and sizes (see page 42).
Fototype, Inc. (Fototype)
Presto Process Co. (Presto Paper Type)
Tecnifax Corp. (Fototype)
Volk Corp. (Clip Book of Lettering)

LETTERS, PASTE-UP (TRANSPARENT TYPE). Removable opaque letters, symbols, numerals, etc. printed on the back side of a thin transparent acetate sheet. Will adhere to most surfaces. Available in black, white, and colors (see page 40).
Artype, Inc. (Artype)
Dick Blick Co. (Artype)
Arthur Brown & Bro., Inc. (Add-A-Type, Craft-Type, and Presto-Type)
Chart-Pak, Inc. (Spaced Lettering)
Concord Artists' Materials (Ad-Letter, Add-A-Type, Craf-Type, and Presto-Type)
Craftint Mfg. Co. (Craf-Type)
Crane-Gallo Artist Supplies (Artype and Cello-Tak)
Lewis Artist Supply Co. (Artype, Ad-Letter, Craf-Type, Para-Tipe, and Quillo)

Jay G. Lissner
Para-Tone, Inc. (Para-Tipe)
Presto Process Co. (Presto-Type)

LETTERS, PRE-CUT CARDBOARD. Die-cut from cardboard. Available in many styles, colors, and sizes (see 2-12).
ABC School Supply, Inc.
Beckley-Cardy Co. (Cut-Out Letters)
Dick Blick Co. (die-cut display letters)
Arthur Brown & Bro., Inc. (Hallcraft)
Duro Art Supply Co.
Ideal School Supply Co.
Kenworthy Educational Services, Inc.
Lewis Artist Supply Co.
Maggie Magnetic Visual Aids Corp.
Harry Mich Co.
Mutual Aids
Redikut Letter Co.
Stick-a-Letter Co.

LETTERS, PRE-CUT MAGNETIC. Die-cut magnetized letters, numerals, etc. Also available with magnets attached to back.
Demco Library Supplies
Educational Services
Charles Mayer Studios, Inc.
Maggie Magnetic Visual Aids Corp.

LETTERS, PRE-CUT GUMMED-BACK. Die-cut gummed-backed cardboard or paper letters and numerals; applied like postage stamps (see 2-9).
Dick Blick Co.
Demco Library Supplies (gummed letters)
Dennison Mfg. Co.
Holes Webway Co.
Horder's Stationary Stores, Inc. (Lettersets)
Oravisual Co., Inc. (gummed letters)
Stick-a-Letter Co.
Tablet & Ticket Co.

LETTERS, PRE-CUT PLASTIC OR TILE. Molded plastics or tile letters and numerals. Available in plain, sanded-back, pin-back, and track (Trac) (see 2-13).
ABC School Supply Co.
Beckley-Cardy Co.
Arthur Brown & Bro., Inc., (Hernard)
Dick Blick Co. (Hernard and Plexiglass)
Demco Library Supplies
Gaylord Bros., Inc. (plastic display letters)
Hernard Mfg. Co.
Mitten's Display Letters
Morilla Co., The (Micro Plastic)
Mutual Aids (Micro Sign)
W. L. Stensgaard & Associates, Inc.

LETTERS, PRE-CUT PLIABLE PLASTIC. Die-cut letters and numerals made from a pliable plastic that sticks on contact to most smooth surfaces (see 2-10 and page 36).
Clingtite Letters (Clingtite)
Charles Mayer Studios, Inc. (Planotype)
Ozalid (Planotype)
Planoscope Corp. (Planotype)

LETTERS, PRE-CUT SELF-ADHERING CARDBOARD OR PAPER. Die-cut cardboard or paper letters and numerals with a pressure-sensitive back that will adhere to most smooth surfaces (see 2-11).
Dick Blick Co. (Con-Tak)
Deninson Mfg. Co.
Harry Mich Co.

LETTERS, RUBBER STAMP. Large rubber letters, numerals, and symbols mounted on easy-to-hold wood blocks (see page 28).
ABC School Supply ,Inc.
Beckley-Cardy Co. (B-C Chart Printer)
Goldsmith Bros. (Fulton Sign Maker)
Horder's Stationary Stores, Inc.
Kurtz Bros. (printing set)

LETTERS, STENCIL TRACING (CARDBOARD). Die-cut lettering guides, usually made of oiled cardboard, containing cut-out letters which can be traced with a variety of lettering and drawing devices. (see page 30).
ABC Pattern & Stencil Co.
ABC School Supply, Inc. (oilboard stencil)
Alvin & Co., Inc. (Stenso)
Dick Blick Co. (Stenso)
Duro Art Supply Co. (oilboard stencil)
E-Z Letter Stencil Co.
Horder's Stationary Stores, Inc. (Stenso)
Lewis Artist Supply, Inc. (Stenso)
Oravisual Co., Inc. (Stenso)
Salt Lake Stamp Co.
Speedry Products, Inc. (Magic Marker Lettering Templates)
Stenso Lettering Co. (Stenso).

LETTERS, STENCIL TRACING (PLASTIC) Transparent plastic lettering guides containing cut-out letters which are traced with a special lettering pen or stylus (see page 44).
American Optical Co. (Letter-Rite)
Alvin & Co., Inc. (C-Thru, Tech-Letter Guides, Do-All, and Typo)
Dick Blick Co. (lettering guides)
Arthur Brown & Bro., Inc. (Wrico and Koh-I-Noor Rapido Guides)
Charles Bruning Co., Inc. (Wrico)
Dick Blick Co. (lettering guides)
C-Thru Ruler Co. (C-Thru)
Concord Artists' Materials (Wrico)
Craftint Mfg. Co. (C-Thru)
Koh-I-Noor, Inc. (Rapido Guides)
Lewis Artist Supply Co. (Wrico)
Oravisual Co., Inc. (Wrico)
Wood-Regan Instrument Co. (Wrico)

LETTERS, TRANSFER (DRY TRANSFER). Letters, numerals, etc., printed on a plastic sheet and transfers from the sheet to acetate, wood, glass, paper, metal, and film with a slight pressure. Available in gold and assorted colors (see page 38).
Alvin & Co., Inc. (Cello-Tak Transfer Type)
Dick Blick Co. (Prestype)
Arthur Brown & Bro., Inc. (Instant Lettering)
Cello-Tak Lettering Corp. (Cello-Tak)
Concord Artists' Materials (Instant Lettering)
Crane-Gallo Artist Supply Co. (Prestype and Cello-Tak Transfer Type)
A. I. Friedman, Inc. (Cello-Tak Transfer Type)
H. T. Herbert Co. (Cello-Tak Transfer Type)

Lewis Artist Supply Co. (Instant Lettering and Letraset)
Morilla Co., The (Instant Type)
Prestype, Inc. (Prestype)
Tecnifax Corp. (Instant-Type)

LIQUID COLOR, SPRAY-CAN. Enamel and fluorescent paints in pressure-packed spray cans (see pages 33 and 34.)

ABC School Supply, Inc.
Dick Blick Co. (Quick-Spray, Krylon, Spray-Hue and Spray-O-Namel)
Arthur Brown & Bro., Inc. (Krylon)
Craftint Mfg. Co. (Spray-Glo)
Crane-Gallo Artist Supplies
Krylon, Inc.
Lewis Artist Supply Co. (Krylon and Quick-Spray)
Precision Paint Corp. (Instant-Coat)
Sheffield Bronze Paint Corp. (Quick-Spray)

LIQUID COLOR, TRANSPARENT WATER COLOR STAMP BOOK. Water soluble leaves (pages) of transparent colors. Color is obtained by touching wet brush or cotton swab to color pages or by dissolving page in water (see page 75).

Arthur Brown & Bro., Inc. (Peerless Transparent Water Colors)
Concord Artists' Materials (Peerless Transparent Water Colors)
Crane-Gallo Artist Supplies (Peerless Transparent Water Colors)
Peerless Color Laboratories (Peerless Transparent Water Colors)
Grand Central Artists' Materials, Inc. (Peerless Transparent Water Colors)

LIQUID COLOR, TRANSPARENT WATER COLORS. Transparent water colors in liquid form. Can be mixed or extended with water (see pages 64 and 75)

B. Aronstein & Co. (Dr. PH. Martin)
Arthur Brown & Bro., Inc. (Luma)
Concord Artists' Materials (Luma, Dr. PH. Martin, Col-O-Tone, and Steig)
Craftint Mfg. Co.
A. I. Friedman, Inc.
Lewis Artist Supply Co. (Luma, Dr. PH. Martin and Webster)
Morilla Co., The (Dr. PH. Martin)
Passche Airbrush Co.
Thayer & Chandler
Webster Bros. Lab. (liquid photo colors)
Winsor & Newton, Inc. (Photo Tints)
Wold Air Brush Mfg. Co.

MAGNETS. Metal and rubber magnets that can be attached to letters, objects, etc. Will work on any metal surface. Available in a variety of shapes and sizes. Rubber magnets can be easily cut with scissors or knife. (see 2-12)

Arthur Brown & Bro. Inc. (bar magnet)
Educational Service (bar magnets)
Ideal School Supply Co. (bar magnets)
Maggie Magnetic Visual Aid Corp.
Magnet Sales Co.
Charles Mayer Studios, Inc. (CMS Rubber Magnets and Alnico)

MOUNT FLAPS AND MASKS. Flaps are designed and constructed to match the sturdiness of commercial mounts; masks are made from heavy white plastic sheets for use as hinged or sliding masks for large transparencies (see 5-106 and 5-107).

Charles Beseler Co. (Flaps)
Tecnifax Corp. (white plastic masks)

MOUNTING BOARD. A pressed-paper board suitable for mounting purposes. Available in several thicknesses.

Dick Blick Co.
Arthur Brown & Bro., Inc.
Concord Artists' Materials
Crane-Gallo Artist Supplies
Crescent Cardboard Co.
A. I. Friedman, Inc.
H. T. Herbert Co.
Lewis Artist Supply Co.
National Card, Mat & Board Co.
Steiner Paper Co.

OPAQUE PROJECTORS. Projects an enlarged image of opaque copy, drawing, photographs, etc. (see 3-2).

American Optical Co.
Bausch & Lomb Optical Co.
Charles Beseler Co.
Arthur Brown & Bro., Inc. (Artscope—accepts originals up to 6-by 6-inches)

OVERHEAD PROJECTORS. Projects an enlarged image of transparent copy, drawings, photographs, etc. (see 3-4).

American Optical Co.
Bausch & Lomb Optical Co.
Charles Beseler Co. (Vu-Graph)
Robert J. Brady Co. (Visual Cast)
Buhl Optical Co. (Koolite)
Projection Optics Co.
Tecnifax Corp. (Transpaque)
Three-M Co. (3M)
Victorlite Industries

PENCILS, DRAWING, Black and colored leads for use on paper, frosted (matte) acetate or glass (see 3-43).

Alvin & Co., Inc.
Dick Blick Co.
Arthur Brown & Bro., Inc.
Concord Artists' Materials
Crane-Gallo Artist Supplies
Eagle Pencil Co.
A. I. Friedman, Inc.
Horder's Stationary Stores, Inc.
Koh-I-Noor, Inc.
Lewis Artist Supply Co.
Venus Pen & Pencil Co.
F. Weber Co.

PENCILS, MARKING (GREASE OR CHINA). Writes on all surfaces, rough, smooth, or slick (see 3-45).

Alvin & Co., Inc. (Mark-All)
American Optical Co.
Charles Beseler Co. (Vu-Graph and All Stabi-lo)
Dick Blick Co. (All Stabilo)
Buhl Optical Co.

Arthur Brown & Bro., Inc. (All Stabilo and China Marking)
Robert J. Brady Co.
Goldsmith Bros. (Blaisdell)
Koh-I-Noor, Inc. (Kok-In-All)
Krutz Bros. (Marker)
Morilla Co., The (Listo, Blaisdell, and Chinagraph)
Ozalid (Acetate Mechanical and All Stabilo)
Venus Pen and Pencil Corp.

PENCILS, TRANSPARENT COLOR (LUMACHROM). Pencils with leads of rich transparent color for use on frosted (matte) acetate (plastic) and glass. "Mars-Omnichrom" pencils will work on special-surfaced acetate (see 3-44).

Charles Beseler Co. (Clear-A-Slide)
Ozalid (Drafton)
Tecnifax Corp (Mars-Omnichrom)

PENS, BALL POINT. Special ink-control ball-point pen designed for smooth lettering and drawing. Ideal for use with cardboard and plastic stencil lettering guides. Several ink colors are available (see 3-41 and 3-46).

Alvin & Co., Inc. (Taubman's Ball Point)
Goldsmith Bros.
Horder's Stationary Stores, Inc. (Lindy)
Koh-I-Noor, Inc. (Koh-I-Ball)
Krutz Bros.
Morilla Co., The (Jumbo Ball Pen)
Ozalid (Opaque Pen)
Wood-Regan Instrument Co. (Wrico Ball Pen)

PEN CLEANER. A liquid cleaning solution for removing dried ink from pens and drawing instruments (see 2-40).

Alvin & Co., Inc. (Disolv-All)
Dick Blick Co. (Higgins)
Arthur Brown & Bro., Inc. (Higgins)
Charles Bruning Co., Inc. (Higgins) and (Wrico)
Concord Artists' Materials (Higgins)
A. I. Friedman, Inc. (Higgins)
Goldsmith Bros. (Higgins)
Koh-I-Noor, Inc. (Rapido-Eze)
Letterguide Co. (cleaning fluid)
Lewis Artist Supply Co. (Wrico and Higgins)
Tecnifax Corp.
Varigraph Co. (cleaning fluid)
Winsor & Newton, Inc. (Higgins)
Wood-Regan Instrument Co. (Wrico)

PENS, CROWQUILL. For drawing and lettering where a fine line is desired (see 3-31).

Alvin & Co., Inc.
Dick Blick Co.
Arthur Brown & Bro., Inc.
Charles Bruning Co., Inc.
Concord Artists' Materials
Craftint Mfg. Co.
Crane-Gallo Artist Supplies
A. I. Friedman, Inc.
Krutz Bros.
Lewis Artist Supply Co.
Morilla Co., The
F. Weber Co.

PENS AND MARKERS, FELT-POINT. Felt-point "fountain pens" for writing on any surface. Uses waterproof oil-based inks. Assorted nibs (points or tips) available (see 3-33).

ABC School Supply, Inc. (Marsh)
Alvin & Co., Inc. (Marsh)
Charles Beseler Co. (Vu-Graph Transparent Marker)
Dick Blick Co. (Marsh)
Arthur Brown & Bro., Inc. (Flo-Master and Magic-Marker)
Concord Artists' Materials (Flo-Master and Magic-Marker)
Craftint Mfg. Co. (Grifhold)
Crane-Gallo Artist Supplies (Flo-Master and Magic Marker)
A. I. Friedman, Inc. (Flo-Master)
Horder's Stationary Stores, Inc. (Cado, Flo-Master, Sanford, and Carter)
Koh-I-Noor, Inc. (Koh-I-Quick)
Krutz Bros. (Cado)
Lewis Artist Supply Co. (Dri Mark)
Marsh Stencil Machine Co. (Marsh)
Morilla Co., The (Cado)
Oravisual Co., Inc. (Dri-Marker and Magic Marker)
Tecnifax Corp. (Cado-Marker and Flo-Master)

PENS, METAL BRUSH. A flexible metal lettering and drawing pen that strokes like a brush. Available in widths, in some makes, from 1/16 to 1 inch (see 3-38).

ABC School Supply, Inc. (Speedball Steel Brush)
Alvin & Co., Inc. (Coit)
Dick Blick Co. (Coit, and Speedball Steel Brush)
Arthur Brown & Bro., Inc. (Coit and Speedball Steel Brush)
Craftint Mfg. Co. (Speedball Steel Brush)
Crane-Gallo Artist Supplies (Coit)
Concord Artists' Materials (Coit and Speedball Steel Brush)
C. Howard Hunt Pen Co. (Speedball Steel Brush)
Kurtz Bros. (Speedball Steel Brush)
Lewis Artist Supply Co. (Coit and Speedball Steel Brush)
Morilla Co., The (Speedball Steel Brush)
F. Weber Co. (Speedball Steel Brush)

PENS, RESERVOIR, Fountain-type pens designed for India and drawing inks. Used in mechanical lettering scribers and for fill-in lettering and artwork (see 2-46).

Keuffel & Esser Co.
Letterguide Co.
Tecnifax Corp.

PENS, SPEEDBALL. Metal lettering and drawing pens. Available in four point styles (see 3-40).

ABC School Supply, Inc.
Alvin & Co., Inc.
Dick Blick Co.
Arthur Brown & Bro., Inc.
Charles Bruning Co., Inc.
C. Howard Hunt Pen Co.
Concord Artists' Materials

Craftint Mfg. Co.
Crane-Gallo Artist Supplies
A. I. Friedman, Inc.
Krutz Bros.
Lewis Artist Supply Co.
Morilla Co., The
F. Weber Co.

PENS, TECHNICAL FOUNTAIN (FOR ACETATE INKS). A non-clogging fountain pen that uses acetate (plastic) inks in addition to regular drawing and India inks (see 3-32).

Sam Flax Artist Materials (Flax Pen)
Robert J. Brady Co. (RTB))
A. I. Friedman, Inc. (Acetograph)
Gaylord Library Supplies (Acetograph)
Koh-I-Noor, Inc. (Acetograph)
Ozalid (Grafika and Rapidograph)
Tecnifax Corp. (Acetograph)

PENS, TECHNICAL FOUNTAIN (FOR REGULAR INDIA AND DRAWING INKS). A non-clogging fountain pen that uses regular India and drawing inks. Some models are available with interchangeable points or nibs (see 3-32 and 3-35).

Dick Blick Co. (Rapidograph)
Arthur Brown & Bro., Inc. (Rapidograph, Pelikan Graphos, and Speedball Auto-Feed)
Charles Bruning Co., Inc. (Rapidograph)
Concord Artists' Materials (Rapidograph and Pelikan Graphos)
Crane-Gallo Artist Supplies (Rapidograph, Higgins, Artist, and Pelikan Graphos)
Sam Flax Artist Materials (Flax Pen)
A. I. Friedman, Inc. (Rapidograph, Pelikan Graphos, Boben, and Speedball Auto-Feed)
Higgins Ink Co. (Higgins)
C. Howard Hunt Pen Co. (Auto-Feed)
Koh-I-Noor, Inc. (Rapidograph)
Lewis Artist Supply Co. (Rapidograph)
Morilla Co., The (Rapidograph, Talens Chin-O-Graph, Higgins, and Pelikan)
Varigraph Co. (Rapidograph)

PHOTOGRAPHIC CONTACT PRINT FRAME. Made of sturdy wood or metal; designed for making paper contact prints from photographic negatives and for making diazo transparencies from prepared masters (see page 91).

Burke & James, Inc.
Eastman Kodak Co.
Hudson Photographic Industries, Inc. (HPI Film Proofer)
Mioplex Products, M.P. Mfg. Co. (Mioplex Printer)
Photo Materials Co. (Premier Printers)
Tecnifax Corp. (photo printing frame)

PHOTOGRAPHIC ENLARGER. Photographic device for enlarging photographic negatives; can also be used to prepare large visuals (see 3-8).

Altman Camera Co.
Burke & James, Inc. (Solar)
Charles Beseler Co.
Federal Mfg. & Engineering Co.
Montgomery Ward, Inc.
Sears, Roebuck & Co.
Simmon Bros., Inc. (Omega)
Testrite Instrument (Fotolarger)

PHOTOGRAPHIC PRINT DRYERS. Photographic device used to dry photographic prints; can be used to mount dry mounting cloth to the back of a print or similar materials (see 1-31).

Altman Camera Co.
Charles Beseler Co.
Burke & James, Inc.
Montgomery Ward, Inc.
Sears, Roebuck & Co.

PICTURE HANGERS (GUMMED-BACK CLOTH). Made of strong cloth with a gummed-back. Ideal for displaying pictures, posters, charts, maps, etc. (see 1-73 and 1-74).

Dennison Mfg. Co.
Horder's Stationary Stores, Inc.
Jiffy Enterprises, Inc.

PLASTIC SPRAY: A transparent acrylic fixitive that gives photos, drawings, artwork, etc., the protection of glass without its disadvantages. Used in the preparation of large transparencies (see 3-17, 5-9, 5-17, 5-34, and 5-82).

Acrolite Products, Inc. (Acrolite)
Alvin & Co., Inc. (Acrolite)
Beckley-Cardy Co. (Plasti-Kote)
Charles Beseler Co. (Clear-O-Slide)
Dick Blick Co. (Dick Blick, Krylon, and Spray-Fix)
Arthur Brown & Bro., Inc. (Marshall Spray-Glass, Krylon, and Agrolite)
Charles Bruning Co., Inc. (Krylon)
Concord Artists' Materials (Krylon, Acrolite, and Marshall Spray-Glass)
Craftint Mfg. Co. (Spray-Art)
Crane-Gallo Artist Supplies (Krylon and Spray-Fix)
Demco Library Supplies (Demcote)
A. I. Friedman, Inc. (Krylon and Spray-Fix)
Gaylord Bros., Inc. (Spraylon)
Krylon, Inc.
Kurtz Bros. (Delkote Bookote)
Lewis Artist Supply Co. (Krylon)
John G. Marshall Mfg. Co., Inc. (Spray Glass)
Morilla Co., The (Krylon and Spray-Fix)
Sheffield Bronze Paint Corp. (Quick Spray)

POLAROID EQUIPMENT AND MATERIALS. Polaroid camera, projector, Copymaker, chemicals and films required for making Polaroid transparencies. (see page 92).

Polaroid Corp.

POSTER BOARD (SHOW CARD). A pressed-paper board suitable for lettering, visuals, etc. Available in several thicknesses and a variety of colors.

Dick Blick Co.
Arthur Brown & Bro., Inc.
Concord Artists' Materials
Crane-Gallo Artist Supplies
A. I. Friedman, Inc.
H. T. Herbert Co.
Lewis Artist Supply Co.
Morilla Co., The

RUBBER CEMENT. A liquid adhesive made from a special premium quality treated rubber, blended to a formula best suited for joining various types of materials together (see pages 2, 42, and 78).
- Alvin & Co., Inc. (Columbia)
- Dick Blick Co. (Dick Blick and Best-Test)
- Arthur Brown & Bro., Inc. (Best-Test and Columbia)
- Charles Bruning Co., Inc. (Best-Test)
- Concord Artists' Materials (Best-Test and Columbia)
- Craftint Mfg. Co. (Kleen-Stik)
- Crane-Gallo Artist Supplies (Cargo and Best-Test)
- A. I. Friedman, Inc. (Frem's and Best-Test)
- Goldsmith Bros. (Pilot and Best-Test)
- Krutz Bros.
- Lewis Artist Supply Co. (Art-Stroke and Best-Test)
- Morilla Co., The (Best-Test)

RUBBER CEMENT DISPENSERS. An air-tight container for rubber cement. Most containers have adjustable length sliding brush. Available in half pint, one pint, and one quart sizes (see page 42).
- Dick Blick Co.
- Arthur Brown & Bro., Inc. (plastic dispenser)
- Charles Bruning Co., Inc.
- Concord Artists' Materials
- Crane-Gallo Artist Supplies
- A. I. Friedman, Inc.
- Lewis Artist Supply Co.

RUBBER CEMENT THINNER (SOLVENT). A liquid used for thinning or reducing cement and for removing materials that have been mounted with rubber cement (see pages 2 and 79).
- Alvin & Co., Inc. (Thinet)
- Dick Blick Co.
- Arthur Brown & Bro., Inc. (Thinet and Bestine)
- Charles Bruning Co., Inc. (Bestine)
- Concord Artists' Materials (Thinet and Bestine)
- Craftint Mfg. Co. (Kleen-Stik)
- Crane-Gallo Artists Supplies (Cargo and Bestine)
- A. I. Friedman, Inc. (Frem and Bestine)
- Krutz Bros. (Bestine)
- Lewis Artist Supply Co. (Bestine)
- Morilla Co., The (Bestine)

SHADING, CRAFTINT DOUBLETONE (TEXTURE). Drawing paper and tracing vellum with two invisible shading (texture) patterns brought out by two chemical developers (see page 70).
- Arthur Brown & Bro., Inc.
- Concord Artists' Materials
- Craftint Mfg. Co.
- Crane-Gallo Artist Supplies
- A. I. Friedman, Inc.
- Lewis Artist Supply Co.

SLIDE CRAYONS. Specially prepared crayons for applying transparent color to frosted (etched) glass or acetate. Available in several colors (see 3-42).
- Keystone View Co.

SLIDE GLASS (2-by 2-inch to 3¼-by 4-inch). High grade glass, plain and frosted, far preparing slides for projection. Frosted (etched) glass will accept pencil, slide crayon and a special slide ink (see pages 98 and 99).
- Brumberger Sales Corp. (2-by 2-inch and 2¼-by 2¼-inch).
- Erie Scientific Corp.
- Keystone View Co. (3¼-by 4-inch)
- Kimac Co.
- The Optics Mfg. Corp. (Newlo)

SLIDEMOUNTS (2-by 2-inch to 3¼-by 4-inch). Cardboard, metal, and plastic mounts (binders or frames) for slides. Metal and plastic mounts usually come with protective cover glass (pages 98 and 99).
- Altman Camera Co. (Linda—for 2-by 2-inch slide)
- American Library Color Slide Co., Inc. (Titania—2-by 2-inch plastic mounts)
- Brumberger Sales Corp. (interlocking)
- Eastman Kodak Co. (Ready Mounts)
- Erie Scientific Corp. (aluminum binders)
- Emde Products, Inc. (aluminum binders)
- Karl Heitz, Inc. (Lindia)
- Andrew E. Lutz Co. (2-by 2-inch mounts)
- Mansfield Industries, Inc. (Kwik Klik - interlocking)
- Mr.-E-Enterprise (plastic 2-by 2-inch and 2¼-by 2¼-inch)
- Optic Mfg. Corp. (LP35 OPTA-Mounts)
- Sonark Industries (2-by 2-inch and 2¼-by 2¼-inch plastic mounting)
- Spiratone (2-by 2-inch and 2¼-by 2¼-inch in quantity)

SLIDE-O-FILM EQUIPMENT AND MATERIALS. A new photographic film exposed by ultra-violet light or in a slide projector, and developed by heat alone. Designed for making positive slides from negatives, negatives from color slides, etc. (see page 96).
- Charles Beseler Co. (Slide-O-Film Div.)

SLIDE PROJECTORS (2-by 2-inch to 3¼-by 4-inch). Projection devices used to project slides; can also be used to produce large visuals (see 3-5, 3-6, and 5-88).
- American Optical Co.
- Argus, Inc.
- Bausch & Lomb Optical Co., Inc.
- Bell & Howell Co.
- Charles Beseler Co.
- Brumberger Sales Corp.
- Burke & James, Inc.
- Graflex, Inc.
- Montgomery Ward, Inc.
- Polaroid Corp.
- Standard Projector & Equipment Co., nlc.
- Viewlex, Inc.

STAPLE GUNS (TACKING GUN). A powerful high compression stapler; useful in wet-mounting (see 1-35).
- Dick Blick Co. (Hansen and Swingline)
- Arthur Brown & Bro., Inc. (Swingline)

115

Concord Artists' Materials (Swingline)
Crane-Gallo Artists Supplies (Swingline)
A. I. Friedman, Inc. (Arrow Gun Tacker)
Goldsmith Bros. (Swingline)
Krutz Bros. (Swingline)
Lewis Artists Supply Co. (Swingline and Displayman's)

TAPE, BINDING. Cloth, paper, or plastic base tape with a pressure-sensitive side that will stick on contact to most surfaces. Available in several colors (see pages 18, 22, and 23).

ABC School Supply, Inc. (Mystick)
Beckley-Cardy Co. (Mystik)
Dick Blick Co. (Library Binding)
Arthur Brown & Bro., Inc. (Passepartout and Mystic)
Concord Artists' Materials (Passepartout and Mystik)
Crane-Gallo Artist Supplies (Mystik)
Demco Library Supplies (Fastape)
Dennison Mfg. Co. (Passepartout and Scotch Opaque Plastic)
A. I. Friedman, Inc. (Scotch Opaque Plastic)
Gaylord Bros., Inc. (Mystik)
Goldsmith Bros. (Mystik)
Kurtz Bros. (Mystik)
Lewis Artist Supply Co. (Mystik)
Minnesota Mining & Mfg. Co. (Scotch Opaque Plastic)

TAPES, COLOR, PATTERN AND SYMBOLS. Transparent and opaque color, patterns, symbols printed on thin width acetate tape with a pressure-sensitive adhesive backing. Ideal for use on transparencies, charts, graphs, etc. (see page 72).

ACS Tapes, Inc.
A. I. Friedman, Inc. (Graph-A-Plan)
Alvin & Co., Inc. (Graph-A-Plan)
Dick Blick Co. (Zip-A-Line)
W. H. Brady Co. (Quick Line)
Arthur Brown & Bro., Inc. (ACS Chartmaker)
Chart-Pak, Inc. (Chart-Pak)
Concord Artists' Materials (ACS Chartmaker Tapes)
Craftint Mfg. Co., The (Charting Materials)
Fototype, Inc. (Rule-Pak)
Labelon Tape Co. (Graph-A-Plan)
Lewis Artist Supply Co. (ACS Chartmaker Tapes)
Jay G. Lissner (Chartape)

TAPE COMPASS (FOR COLOR, PATTERN, AND SYMBOL TAPES). A device for drawing circular tape-line accurately (see page 72).

Chart-Pak, Inc. (Beam Compass Tape-Pen Holder)
Crane-Gallo Artist Supplies (Chart-Pak Beam Compass Tape-Pen Holder)
Tecnifax Corp. (Radial Tape-Pen)

TAPE CUTTERS (FOR COLOR PATTERN, SYMBOL TAPES). Cutting device for color, pattern, and symbol tapes (see page 72).

ACS Tapes, Inc.
Alvin & Co., Inc. (Graph-A-Plan)
Arthur Brown & Bro., Inc. (ACS Chartmaker)
Chart-Pak, Inc. (scapel, knife and cutter)
Concord Artists' Materials (ACS Chartmaker)
Crane-Gallo Artist Supplies (Chart-Pak)
A. I. Friedman, Inc. (Graph-A-Plan)
Labelon Tape Co. (Graph-A-Plan)
Lewis Artist Supply Co. (ACS Chartmaker)
Tecnifax Corp. (Tecnitape cutter or knife)

TAPE, DOUBLE COATED ADHESIVE. Has adhesive on both sides; useful for mounting whenever a two-sided adhesive tape is necessary; available with opaque or transparent base (see 1-82).

Beckley-Cardy Co. (Kleen-Stik)
Dick Blick Co.
Arthur Brown & Bro., Inc.
Concord Artists' Materials
Crane-Gallo Artist Supplies
Demco Library Supplies
Fototype, Inc.
A. I. Friedman, Inc. (Scotch)
Gaylord Bros., Inc.
Lewis Artist Supply Co.
Minnesota Mining & Mfg. Co.

TAPE, MASKING (DRAFTING). Extra strong, heavy weight paper base tape with a pressure-sensitive adhesive side that sticks to most surfaces with a slight hand pressure. (see 22, 42, and 48).

Dick Blick Co.
Arthur Brown & Bro., Inc.
Concord Artists' Materials
Crane-Gallo Artist Supplies
A. I. Friedman, Inc.
Goldsmith Bros.
Lewis Artist Supply Co.
Minnesota Mining & Mfg. Co.

TAPE-PEN (FOR COLOR, PATTERN AND SYMBOL TAPES). A device for drawing straight or curved tape lines accurately (see page 72).

Alvin & Co., Inc. (Graph-A-Plan)
W. H. Brady Co. (Quick Line)
Crane-Gallo Artist Supplies (Chart-Pak)
A. I. Friedman, Inc. (Graph-A-Plan)
Labelon Tape Co. (Graph-A-Plan)
Jay G. Lissner (Tapetool)
Tecnifax Corp. (Tape-Pen)

TAPE, SLIDE BINDING. Gummed paper or pressure-sensitive cloth-base tape designed for slide binding (see 5-96).

Eastman Kodak Co. (Yellow)
Keystone View Co.

TEXTURE SHEETS (SHADING). Texture (shading) patterns printed on the underside of a pressure-sensitive transparent acetate sheet, that can be transferred to most surfaces. Available in a variety of patterns and colors (see page 68).

Dick Blick Co. (Zip-A-Tone and Bourges)
Bourges, Inc. (Bourges Tex)
Arthur Brown & Bro., Inc. (Craft-Tone, Pres-Tone, Add-A-Tint, and Zip-A-Tone)
Cello-Tak Lettering Corp. (Cello-Tak)
Chart-Pak, Inc.
Concord Artists' Materials (Craf-Tone, Pres-Tone, Add-A-Tint, and Zip-A-Tone)
Craftint Mfg. Co. (Craf-Tone)

Crane-Gallo Artist Supplies (Craf-Tone, Contak, Artype, and Zip-Type)
A. I. Friedman, Inc. (Cello-Tak)
H. T. Herbert Co. (Cello-Tak)
Lewis Artist Supply Co. (Artype, Contak, and Zip-A-Tone)
Jay G. Lissner
Para-Tone, Inc. (Zip-A-Tone)
Tecnifax Corp.
Webster Bros. Laboratory
Winsor & Newton, Inc. (Bourges Tex)

THERMO-FAX EQUIPMENT AND MATERIALS. A dry heat photo process which reproduces transparencies from opaque or transparent originals; can be used to laminate originals (see pages 12, 82, and 88).
Three-M Company (3M)

THUMB SPOTS, SLIDE. Gummed-paper markers used as a projection guide in transparent slide presentations (see 5-91).
I. D. Tabs (Slide Indexers)
Sanders Co. (Numbatabs)

TRACING PAPER. A high quality translucent paper for all tracing purposes (see pages 56 and 59).
Alvin & Co., Inc.
Dick Blick Co.
Arthur Brown & Bro., Inc.
Concord Artists' Materials
Craftint Mfg. Co.
Crane-Gallo Artist Supplies
A. I. Friedman, Inc.
H. T. Herbert Co.
Kurtz Bros.
Lewis Artist Supply Co.
Morilla Co., The
Winsor & Newton, Inc.

TRACKS, TRANSPARENCY. Plastic "tracks" for sliding masks; used on overhead transparencies (see 1-107).
Tecnifax Corp. (Plastic Tracks)

TRANSFER TRACING PAPER (CARBON). Special colored carbon paper for transferring lettering, visuals, etc., in color, on various surfaces; available in several colors (see pages 56 and 59).
S. B. Albertis Paper Co. (Saral)
Dick Blick Co. (colored transfer paper)
Arthur Brown & Bro., Inc. (Saral)
Concord Artists' Materials (Saral)
Craftint Mfg. Co., The (Saral)
H. T. Herbert Co.
Lewis Artist Supply Co. (Saral)
Morilla Co., The
Saral Paper Co. (Saral)

TRANSPARENCY MOUNTS (3¼-by 4-inch and LARGER). Die-cut pressed-board "frames" for transparencies (projectuals). (see pages 100 and 101).
American Optical Co.
Charles Beseler Co. (Vu-Graph Mounts)
Robert J. Brady Co. (All Plastic and white pressboard)
Gestener Duplicator Corp. (10 3/4-by 14-inch and 10½-by 1-2inch)
Keuffel & Esser Co. (Gemini)
Ozalid (Projecto Mounts)
Tecnifax Corp. (Projectual Mounts)
Three-M Company (3M mounting frames)
Victorlite Industries, Inc.

TRANSPARENT CURVES. Transparent drafting devices used for making curves that cannot be made with a compass (see 3-54).
Alvin & Co., Inc.
Dick Blick Co.
Arthur Brown & Bro., Inc.
Charles Bruning Co., Inc.
Concord Artists' Materials
Craftint Mfg. Co.
Crane-Gallo Artist Supplies
C-Thru Ruler Co.
A. I. Friedman, Inc.
Goldsmith Bros.
Lewis Artist Supply Co.
Morilla Co., The

T-SQUARES. Drafting instrument made of wood, plastic or metal for drawing accurate straight lines; also used to hold lettering guides in place (see pages 4, 6, and 50).
Alvin & C., Inc.
Arthur Brown & Bro., Inc.
Charles Bruning Co., Inc.
Concord Artists' Materials
Craftint Mfg. Co.
Crane-Gallo Artist Supplies
C-Thru Ruler Co.
Dick Blick Co.
A. I. Friedman, Inc.
Letterguide Co. (Cam-Loc)
Lewis Artist Supply Co.
Morilla Co., The
Varigraph Co. (Boardlock)

WHEAT PASTE FLOUR. A special formula flour designed for preparing the paste used for wallpaper hanging. Ideal for wet-mounting (see page 15).
Huron Milling Co. (Red Stave)
Krause Milling Co. (Golden Harvest)

XEROGRAPHIC EQUIPMENT AND MATERIALS. Electrostatic photographic copying process. Will enlarge or reduce anything written, printed, typed or drawn (see 5-57).
Xerox Corp.

REFERENCE D

ADDRESSES OF DISTRIBUTORS, MANUFACTURERS, PRODUCERS, AND PUBLISHERS

A

ABC Pattern & Stencil Company, 207 Willard Avenue, Michigan City, Indiana.
ABC School Supply, Incorporated, 34 East Andrews Drive, N.W., Atlanta 5, Georgia.
Acrolite Products, Incorporated, 106 Ashland Avenue, West Orange, New Jersey.
ACS Tapes, Incorporated, 217 California Street, Newton 58, California.
Addressograph-Multigraph Corporation, Cleveland 17, Ohio.
Albertis, S. B. Paper Company, 5 Tudor City Place, New York 17, New York.
Altman Camera Company, 16 S. Wabash Avenue, Chicago 3, Illinois.
Alvin & Company, Incorporated, 611 Palisado Avenue, Windsor, Connecticut.
American Book Company, 55 Fifth Avenue, New York 3, New York.
American Library Color Slide Company, Incorporated, 222 W. 23rd Street, New York 11, N. Y.
American Optical Company, Instrument Division, Box A, Buffalo 15, New York.
American Photocopy Equipment Company, 2100 W. Dempster Street, Evanston, Illinois.
Ampto, Incorporated, Hix Avenue, Newton, New Jersey.
Argus, Incorporated, Ann Arbor, Michigan.
Aronstein B. & Company, Flushing, New York.
Artype, Incorporated, 127 S. Northwest Highway, Barrington, Illinois.

B

Bausch & Lomb Optical Company, Incorporated, 635 St. Paul Street, Rochester 2, New York.
Beckley-Cardy Company, 1900 N. Narragasett, Chicago 39, Illinois.
Bee Paper Company, P. O. Box 1016 100 8th Street, Passaic, New Jersey
Bell & Howell Company, 7100 McCormick Road, Chicago 45, Illinois.
Beseler, Charles Company, 219 S. 18th Street, East Orange, New Jersey.
Best Plastic Products, Incorporated, 751 East 92nd Street, Chicago 19, Illinois.
Blick, Dick Company, Gailesburg, Illinois.
Bourges, Incorporated, 80 Fifth Avenue, New York 11, New York.
Brady, Robert J. Company, 3227 M. Street, N.W., Washington 7, D. C.
Brady, W. H. Company, 727 W. Glendale Avenue, Milwaukee 9, Wisconsin.
Bradywine Photo Chemical Company, Box 298, Avondale, Pennsylvania.
Brigham Young University, Audio-Visual Center, Provo, Utah.
Brooks Manufacturing Company, P.O. Box 156, Cincinnati 31, Ohio.
Brown, Arthur & Brother, Incorporated, 2 W. 46th Street, New York 36, New York.
Brown, William C. Company, Publishers, 135 S. Locust Street, Dubuque, Iowa.
Brumburger Sales Corporation, 68-34th Street, Brooklyn 32, New York.
Buhl Optical Company, 1009 Beech Avenue, Pittsburgh 33, Pennsylvania.
Bruning, Charles, Incorporated, Mount Prospect, Illinois.
Burke & James, Incorporated, 321 S. Wabash Avenue, Chicago 4, Illinois.

C

Carr Plastics Corporation, 3030 Euclid Avenue, Cleveland 15, Ohio.
Cello-Tak Lettering Corporation, 35 Alabama Avenue, Island Park, L. I., New York.
Chandler Publishing Company, 604 Mission Street, San Francisco 5, California.
Chart-Pak Incorporated, 1 River Road, Leeds, Massachusetts.
Chilton Company, Book Division, 56th & Chestnut Streets, Philadelphia 39, Pennsylvania.
Clingtie Letters, 886 N. Wabash Avenue, Chicago 11, Illinois.
Color Stik, 219 South 18th Street, East Orange, New Jersey.
Concord Artists' Materials, 181 Lexington Avenue, New York 16, New York.
Craftint Manufacturing Company, The, 18501 Euclid Avenue, Cleveland 12, Ohio.
Crane-Gallo Artist Supplies, 110 W. 31st Street, New York 1, New York.
Cresent Cardboard Company, 1240 N. Homan Avenue, Chicago 51, Illinois.
Crowell, Thomas Y. Company, 432 Park Avenue, New York 16, New York.
C-Thru Ruler Company, 823-827 Winsdor Street, Hartford 1, Connecticut.

D

Davis Publications, Printers Building, Worcester, Massachusetts.
Demco Library Supplies, Box 1488, Madison 1, Wisconsin.
Dennison Manufacturing Company, Framingham, Massachusetts.
Dick, A. B. Company, 5700 W. Touhy Avenue, Chicago 48, Illinois
Ditto, Incorporated, 6800 McCormick Road, Chicago 45, Illinois.
Dot & Company, 85-47 Little Neck Parkway, Floral Park, New York.
Duro Art Supply Company, 1832 Juneway Terrace, Chicago 26, Illinois.

E

Eagle Pencil Company, Danbury, Connecticut.
Educational Service, 1730 Eye Street, N. W., Washington, D.C.
Esterbrook Pen Company, The, Delaware Avenue & Copper Street, Camden 1, New Jersey.
Eastman Kodak Company, 343 State Street, Rochester 4, New York.
Emde Products, Incorporated, 2040 Stoner Avenue, Los Angeles 25, California.
Erie Scientific Corporation, 693 Seneca Street, Buffalo 10, New York.
E-Z Buckle, Incorporated, 418 Lafayette Street, New York 3, New York.
E-Z Stencil Company, 6029 Berkeley Avenue, Baltimore 9, Maryland.

F

Federal Manufacturing & Engineering Corporation, 1055 Stewart Avenue, Garden City, New York.
Flax, Sam Artist Materials, 25 E. 28th Street, New York 16, New York.
Florida State University, Audio-Visual Center, Tallahassee, Florida.
Fototype, Incorporated, 1414 Roscoe Street, Chicago 13, Illinois.
Friedman, A. I. Incorporated, 25 W. 45th Street, New York 36, New York.

G

Gaylord Brothers, Incorporated, 155 Gifford Street, Syracuse 1, New York.
General Binding Corporation, Northbrook, Illinois.
Gestetner Duplicator Corporation, 216 Lake Avenue, Yonkers, New York.
Golden Press, Incorporated, 850 Third Avenue, New York 22, New York.
Goldsmith Brothers, 77 Nassau Street, New York 8, New York.
Grafic Tools, 715 S. Cedar Street, Roswell, New Mexico.
Graflex, Incorporated, 3750 Monroe Avenue, Rochester 3, New York.
Grand Central Artists' Materials, Incorporated, 3 East 40th Street, New York 16, New York.

H

Harper & Brothers, 49 E. 33rd Street, New York 16, New York.
Heitz, Karl, Incorporated, 480 Lexington Avenue, New York 17, New York.
Herbert, H. T. Company, 10-63 Talkson Avenue, Long Island City, New York.
Hernard Manufacturing Company, Incorporated, 21 Saw Mill River Road, Yonkers, New York.
Heyer, Incorporated, 1850 Kostner Avenue, Chicago 23, Illinois.
Higgins Ink Company, Incorporated, 271 Ninth Street, Brooklyn 15, New York.
Holes Webway Company, The, St. Cloud, Minnesota.
Holliston, Mills, Incorporated, Norwood, Massachusetts.
Holt, Rinhart and Winston, Incorporated, 383 Madison Avenue, New York 17, New York.
Horder's Stationery Stores, Incorporated, 231 S. Jefferson Street, Chicago 6, Illinois.
Hunt, C. Howard Pen Company, P. O. Box 560, Camden, New Jersey.
Huron Milling Company, Harbor Beach, Michigan.

I

Ideal School Supply Company, 8312-46 Birkhoff Avenue, Chicago 20, Illinois.
I. D. Tabs, 7014 165th Street, Flushing, New York.
Indiana University, Audio-Visual Center, Bloomington, Indiana.
International Sales Company, Incorporated, 17-19 W. Baltimore Street, Baltimore 1, Maryland.
International Cooperation Administration, Office of the Deputy for Operation, Washington, D. C.
Iowa, University of, Bureau of Audio-Visual Instruction, Iowa City, Iowa.

J

Jiffy Enterprises, Incorporated, 146-48 50 N. 13th Street, Philadelphia 7, Pennsylvania.
Judy Company, 310 N. Second Street, Minneapolis 1, Minnesota.

K

Kees, F. D. Manufacturing Company, 700 Park Street, Beatrice, Nebraska.
Kenworthy, Educational Service, Incorporated, 138 Allen Street, Buffalo 1, New York.

Keystone View Company, Meadville, Pennsylvania.
Keuffel & Esser Company, Audio-Visual Division, 300 Adams, Hoboken, New Jersey.
Kimac Company, The, Old Greenwich, Connecticut.
Koh-I-Noor, Incorporated, North Street, Bloomsbury, New Jersey.
Krause's Milling Company, Milwaukee, Wisconsin.
Krylon, Incorporated, 18 W. Airy Street, Norristown, Pennsylvania.

L

Labelon Tape Company, Incorporated, Rochester 9, New York.
Lea A-V Service, 240 Audley Drive, Sun Prairie, Wisconsin.
Letterguide Company, Box 99, State House Station, Lincoln 9, Nebraska.
Lewis Artist Supply Company, 6408 Woodward Avenue, Detroit 2, Michigan.
Lissner, Jay G., 3417 W. 1st Street, Los Angeles 37, California.
Ludwig, F. G., Incorporated, Coulter Street, Old Saybrook, Connecticut.
Lutz, Andrew E. Company, P. O. Box 5, Syracuse 11, New York.

M

Magnet Sales Company, 3935 S. Vermont, Los Angeles 37, California.
Maggie Magnetic Visual Aids Corporation, 39 W. 32nd Street, New York 1, New York.
Maker Products, Incorporated, Irvington-on-Hudson, New York.
Mansfield Industries, Incorporated, 1227 Loyola Avenue, Chicago 26, Illinois.
Major Services, 1740 W. Columbia Avenue, Chicago 26, Illinois.
Marshall, John G. Manufacturing Company, Incorporated, 167 N. 9th Street, Brooklyn 11, New York
Marsh Felt-Point Pen Division, 707 East "B" Street, Belleville, Illinois.
Mayer, Charles Studios, Incorporated, 766 Commins Street, Akron 7, Ohio.
McGraw-Hill Book Company, Incorporated, (For Films, Text-Film Department) 330 W. 42nd Street, New York 36, New York.
McManus & Morgan, Incorporated, 2506 W. 7th Street, Los Angeles 57, California.
Mich, Harry Company, 216 W. Ontario Street, Chichago 10, Illinois.
Milo Harding Company, Monterey Park, California.
Mioplex Products, M. P. Manufacturing Company, P. O. Box 79, 1809 W. 12 Street, Brooklyn 23, New York.
Mitten's Display Letters, 39 W. 60th Street, New York 23, New York.
Montgomery Ward, Incorporated, Baltimore 32, Maryland.
Morilla Company, The, 328-332 E, 23rd Street, New York 10, New York.
MR-E-Enterprises, P. O. Box 45586, Los Angeles 45, California.
Mutual Aids, 1946 Hillhurst Avenue, Los Angeles 27, California.

N

National Card, Mat & Board Company, 4318-36 Carroll Avenue, Chicago 24, Illinois.
Nostrand, D. Van Company, Incorporated, 120 Alexander Street, Princeton, New Jersey.

O

Ohio State University, Teaching Aids Laboratory, Columbus 10, Ohio.
Optics Manufacturing Corporation, Amber & Willard Streets, Philadelphia 34, Pennsylvania.
Oravisual Company, Box 11150, St. Petersburg 33, Florida.
Ozalid, Johnson City, New York.

P

Paasche Airbrush Company, 1909 Diversey Parkway, Chicago 14, Illinois.
Para-Tone, Incorporated, 512 W. Burlington Avenue, LaGrange, Illinois.
Penn Products Company, 963 Newark Avenue, Elizabeth 3, New Jersey.
Peerless Color Laboratories, 11 Diamond Place, Rochester 9, New York.
Photo Materials Company, 2100 W. Fulton Street, Chicago 12, Illinois.
Photorapid Corporation, 3620 Oakton St., Skokie, Illinois.
Planoscope Corporation, 551 5th Avenue, New York 17, New York.
Polaroid Corporation, Main Street, Cambridge 39, Massachusetts.
Precision Paint Corporation, Chamblee, Georgia.
Prentice-Hall, Incorporated, Englewood Cliffs, New Jersey.
Presto Process Company, 183 St. Paul Street, Rochester 4, New York.
Prestype, Incorporated 136 W. 21st Street, New York 11, New York.
Projection Optics Company, 271 Eleventh Avenue, East Orange, New Jersey.

R

Radio-Mat Slide Company, Incorporated, 222 Oak Ridge Boulevard, Daytona Beach, Florida.
Redikut Letter Company, 185 N. Prairie Avenue, Hawthorne, California.
Rogers Litho, 322 N. Avenue P, Lubbock, Texas.
Ronald Press Company, The, 15 E. 26 Street, New York 10, New York.
Rosco Laboratories, Incorporated, 29 Moore Street, Brooklyn, 6, New York.

S

Salt Lake Stamp Company, 43 West 3rd South, Salt Lake City, Utah.
Sanders Company, Box 111, Rochester 1, New York.
Sanford Ink Company, 2740 Washington Boulevard, Bellwood, Illinois.
Saral Paper Company, 5 Tudor City Place, New York 17, New York.
Seal, Incorporated, 8 Broad Street, Shelton, Connecticut.
Sheffield Bronze Paint Corporation, Cleveland 19, Ohio.
Shiva Artists' Colors, 435 W. Goethe Street, Chicago 10, Illinois.
Simmons Brothers, Incorporated, 30-28 Starr Avenue, Long Island City 1, New York.
Slidecraft Company, Mountain Lakes, New Jersey.
Sonark Industries, 10401 Virginia Avenue, Culver City, California.
Speedry Products, Incorporated, Richmond Hill 18, New York.
Spiratone, 135-06 Northern Boulevard, Flushing 54, New York.
Standard Projector and Equipment Company, Incorporated, 7433 N. Harlem Avenue, Chicago, Illinois.
State College of Washington, Community College Service, Pullman, Washington.
Steiner Paper Corporation, 601 W. 26th Street, New York, 1, New York.
Stensgaard, W. L. & Associates, Incorporated, 346 N. Justine Street, Chicago 7, Illinois.
Stenso Lettering Company, 1101 E. 25th Street, Baltimore, Maryland.
Stewart, Henry, Incorporated, 210 Ellicott Street, Buffalo, New York.
Stick-a-Letter Company, Rt. 2, Box 1400, Escondida, California.

T

Tablet & Ticket Company, The, 1021 W. Adams Street, Chicago 7, Illinois.
Teaching Aids Laboratory, College Road Annex, The Ohio State University, Columbus 10, Ohio.
Tecnifax Corporation, Holyoke, Massachusetts.
Testrite Instrument Company, Incorporated, 135 Monroe Street, Newark 5, New Jersey.
Texas, University of, Visual Instruction Bureau, Austin 12, Texas.
Thayer & Chandler, 331 S. Peoria Street, Chicago 7, Illinois.
Three-M Company (3M), 900 Bush Avenue, St. Paul 6, Minnesota.
Tudor Publishing Company, 221 Park Avenue South, New York 3, New York.

U

Union Rubber and Asbestos Company, Trenton 6, New Jersey.

V

Varigraph Company, 841 W. Lakeside Street, Madison 1, Wisconsin.
Venus Pen and Pencil Corporation, Lewisburg, Tennessee.
Victor Animatograph Corporation, Plainesville, Connecticut.
Victorlite Industries, Incorporated, 4117 W. Jefferson Boulevard, Los Angeles 16, California.
Viewlex, Incorporated, Holbrook, Long Island, New York.
Volk Corporation, Pleasantville, New Jersey.

W

Watson-Guptill Publications, Incorporated, 24 W. 40th Street, New York 18, New York.
Weber, F. Company, 1200 Buttonwood Street, Philadelphia 23, Pennsylvania.
Webster Brothers Laboratory, 2040 W. Chase Avenue, Chicago 45, Illinois.
Winsor & Newton, Incorporated, 902 Broadway, New York 10, New York.
Wold Air Brush Manufacturing Company, The, 2171 N. California Avenue, Chicago 47, Illinois.
Wood-Regan Instrument Company, Nutley 10, New Jersey.

X

X-Acto, Incorporated, 48-41 Van Dam Street, Long Island City 1, New York.
Xerox Corporation, Haloid Street, Rochester 3, New York.

REFERENCE E

VISUAL INDEX
This is a quick reference for locating recommended techniques for preparing visual instructional materials.

INSTRUCTIONAL MATERIAL	MOUNTING	LETTERING	VISUALS	COLOR AND TEXTURE	PHOTOGRAPHIC AND NON-PHOTOGRAPHIC TRANSPARENCIES
Charts, Graphs, Maps	2, 4, 6, 8, 10, 12, 14, 16, 22, 23, 24	28, 30, 32, 36, 38, 40, 42, 44, 46, 48, 50	54, 56, 58, 60, 62, 64	66, 68, 72, 74	86, 88, 90, 94, 95
Diazo Masters		36, 38, 40, 42, 44, 46, 48, 50	58, 62, 64	68, 72	78, 80, 82, 84, 86, 92, 94, 96
Displays and Exhibits	2, 4, 6, 8, 10, 12, 14, 16, 18, 20, 22, 23, 24	28, 30, 32, 34, 36, 38, 44, 46, 48, 50	54, 56, 58, 60, 62, 64	66, 68, 72, 74	78, 80, 82, 84, 86, 88, 90, 95
Filmstrips		28, 36, 38, 40, 42, 44, 46, 48, 50	56, 58, 60, 62, 64	66, 68, 70, 72, 74	For Overlays and Titles 86, 88, 90
Flash Cards		28, 30, 32, 44, 46, 48			
Fluid and Wax Stencils		44, 46, 48	58, 60, 62		
Mounted Materials	2, 4, 6, 8, 10, 12, 14, 16, 18, 20, 22, 23, 24				
Offset Masters		38, 40, 42, 44, 46, 48, 50,	58, 60, 62, 64		90, 92

HOW TO USE THE VISUAL INDEX

First, select the instructional material desired, then read opposite the material for the pages of recommended techniques for its preparation.

MOUNTING	LETTERING	VISUALS	COLOR AND TEXTURE	PHOTOGRAPHIC AND NON-PHOTOGRAPHIC TRANSPARENCIES	INSTRUCTIONAL MATERIAL
2, 4, 14, 16, 22, 23, 24	28, 30, 32, 34, 36, 38, 44, 46, 48, 50	54, 56, 58, 60, 62, 64	66, 68, 72, 74	86, 90	Posters
	28, 32, 36, 38, 40, 42, 44, 46, 48, 50	54, 56, 58, 60, 62, 64	66, 68, 72, 74	86, 88, 90	Projected Titles
2, 4, 6, 20, 24	36, 38, 40, 42, 44, 46, 48, 50	54, 56, 58, 60, 62, 64	66, 68, 70, 72, 74		Publication Art
	28, 30, 32, 34, 36, 38, 40, 42, 44, 46, 48, 50		66, 68, 72, 74	86, 90	Signs
	38, 40, 42, 46, 48, 50	54, 56, 58, 60, 62			Silkscreen Art
98, 100	28, 32, 36, 38, 40, 42, 44, 46, 48, 50	58, 60, 62, 64	66, 68, 72, 74	78, 80, 82, 84, 86, 88, 90, 92, 94, 96,	Slides and Large Transparencies
22	28, 32, 36, 38, 40, 42, 44, 46, 48, 50	54, 56, 58, 60, 62, 64	66, 68, 72, 74	86, 88, 90	Television Titles
2, 4, 6, 8, 10, 12, 14, 16, 18, 20, 22, 23, 24			66, 68, 72, 74	78, 80, 82, 84, 86, 88, 90, 92, 94, 95, 96	Visuals

123